MODERN ARCHITECTURE

Modern Architecture: The Basics examines technological, stylistic, socio-political, and cultural changes that have transformed the history of architecture since the late 18th century. Broad definitions of modernity and postmodernity introduce the book, which comprises 24 short thematic chapters looking at the concepts behind the development of modern and postmodern architecture. These include major historical movements, key figures, and evolving building typologies. There is also an emphasis on the changing city during the 19th and 20th centuries. Approaches to representation and its impacts on architecture are studied, along with the changing global role of architecture as cultural expression. The book introduces new topics, including gender, race, postcolonialism, and indigeneity. An undaunting, contemporary, and inclusive account of modern architectural history, this is a must-read for all students of architecture as well as those outside the discipline approaching the subject for the first time.

Graham Livesey is Emeritus Professor in the School of Architecture, Planning and Landscape at the University of Calgary.

W0234780

The Basics Series

The Basics is a highly successful series of accessible guidebooks which provide an overview of the fundamental principles of a subject area in a jargon-free and undaunting format.

Intended for students approaching a subject for the first time, the books both introduce the essentials of a subject and provide an ideal springboard for further study. With over 50 titles spanning subjects from artificial intelligence (AI) to women's studies, *The Basics* are an ideal starting point for students seeking to understand a subject area.

Each text comes with recommendations for further study and gradually introduces the complexities and nuances within a subject.

SIMONE DE BEAUVOIR
Megan Burke

INTERVIEWING: THE BASICS
Mark Holton

SHAKESPEARE (FOURTH EDITION)
Sean McEvoy

DREAMS
Dale Mathers and Carola Mathers

JEWISH ETHICS
Geoffrey D. Claussen

MODERN ARCHITECTURE
Graham Livesey

For a full list of titles in this series, please visit www.routledge.com/The-Basics/book-series/B

MODERN ARCHITECTURE

THE BASICS

Graham Livesey

Drawings by Mohammad Moezzi

Routledge
Taylor & Francis Group
LONDON AND NEW YORK

Designed cover image: Solomon R. Guggenheim Museum,
Credit: Mondadori Portfolio

First published 2025
by Routledge
4 Park Square, Milton Park, Abingdon, Oxon OX14 4RN

and by Routledge
605 Third Avenue, New York, NY 10158

Routledge is an imprint of the Taylor & Francis Group, an informa business

© 2025 Graham Livesey

British Library Cataloguing-in-Publication Data
A catalogue record for this book is available from the British Library

ISBN: 978-1-032-51796-4 (hbk)
ISBN: 978-1-032-51794-0 (pbk)
ISBN: 978-1-003-40397-5 (ebk)

DOI: 10.4324/9781003403975

Typeset in Bembo
by Apex CoVantage, LLC

For Product Safety Concerns and Information please contact our EU representative:
GPSR@taylorandfrancis.com
Taylor & Francis Verlag GmbH, Kaufingerstraße 24, 80331 München, Germany

CONTENTS

ACKNOWLEDGEMENTS

I would like to acknowledge the support I have received from various people who were essential to the realization of this book. I am indebted to my training at McGill University, which was shaped by two important architectural historians: Prof. Peter Collins and Dr. Alberto Pérez-Gómez. I would like to thank the many students I taught at the University of Calgary; they have been a continuous source of inspiration. I would like to express deep gratitude to my esteemed colleague and friend Julia Gersovitz, O.C., who graciously agreed to review and edit the text. The book would not have been the same without the evocative drawings created by Mohammad Moezzi. I am also grateful to the staff at Routledge, especially Lydia Kessell and Jake Millicheap, who made the task of producing the book very easy. The libraries at the University of Calgary and Queen's University (Kingston, Ontario) provided research material for the book. Finally, I could not have undertaken this project without the loving support of my wife, Allison (and her family), and my sons, Aidan and Ellis.

ACKNOWLEDGMENTS

MODERNISM AND POSTMODERNISM

We tend to associate the terms "modern" and "modernity" with meaning up to date, as opposed to belonging to the past. However, they also can imply a break with tradition or history. Although we typically think of "modernism" as a style of the 20th century, the origins of the modern world began during the European Renaissance. This book will examine the development and evolution of modern architecture from the late 18th century. It will focus primarily on concepts that shaped the emergence of a new international architecture in the 1920s and 1930s. It will also examine the "postmodern" period, beginning in the 1950s, that challenged the fundamental premises of modernity.

This history of modern architecture begins around 1775, during the period often referred to as the Enlightenment. Peter Gay expresses the ambitions of the period as follows:

> The men of the Enlightenment united on a vastly ambitious program, a program of secularism, humanity, cosmopolitanism, and freedom, above all, freedom in its many forms – freedom from arbitrary power, freedom of speech, freedom of trade, freedom to realize one's talents, freedom of aesthetic response, freedom, in a word, of moral man to make his own way in the world.[1]

The Enlightenment was characterized by the rationalism and methodological empiricism that emerged from the Scientific Revolution. It also demonstrated a tendency towards secularism, the pursuit of knowledge, the triumph of modern views over traditional ones, the

DOI: 10.4324/9781003403975-1

belief in the marketplace, and a focus on liberalism, egalitarianism, and humanitarianism. It was also a period of great political, social, and technological revolutions. A key example of an Enlightenment project was the *Encyclopédie* (or the *Encyclopedia, or a Systematic Dictionary of the Sciences, Arts, and Crafts*), edited by philosophers Denis Diderot and Jean le Rond d'Alembert and published between 1751 and 1772 in 28 volumes. The *Encyclopédie* was intended to be a comprehensive effort to describe all human knowledge in text and images.

In his book *All That is Solid Melts Into Air: The Experience of Modernity*, political scientist Marshall Berman outlines the history of modernism and describes its paradoxical nature. Berman identifies three phases of modernity.[2] The first started at the beginning of the 16th century and ended in the late 18th century, this phase encompassed the lives of influential figures like Leonardo da Vinci (1452–1519), Nicolaus Copernicus (1473–1543), René Descartes (1596–1650), Sir Isaac Newton (1643–1727), Jean-Jacques Rousseau (1712–1778), and Adam Smith (1723–1790). These men were part of a scientific and intellectual revolution that challenged the religious teachings of the age that placed humans at the centre of the universe. They personified an age of human invention and exploration that led to discoveries at all scales, from the microscopic to the cosmic.

The second phase of modernity started at the end of the 18th century and coincided with the American and French Revolutions and the Industrial Revolution. This second phase ended in the 1890s. The revolutions launched enormous political, social, and technological changes and would draw America into a central role in the modern project. The third phase coincided with the 20th century, as the forces of modernism created new modes of living and new styles. At this point, modernity had spread across the world through colonization and conquest. Its imposition on numerous non-Western cultures led to its adaptation to differing cultural situations.[3] As Berman suggests, to be modern is to live in an age full of both promise and destruction. He writes of its characteristics:

> The maelstrom of modern life has been fed from many sources: great discoveries in the physical sciences, changing our images of the universe and our place in it; the industrialization of production, which transforms scientific knowledge into technology, creates new human environments and destroys old ones, speeds up the whole tempo of life, generates new forms of corporate power and class struggle; immense demographic upheavals, severing millions from their ancestral habitats, hurtling them half way across the world into new lives; rapid and often cataclysmic

urban growth; systems of mass communication, dynamic in their development, enveloping and binding together the most diverse people and
societies; increasingly powerful nation states, bureaucratically structured
and operated, constantly striving to expand their powers; mass social
movements of people, and peoples, challenging their political and economic rulers, striving to gain some control over their lives; finally, bearing
and driving all these people and institutions along, an ever-expanding,
drastically fluctuating capitalist world market.[4]

The factors that Berman describes had a significant impact on society
as many traditional practices were challenged; this was the case with
architecture, particularly during the 19th and early 20th centuries.

★ ★ ★

In the 1950s and 1960s, modernity itself came under attack from
multiple vantage points. Some cultural theorists describe this period
as a late stage of modernism; others describe this new era as "postmodern," defined by factors that are opposite to the tendencies of
modernism. In this book, postmodernism is accepted as a new historical period. Beverley Brown has characterized postmodernism as:

pastiche, self-referentiality, fragmentation, hybridization of styles, linguistic multiplicity, and as a movement in philosophy registering a crisis in
the legitimation of Western knowledge through a breakdown of meta-
narratives and the consequent end therefore of metaphysics and of all
thought attempting to ground itself in first principles or final causes,
such as God, Nature, Spirit. Similarly, "postmodernity" has been vari-
ously defined as the Age of the Hyperreal, where all distinctions between
truth and appearance, depth and surface, latent and manifest have broken down . . . as an era of capitalist expansion where spatial and tem-
poral compression of the globe (through new information technologies,
search for new markets, financial development) is producing a crisis in
traditional conceptualizations of identity and history; as a new political
age of "difference" where notions of democracy and consensus have
failed under pressure from the emerging voices of those 'others' whose
exclusion has facilitated the establishment of the dominants as part of an
ostensible regime of truth, not one of power.[5]

We can break down various key ideas embedded in this quotation. The
notion of "pastiche, self-referentiality, fragmentation, hybridization
of styles, linguistic multiplicity" is found particularly in postmodern
architecture. Starting in the 1960s, hybrid designs were often created which referenced the history of architecture and popular culture
and questioned the dominance of modernism.[6] The "breakdown of

meta-narratives" is a concept developed by the French philosopher Jean-François Lyotard to explain the end of large, over-arching ideas such as those contained in religious and political systems.[7] The "Age of the Hyperreal" refers to the work of another French philosopher, Jean Baudrillard, and his accusation that the postmodern era emphasizes surfaces, screens, spectacles, and simulations over the real.[8]

There is no doubt that since the 1950s, increasing globalization has resulted from the dominance of capitalism and the rise of communication and information technologies that have compressed space and time into what media theorist Marshall McLuhan termed the "global village."[9] Not only are information, capital, and trends moving at lightning speed across the world, but in recent decades, there has been the proliferation of new voices and communities that have not had any power or presence in the modern age. Identity factors such as gender, race, religion, and sexual orientation are increasingly being accepted on their own terms.

★ ★ ★

This book begins towards the end of the 18th century, coinciding with the beginning of Berman's second phase, as the great political and industrial revolutions take hold. It examines the development of modern architecture using a format that focuses on the vital concepts that define modern and postmodern architecture until the beginning of the 21st century. Like all histories, this book presents a particular interpretation of the vast historical resources available on the subject. This book is an introduction to the concepts and ideas that shaped architecture since the late 18th century and is intended to bring in diverse contributors to the story. History remains important as a subject, as José Ortega y Gasset states:

> one must recognize that the past is here among us, that we are its summing up, that our present is made out of the material of that past, which past is therefore the moment at hand, the heart, the hidden core, of the present.[10]

As far as possible, the book will attempt a global approach to the subject and will generally follow an overall historical chronology. The text is intended to give an overview of modern and postmodern architecture by presenting key concepts that shaped the evolution of architecture. Each section will present key concepts and provide a short historical overview. The book will also be inspired by the writings of important architectural historians and by various other thinkers. It will strive to provide a new approach to the history of modern architecture while recognizing that certain historical narratives are widely accepted. The suggested readings at the end of each section will provide the reader with sources that can provide more detail on specific architects, types of buildings, materials, and periods. The date included for each building is the completion date, which does not necessarily take into account that some buildings have a long gestation period.

In his essay "The Beholding Eye: Ten Versions of the Same Scene," geographer D.W. Meinig demonstrates that a landscape can be viewed as nature, habitat, artefact, system, problem, wealth, ideology, history, place, and aesthetic.[11] If this model is transposed to architecture, it can be suggested that a building plays a complex role in any society of which it is a part. A building belongs to a physical and cultural context; it provides a shelter for a broad range of human activities, and it is a tangible construction that involves materials and techniques. Buildings can solve problems but can also create problems, such as global warming. Buildings represent an investment on the part of those who build and maintain them. Buildings also use a wide range of resources. Every building involves political and social expression and occupies a place in the small and large histories that shape communities and their inhabitants. Finally, a building belongs to an aesthetic or cultural order that influences its appearance. This book attempts to be conscious of these complex concepts that shape modern and postmodern architecture.

NOTES

1 Peter Gay, *The Enlightenment* (New York: W.W. Norton & Co., 1995), p. 3.
2 See Marshall Berman, *All That Is Solid Melts Into Air* (New York: Viking Penguin Inc., 1988), pp. 16–17.
3 Ibid.
4 Ibid., p. 16.
5 Beverley Brown, "Postmodernism," in Elizabeth Wright et al., eds., *Feminism and Psychoanalysis: A Critical Dictionary* (Oxford: Blackwell, 1992), pp. 341–342.
6 See Charles Jencks, *The Language of Post-Modern Architecture* (New York: Rizzoli, 1991).
7 See Jean-François Lyotard, "Answering the Question: What Is Postmodernism?" in Charles Jencks, ed., *The Post-Modern Reader* (London: Academy Editions, 1992), pp. 138–150.

8 See Jean Baudrillard, "The Ecstasy of Communication," in Hal Foster, ed., *Postmodern Culture* (London: Pluto Press, 1985), pp. 126–134.

9 See Marshall McLuhan, *Understanding Media: The Extensions of Man* (New York: McGraw-Hill, 1964).

10 J. Ortega y Gasset, *Man and Crisis* (London: George Allen & Unwin Ltd., 1959), p. 53.

11 See D.W. Meinig, "The Beholding Eye: Ten Versions of the Same Scene," in D.W. Meinig, ed., *The Interpretation of Ordinary Landscapes* (New York: Oxford University Press, 1979), pp. 33–48.

SUGGESTED READING

Berman, Marshall. *All That Is Solid Melts Into Air: The Experience of Modernity.* New York: Penguin Books, 1988.

Foster, Hal, ed., *Postmodern Culture.* London: Pluto Press, 1985.

Jencks, Charles, ed. *The Post-Modern Reader.* London: Academy Editions, 1992.

McLeod, Mary. "Modernism," in Iain Borden, Murray Fraser, and Barbara Penner, eds., *Forty Ways to Think About Architecture: Architectural History and Theory Today.* New York: John Wiley & Sons, 2014.

Weston, Richard. *Modernism.* London: Phaidon, 1996.

2

REVOLUTION AND REPUBLICANISM

The concept of "revolution" has been essential to the development of modern architecture. This occurred politically, culturally, technologically, and stylistically. A revolution implies a sudden and significant change in a situation. A political revolution can be defined as "the forcible overthrow of a government through mass mobilization (whether military or civilian or both) in the name of social justice, to create new political institutions."[1] According to historian Jack A. Goldstone, there are five conditions necessary for a political revolution, "economic or fiscal strain, alienation and opposition among the elites, widespread popular anger at injustice, a persuasive narrative of resistance, and favorable international relations."[2] This section will concentrate on how architecture has expressed political systems in two major revolutions, which both attempted to remove the authority of the monarch and to install more democratic forms of republican government: the American Revolution (1765–1783) and the French Revolution (1789–1799).

The concept of a monarchy has a king or queen as the head of state, either as an absolute authority or in a more restricted role defined by a constitution. A good example of an absolute monarch was Louis XIV (1638–1715), who ruled as the king of France for 72 years and was responsible for the creation of the enormous palace and gardens at Versailles. The counterposition of monarchy is democracy, in which power is held by the people based on free elections and the principle of equality. Democracy was first developed in ancient Athens, where a limited form of vote was given to property-owning

DOI: 10.4324/9781003403975-2

male citizens. The concept of democracy gained momentum with the English Civil War (1642–1651), which removed power from the monarch, and with the American Revolution, which resulted in a republic. A republic involves elected representatives, usually under a president. In the aftermath of the American War of Independence, a democratic republic was established, while the French Revolution ultimately failed with the rise of Napoleon Bonaparte (1769–1821), who seized power in 1799 and crowned himself emperor in 1804.

The role of architecture role in supporting various political systems is central, both in the functional definition of institutions and in the expression of political order. As French philosopher Michel Foucault suggests, "power" informs all relationships and can emanate from anywhere in a system.[3] All forms of government exercise power represented through the architecture of governing institutions: palaces, parliaments, congresses, presidential homes, etc. Power is exercised by national governments, something that has emerged since the 18th century. The state exerts totalizing and individualizing forms of power.[4] States have a multitude of modes for exerting power on individuals, including economic factors, laws, systems of surveillance, violence, and architecture. Democratic political systems tend to use two chambers (elected and appointed) as part of a governing structure, typically with a president or a prime minister and various political parties. The selection of various architectural styles to represent government often looks to the past, often to a time of imagined or real glory in a nation's past. Architects, whether knowingly or not, often become involved in the activities perpetuated by the regime in power.

★ ★ ★

In late 18th century America, where tensions had brewed for years between the emerging American nation and Britain, war erupted in 1775. On July 4, 1776, the Second Continental Congress issued the United States Declaration of Independence, initially drafted by future US President and architect Thomas Jefferson (1743–1826). The document famously states "that all men are created equal" and cites many grievances against the British before claiming independence. The American Revolutionary War would last until 1783 when the terms of independence from Britain were ratified by the Treaty of Paris. The Constitution of the United States came into effect on March 4, 1789. In this document, one of the most important in history, the structure of the republic was defined with the office of the president and the Congress. The document contains a Bill of Rights and has been amended 27 times. As a result of revolution, there came the enormous task of building a nation, including its capital city and major governmental institutions.

A key figure in the definition of the new nation was Thomas Jefferson, statesman, architect, and slave owner. Jefferson began his interest in architecture as a young man when he started work on his own neo-Palladian house, Monticello, in Virginia, as early as 1769, a project he continued to develop for the next three decades. As a plantation owner, he owned dozens of black slaves who built his property as the centre of a carefully controlled world. Jefferson served a term as the governor of Virginia from 1779 to 1781, during which he was also asked to design the State Capitol in Richmond. In 1784, he was appointed the American Minister to France, where he would remain for five years. While in France, he befriended various architects and visited the Maison Carrée, a well-preserved Roman temple in southern France. This ancient monument provided Jefferson with a model for the Virginia State Capitol, which was eventually completed according to Jefferson's design in 1796. The scheme incorporated the House of Delegates and Senate, along with rooms for committees and clerks. Jefferson's design was intended to provide a model for future American institutional buildings based closely on ancient Roman architecture.

Jefferson's third significant architectural project was his design for the campus of the University of Virginia (1826), which he developed after the two terms of his presidency (1801–1809).[5] Based on the concept of the "academical village," the campus includes a rotunda building to house the library, ten pavilions housing classrooms and offices, a common green space, and "hotels" for students. The campus design relied heavily on black labour for its construction and maintenance. As historian Louis P. Nelson demonstrates, the original scheme did not adequately allow for the accommodation of the enslaved workers, but this changed over time. The area between the teaching pavilions and student hotels (transformed into gardens between 1948 and 1964) was separated by walled work yards where slaves prepared food and undertook other tasks, altering our understanding of the ideal nature of the original plan.[6]

As architectural historian Mabel O. Wilson shows, despite his writings, Jefferson considered blacks and indigenous peoples as being inferior to whites, although blacks, both free and enslaved, built many of the nation's key monuments. Wilson writes that Jefferson carefully sited his buildings so that "the white-columned Neoclassical buildings appeared to visitors as idyllic beacons of democratic values overlooking sublime nature unsullied by the presence of those spaces in which unsightly slaves toiled to make the land fertile and the lives of white citizens comfortable."[7] At the heart of the American Revolution were significant injustices and contradictions, which architecture underscored. The burgeoning American democracy did not grant the right to vote for black men until after the American Civil War (1870), and women did not until 1920.

In 1790 the decision was made to establish a new capital city on the banks of the Potomac River. The city of Washington, D.C., was laid out according to the Baroque designs of a French engineer and soldier named Pierre Charles l'Enfant (1754–1825). Featuring wide avenues, many on a diagonal, and focal points, the heart of the plan is the Mall, which is prominently located at the future President's House and the Capitol. The design for the landmark White House was by the architect James Hoban (1756–1821). Following in Jefferson's footsteps, it was also inspired by Roman architecture. L'Enfant's plan provided a framework for the long-term development of the city. Today, the Mall is lined with many national institutions; it is one of the world's great expressions of government and nationalism.

The Capitol is organized around its two primary spaces of government, the Senate and the House of Representatives (and originally the Supreme Court), where elected senators and representatives develop federal policies and laws. An unsuccessful competition was held in 1792 for the design of the Capitol. The commission was awarded to William Thornton (1759–1828) the following year, a doctor and amateur architect. Thornton was supported by Etienne (Stephen) Sulpice Hallett (1755–1825), a French-born architect. Years of conflict over the design followed, which impeded progress. After a fire in 1814, Charles Bullfinch (1763–1844) and Benjamin Latrobe (1794–1820), two of the most important early American architects, were involved in the completion of the initial building. Later in the century, the Capitol underwent further expansion, including the completion of the great cast-iron dome over the Rotunda by Thomas U. Walter (1804–1887) in 1868.

The governmental buildings of Washington were designed to express the democratic aspirations of a new democratic republic in which an elected president and Congress governed the nation. This expression of government would extend to state capitols such as the Massachusetts State House (1798) by Charles Bullfinch and

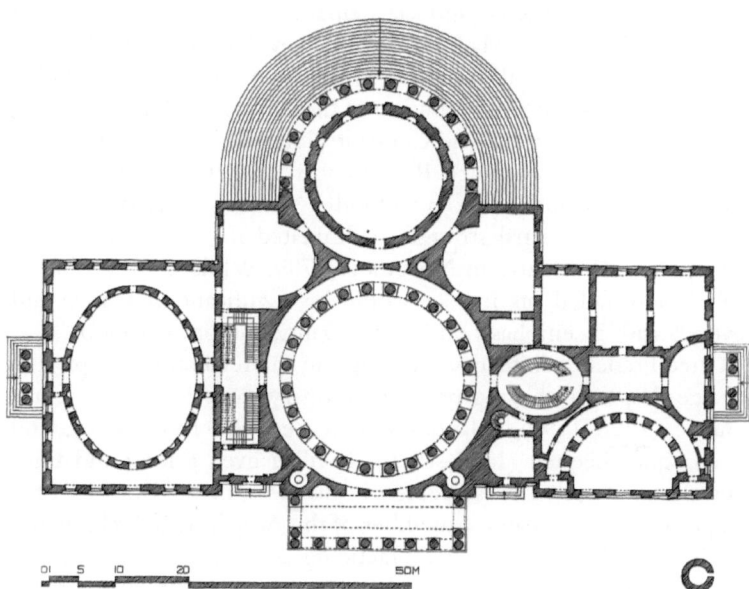

Figure 2.1 Main Floor Plan, William Thornton, United States Capitol, c. 1793–1797, Washington, D.C., USA. This early plan was organized around a central rotunda, with the House of Representatives located to the left and the smaller Senate chamber to the right; the second central circular space above the rotunda was deleted in later schemes. Drawing by Mohammad Moezzi.

the Nebraska State Capitol (1932) by Bertram Grosvenor Goodhue (1869–1924). The impact of the American Revolution would be wide-reaching, as historian Gordon S. Wood states:

> The Revolution not only radically changed the personal and social relationships of people, including the position of women, but also destroyed the aristocracy as it had been understood in the Western world for at least two millennia . . . it actually reconstituted what Americans meant by public or state power and brought about an entirely new kind of popular politics and a new kind of democratic officeholder . . . it made the interests and prosperity of ordinary people – their pursuits of happiness – the goal of society and government.[8]

★ ★ ★

In France, the Revolution was shorter lived. One notable event was the execution of the monarch Louis XIV and his family in 1793.

As a result of economic and class turmoil in France, the French Revolution started in May 1789. The Revolution involved many, often violent, historical twists and turns. Important events included the publication of the "Declaration of the Rights of Man" in August 1789, the ratification of a new constitution in 1791, and the establishment of the First French Republic in 1792. However, this was followed by the infamous and bloody "Reign of Terror" (1793–1794). Various internal struggles culminated in the rise to power of Napoleon Bonaparte in November 1799. While the Revolution itself largely failed, its impact would be significant in France and beyond, with its emphasis on liberty, egality, and brotherhood.

Three French architects would capture the revolutionary spirit of the age despite all having pre-revolutionary careers: Etienne-Louis Boullée (1728–1799), Claude-Nicolas Ledoux (1736–1806), and Jean-Jacques Lequeu (1757–1826). Boullée lived a long and uneventful life. Despite the radicalness of his ideas, he held various official positions and became a member of the Académie d'Architecture in 1762. Boullée's output as a practicing architect was limited to a few domestic works. He is best remembered for his sublime "visionary" or "theoretical" drawings that depict the institutions of a new city and various funerary monuments. His renderings of funerary monuments were celebrated, as was his cenotaph project to Sir Isaac Newton (1784), the great British scientist. In this unrealized project, an immense spherical structure intended to represent the cosmos is rendered in dramatic shadow and light.

Boullée expressed his core ideas in an unpublished manuscript, "Architecture, Essay on Art," in which he argues that buildings should be "poems" that "should arouse in us sensations that correspond to the function of the building in question."[9] In this essay, he also describes institutions for a city in text and drawings. These include a basilica, a theatre, a palace of justice, a national palace, a municipal palace, a coliseum, a public library, a city entrance, etc. The drawing of the National Palace (1785) depicts a building with constitutional laws inscribed into its façade, a tangible way of describing the purpose of the building.

Claude-Nicolas Ledoux, arguably the greatest French architect of the second half of the 18th century, was an architect who devised a recognizable style and tackled new challenges. Ledoux came from a humble background. After he completed his education, he quickly established himself as an architect with wealthy and influential clients. Important designs included the Hôtel Guimard (1771), a house for a famous dancer, and various works for Mme du Barry, the official mistress to King Louis XV. With his patrons' support, Ledoux was appointed inspector of saltworks and became a member of the Academy in 1773, giving him the title of "Architecte du Roi" or architect to the king.

His first important public commission was the saltworks at Arc et Senans (1779), near the forest of Chaux in eastern France. Salt was a vital and expensive commodity that was produced from saline springs that required large quantities of wood to boil down the salty liquid. Ledoux's design is an early work of industrial architecture. The complex is organized in a semi-circle around the house of the director from which operations could be monitored. Flanking the house of the director are sheds where the evaporation process occurred. Arranged around the semi-circle are storage buildings, apartments for workers, offices, and a grotto-like entry building. Like Boullée, Ledoux was also an advocate for the use of primary forms. His design is a prime example of "architecture parlante," a concept often attached to Ledoux's work. This means that the architect uses techniques that "speak" to the function of the building. This concept was important as a wide range of new building types were emerging at the time.

In the 1780s, Ledoux was again employed by the governmental agency responsible for collecting customs and monitoring the tobacco and salt industries. He designed offices for the organization and the controversial custom/toll houses, or *barrières*, that were constructed around Paris. This commission involved the design of over 50 toll houses, each an essay on primary form and on Ledoux's forceful use of the classical orders. Intended to demonstrate the power of the state and to prevent smuggling, the *barrières* would become symbols of government oppression during and after the Revolution. Ledoux became a despised public figure as a result. In 1793, He was imprisoned for a year during the Reign of Terror.

After his release from prison Ledoux developed his visionary text *L'architecture considérée sous le rapport de l'art, des moeurs et de la legislation* (or *Architecture Considered in Relation to Art, Mores, and Legislation*) published in 1804 and 1847. In the text, Ledoux developed his scheme for the Royal Saltworks into a vision of an ideal city. His design doubled the original saltworks plan and scattered throughout a pastoral surrounding landscape a series of novel institutions, each a demonstration of the concept of "architecture parlante." The most explicit example of this is the Oïkéma, or the house of sexual instruction, which features a plan based on the phallus. The scheme, dedicated to "artistic workmen" in an Eden-like setting, featured designs for houses for rural caretakers, coopers, woodcutters, charcoal burners, and the like. Ledoux writes:

> You must come to terms with the site, allowing it to suggest methods of relating the building both to its function and to its position in the plan. Any shape that can be drawn by a single compass stroke is recognized by good taste. The circle and the square are the letters of the alphabet with which the author will spell out his best work. With these, epic poems and elegies, hymns to the gods and simple airs for shepherds, are composed; temples can rise up to Valour, Strength, and Voluptuousness; houses are built as well as the humblest places used by the community.[10]

Jean-Jacques Lequeu is the least known of the three "revolutionary" architects. His legacy is a series of fantastical drawings, including manuscripts for several unpublished treatises, that he deposited in the Bibliothèque Royale (now the national library) just before he died. Celebrated for his meticulous draftsmanship, his design for a "Temple of Equality" (1794) demonstrated his vision for revolutionary architecture.[11]

★ ★ ★

A political revolution, usually triggered by an uprising of people, is intended to result in a better society. Architecture is one mode for expressing the aspirations of revolutionary forces. In America, the use of architecture derived from Roman precedents to express the new republic can be seen as an ironic choice of styles, given that Rome was ruled by emperors. And, as architectural historian Anthony Vidler argues, in the end, there isn't really an architecture that consistently captures the French Revolution. In fact, the destruction of monuments representing the French monarchical system more accurately portrays the revolutionary spirit of the age.[12] Nevertheless, the political revolutions of the late 18th century resulted in many changes that would affect the course of modern architecture.

NOTES

1 Jack A. Goldstone, *Revolutions: A Very Short Introduction* (Oxford: Oxford University Press, 2014), p. 4.

2 Ibid., p. 19.

3 See Richard A. Lynch, "Foucault's Theory of Power," in Dianna Taylor, ed., *Michel Foucault: Key Concepts* (London: Routledge, 2014), pp. 13–26.

4 Michel Foucault, "The Subject and Power," in James D. Faubion, ed., *Michel Foucault: Power* (New York: The New Press, 2000), p. 332.

5 See Lloyd De Witt and Corey Piper, eds., *Thomas Jefferson, Architect: Palladian Models, Democratic Principles, and the Conflict of Ideals* (New Haven: Yale University Press, 2019).

6 Louis P. Nelson, "The Architecture of Democracy in a Landscape of Slavery: Design and Construction of Jefferson's University," in Lloyd De Witt and Corey Piper, eds., *Thomas Jefferson, Architect: Palladian Models, Democratic Principles, and the Conflict of Ideals* (New Haven: Yale University Press, 2019), p. 115.

7 Mabel O. Wilson, "Notes on Thomas Jefferson's Virginia Capitol," *Architect Magazine*, Posted Dec. 28, 2020. https://www.architectmagazine.com/design/notes-on-thomas-jeffersons-virginia-capitol_o. Accessed August 20, 2021.

8 Gordon S. Wood, *The Radicalism of the American Revolution* (New York: Vintage Books, 1993), pp. 7–8.

9 Etienne-Louis Boullée, "Architecture, Essay on Art," in H. Rosenau, ed., *Boullée and Visionary Architecture* (London: Academy Editions, 1976), p. 82.

10 Claude-Nicolas Ledoux, "Architecture Considered in Relation to Art, Mores, and Legislation," in E.G. Holt, ed., *From the Classicists to the Impressionists: Art and Architecture in the Nineteenth Century* (New York: Anchor Books, 1966), p. 242.

11 Lequeu's manuscripts on *Architecture Civile, Nouvelle Methode, Figures Lascives*, and *Figures et Architecture* are reproduced in Philippe Duboy, *Lequeu: An Architectural Enigma* (Cambridge, MA: MIT Press, 1986).

12 See Anthony Vidler, "Researching Revolutionary Architecture," *Journal of Architectural Education*, vol. 44, no. 4 (August 1991), pp. 206–210.

SUGGESTED READING

Bergdoll, Barry. *European Architecture 1750–1890*. Oxford: Oxford University Press, 2000.

De Witt, Lloyd and Corey Piper, eds. *Thomas Jefferson, Architect: Palladian Models, Democratic Principles, and the Conflict of Ideals*. New Haven: Yale University Press, 2019.

Fontana-Giusti, Gordana. *Foucault for Architects*. London: Routledge, 2013.

Reps, John W. *Monumental Washington: The Planning and Development of the Capital Center*. Princeton: Princeton University Press, 1967.

Vidler, Anthony. *Claude-Nicholas Ledoux: Architecture and Utopia in the Era of the French Revolution*. Basel: Birkhäuser, 2020.

3

PICTURESQUE AND SUBLIME

The Picturesque, a popular style of landscape architecture developed in Britain during the 18th century, emphasized naturalistic landscapes that a viewer moved through. In the Picturesque garden, visitors encountered carefully composed views, or "pictures," that were inspired by the landscape paintings of various 17th-century artists.[1] The English approach to landscape was in direct opposition to the French formal tradition of the previous century, with its geometrically composed landscapes and plantings. Ideas developed in landscape design were then transposed to architecture. The great Scottish architect Robert Adam (1728–1792) describes a picturesque architecture:

> Movement is meant to express, the rise and fall, the advance and recess, with other diversity of form, in the different parts of a building, so as to add greatly to the picturesque of the composition. For the rising and falling, advancing and receding, with the convexity and the concavity, and other forms of the great parts, have the same effect in architecture, that hill and dale, fore-ground and distance, swelling and sinking have in a landscape: That is, they serve to produce an agreeable and diversified contour, that groups and contrasts like a picture, and creates a variety of light and shade, which gives great spirit, beauty and effect to the composition.[2]

Adam suggests an architecture that is irregular in form and silhouette, producing "great spirit, beauty and effect." The Picturesque style invoked new concepts of "beauty" and the notion that a garden or a building could evoke a wide range of emotions and sensations, in particular those associated with the "sublime."

DOI: 10.4324/9781003403975-3

Various developments during the 18th century were vital for laying the foundations for the emergence of fully modern architecture at the beginning of the 20th century. Beyond conjuring emotional responses, this involved new ways of composing and moving through landscapes and buildings. These factors are particularly evident in the evolution of the villa, an important building type in the development of modern architecture.[3]

★ ★ ★

A new approach to aesthetics occurred in the 18th century and was inspired by the philosopher John Locke's *Essay on Human Understanding* (1690) and the subsequent writings of Joseph Addison entitled "The Pleasures of the Imagination" (1712). When considering buildings, Addison, an influential writer, places emphasis not on "beautiful proportions" but on how they create thoughts and ideas in the mind of an observer.[4] Both Locke and Addison introduced psychology into design. These ideas were further developed in the philosopher Edmund Burke's *A Philosophical Enquiry into the Origin of Our Ideas of the Sublime and Beautiful* (1757), which presents the new concepts of beauty and the "sublime." In his introductory section on Taste, Burke writes:

> On the whole it appears to me, that what is called Taste, in its most general acceptation, is not a simple idea, but is partly made up of a perception of the primary pleasures of sense, of the secondary pleasures of the imagination, and the conclusions of the reasoning faculty, concerning the various relations of these, and concerning the human passions, manners, and actions.[5]

Burke goes on in the first part to examine a range of human emotions, from pain and pleasure, to delight and pleasure, and joy and grief. He introduces the "sublime" as producing the strongest human emotions, linking it to the sensation of terror. And he introduces the notion of "beauty" as a counterpart, along with behaviours such as sympathy, imitation, and ambition.

The second part of Burke's text is devoted to the concept of the sublime, one of the defining ideas of the 18th century. It is one that captured many of the complexities of the period. The feeling of the sublime, as astonished terror, can be evoked by experiencing the immensity of mountains or the vastness of the ocean; it can be felt around certain animals, such as poisonous snakes, and by being in the presence of vast power. Further, certain conditions, such as darkness, solitude, and silence, can induce feelings of the sublime. The sublime can be manifest in the infinite, in the play of light and dark, and in the impact of certain sounds, smells, and tastes.[6] Often associated with sensations of awe, gloom, and melancholy, the sublime was captured in a series of drawings for enormous funeral monuments produced in the late 18th century by the French visionary architect Etienne-Louis Boullée (1728–1799) that expressed the mood of a changing time in which the role of religion was being questioned.

In the third part of the text on beauty, Burke claims that classical ideals such as proportion, fitness, and perfection are not the basis for the beautiful. He states that beauty is not related to reasoning, nor is it related to measure, geometry, or calculation.[7] In a direct challenge to classical principles, he argues that beautiful humans can have a wide range of proportions, questioning the ideal classical figure of a young man described by the ancient Roman architect Vitruvius (c. 80–15 BC) and famously drawn by the Renaissance artist Leonardo da Vinci around 1487.[8] Further, Burke raises the question of "deformity" and the idea that "ugliness" is the opposite of beauty. In discussing the relationship between utility (fitness) and beauty, Burke states that many useful things are not beautiful, and therefore, utility is not a quality of beauty.[9] Beauty, as opposed to the sublime, encompasses smallness, smoothness, gradual variation, delicacy, and clear colour.[10] Ultimately, he concludes that the sublime is based on pain, while beauty is based on pleasure. In the writings of these British thinkers, new concepts based on human experience challenged tradition and pointed forward to subsequent developments.

★ ★ ★

By abandoning many traditional determinants of good design, 18th century British landscape architects and architects were free to introduce new concepts of beauty and taste. Instead of relying on classical principles, which Vitruvius equated with order, arrangement, eurythmy, symmetry, propriety, and economy,[11] these designers were interested in how the experience of a landscape or building could evoke sensations and emotions. As noted previously, Vitruvius also referenced the human body as the perfect paradigm of design. This association with the human figure is found in the three basic classical orders: the Doric (a mature man), the Ionic (a mature woman), and the Corinthian (a young woman).

The English Picturesque gardens of the 18th century were part of large country estates of the land-owning classes. These vast estates often featured a country house inspired by the influential late Renaissance Italian architect Andrea Palladio (1508–1580). The gardens used carefully placed architectural "follies" to create historical and narrative associations. These were usually classical temples, ruined structures, or grottoes. Architecture was used to support pictorial compositions in the landscape that were experienced as one moved through a garden. The gardens were highly evocative, able to express a broad range of emotions, including the beautiful and the sublime. It is worth noting that in the 18th century, there was an awareness in Britain of Chinese garden design, which traditionally featured naturalistic landscapes, although on a smaller scale.

Garden designers work with the earth, landforms, vegetation, architecture, and water. Garden commentator Thomas Whately's description of the qualities of water in an English garden from his *Observations on Modern Gardening* (1770) demonstrates how Picturesque garden designers could trigger the imagination of those viewing the gardens:

> So various are the characters that water can assume, that there is scarcely an idea in which it may not concur, or an impression which it cannot enforce: a deep stagnated pool, dank and dark with shades which it dimly reflects befits the seat of melancholy . . . a brisker current, which wantons in little eddies over a bright sandy bottom, or babbles among pebbles, spreads cheerfulness all around . . . the roar and rage of a torrent, its force, its violence, its impetuosity, tend to inspire terror; that terror, which, whether as cause or effect, is so nearly allied with sublimity.[12]

The "characters" that Whately describes, including those inspired by artificial architectural ruins, evoke the passing of time and, ultimately, the decay that everything experiences.

The early phase of the English Picturesque garden was defined by the painter and designer William Kent (1685–1748), who often reworked gardens. A significant early work by Kent is his redesign of the Rousham Garden in Oxfordshire (1744), which involved softening the features of the garden, introducing various architectural and sculptural elements, and creating the impression that the garden extended into the surrounding landscape. Kent used a similar approach at the much larger garden at Stowe (1748). A particularly distinctive garden is Stourhead (1783) in Wiltshire, designed by owners Henry Hoare and Richard Colt Hoare, where the visitor to the garden journeys around an artificial lake encountering various carefully composed views. Lancelot "Capability" Brown (1716–1783), who defined the second phase of the English Picturesque garden, was responsible for many gardens that used simple and open designs that were less reliant on a pictorial approach. Ultimately, the English Picturesque garden was the product of a wealthy society prepared to question traditional values and to draw inspiration from a variety of sources.

★ ★ ★

The defining building type during the late 18th and early 19th century, according to architectural historian Peter Collins, was the villa, which would also be a formative building type for modern architects including Frank Lloyd Wright and Le Corbusier.[13] As a more informal type of country house, the villa descends from Roman times. And while most large English country houses of the 18th century were neo-Palladian, various garden designers began to introduce Gothic elements into the garden. Gothic architecture is commonly associated with the great medieval cathedrals of Europe and features the use of elements such as pointed arches, flying buttresses, and steep roofs. It is a style that had largely been out of fashion until it was revived in the 18th and 19th centuries. Further, in the middle of the 18th century, architects also began to consider ordinary buildings, such as cottages, as worthy of study, which introduced rustic features to landscape and building design as well.

Two early neo-Gothic houses were Strawberry Hill (1754) at Twickenham by the writer and politician Horace Walpole (1717–1797) for himself and Fonthill Abbey (1813) in Wiltshire for William Beckford, designed by the architect James Wyatt (1746–1813). Both houses were asymmetrical in design and composition, composed of Gothic elements, and built to create a range of affects. The emergence of neo-Gothic villas in the 18th century responded to the Picturesque, as Gothic was seen as a more varied and flexible style of architecture capable of creating a response to a landscape and evoking feelings of the sublime. As Collins states, "in these structures originated the notion of free planning," resulting in "freely designed shapes."[14] Eventually, this would lead to a relationship which matched form and function (see Chapter 5).

Richard Payne Knight (1750–1824) was a somewhat controversial writer, collector, and politician who inherited family wealth. Like many rich Englishmen of his generation, he travelled to Italy and Europe as part of a "Grand Tour" of historical sites. Knight became one of the late promoters of the Picturesque tradition. His *Analytical*

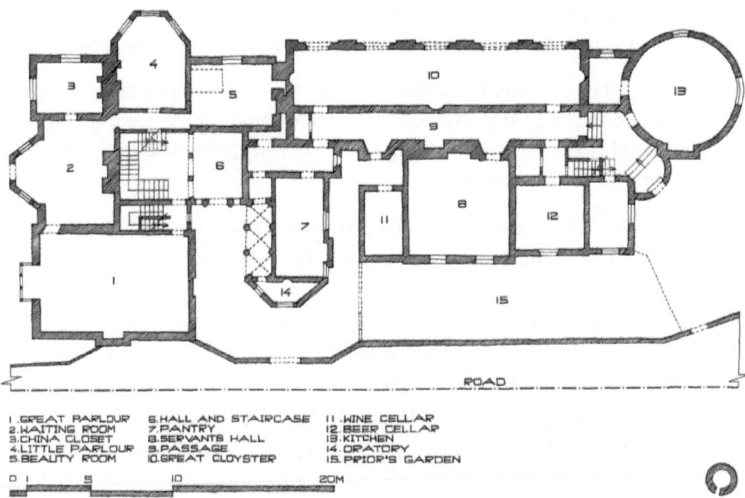

1.GREAT PARLOUR   6.HALL AND STAIRCASE   11.WINE CELLAR
2.WAITING ROOM   7.PANTRY   12.BEER CELLAR
3.CHINA CLOSET   8.SERVANTS HALL   13.KITCHEN
4.LITTLE PARLOUR   9.PASSAGE   14.ORATORY
5.BEAUTY ROOM   10.GREAT CLOYSTER   15.PRIOR'S GARDEN

Figure 3.1 Main Floor Plan, Horace Walpole, Strawberry Hill, 1754, Twicken-ham, England. The design features a series of regular spaces arranged in an irregular and Picturesque manner along a central corridor. Drawing by Mohammad Moezzi.

Inquiry into the Principles of Taste, published in 1805, discusses the concept of the "association of ideas," he writes:

> As all the pleasures of intellect arise from the association of ideas, the more the materials of association are multiplied, the more the sphere of these pleasures be enlarged. To a mind richly stored, almost every object of nature or art, that presents itself to the senses, either excites fresh trains and combinations of ideas, or vivifies and strengthens those which existed before.[15]

This was a development of notions that had been circulating for over a century with an emphasis on ideas over emotions.

Between 1772 and 1778, Knight built Downton Castle in Hertfordshire, England as an expression of his ideas, particularly the radical use of an irregular plan. The design was inspired, it seems, by the medieval castle as an older building type, one that was ideal for expressing qualities of the beautiful and the sublime. However, Knight did not opt for a medieval style in the original design; instead, the building was designed in his interpretation of the Classical style. Gothic additions to the house were undertaken in the mid-19th century. The plan is innovative in that it uses function to create an irregular design. As architectural historian Andrew Ballantyne writes:

> Knight's plan . . . was remarkable. Internally its arrangements abided by the conventions of the day, but the conventional rooms were grouped in a strikingly original effect, giving rise to the irregular and unaccountable appearance of the exterior.[16]

Downton Castle is an early example of picturesque architecture and the use of the irregular plan organized according to function and the site.

The emphasis on dynamic asymmetrical compositions, such as Downton Castle, foreshadows *The International Style* exhibition held at the Museum of Modern Art in New York in 1932 (see chapter 12). According to Henry-Russell Hitchcock and Philip Johnson, the curators of the exhibition, the International Style, as the culmination of modern architectural developments in the 1920s, was defined by volume, regularity, and the avoidance of applied decoration.[17] In the catalogue, Hitchcock and Johnson expand on the idea of "regularity," which involved structural consistency, avoided axial symmetry, diverged from pure functionalism, and sought to create visual interest.[18] Ultimately, modern architects used compositional approaches that were not classical; instead, they employed a functional organization of spaces that resulted in form.[19]

Finally, the picturesque was also adopted in urban design, especially to create dynamic vistas and interesting sequences of spaces in cities. This is found in Georgian cities, such as Bath and Edinburgh, and in John Nash's (1752–1835) transformation of London with Regent's Park and Regent's Street. John Summerson, the important British architectural historian, confirms that Nash took an approach to urban design inspired by landscape design:

> This curious mixture of *laissez-faire* and spasmodic control reflects Nash's philosophy of street design as it evolved in the unique circumstances with which it faced. It was nothing if not realistic. It allowed individual expression by different users but at the same time aimed at shuffling the accidental into picturesque coherence. It was a landscape philosophy brought to bear on townscape.[20]

The concept of carefully composed streetscape design was also a feature of late 19th-century urban design trends, including the City Beautiful and Garden City movements (see Chapter 7).

★ ★ ★

During the 18th century, designers were willing to break from history, redefine beauty, and employ concepts such as the sublime in their work. The notion of expressing feelings of melancholy, sadness, awesomeness, ugliness, and strangeness introduced psychology into design. At the same time, the Picturesque inspired new and dynamic approaches to landscape and building design that would become a hallmark of modern architecture. The concept of the sublime has continued to impact 20th-century thinking. The American abstract expressionist painter Barnett Newman (1905–1970) wrote in 1948, while discussing the sublime, that the "impulse of modern art was this desire to destroy beauty."[21] The sublime has also been taken up by various Postmodern philosophers, including Jean-François Lyotard.[22]

NOTES

1 Such as Nicholas Poussin (1594–1665) and Claude Lorrain (1600–1682).

2 Robert Adam quoted in Robin Middleton, *Neoclassical and 19th Century Architecture* (New York: Harry N. Abrams Inc., 1980), p. 48.

3 See James S. Ackerman, *The Villa: Form and Ideology of Country Houses* (Princeton: Princeton University Press, 1990).

4 Peter Collins, *Changing Ideals in Modern Architecture, 1750–1950* (Montreal: MQUP, 1967), p. 45.

5 Edmund Burke, *A Philosophical Enquiry into the Origin of Our Ideas of the Sublime and Beautiful* (London: Vernor and Hood et al., 1798), p. 30.

6 See Ibid., pp. 41–159.

7 See Ibid., pp. 164–166.

8 See Ibid., pp. 181–183.

9 See Ibid., pp. 191–202.

10 See Ibid., pp. 209–221.

11 Vitruvius, *The Ten Books of Architecture* (New York: Dover Publications Inc., 1960), pp. 13–16.

12 Thomas Whately quoted in John Dixon Hunt and Peter Willis, eds., *The Genius of the Place: The English Landscape Garden 1620–1820* (Cambridge, MA: MIT Press, 1988), pp. 302–303.

13 Collins, *Changing Ideals in Modern Architecture*, pp. 42–43.

14 Ibid., p. 58.

15 Richard Payne Knight quoted in Hunt and Willis, eds., *The Genius of the Place, p.* 348.

16 Andrew Ballantyne, "Downton Castle: Function and Meaning," *Architectural History*, vol. 32 (1989), p. 114.

17 Henry-Russell Hitchcock and Philip Johnson, *The International Style* (New York: W.W. Norton & Co., 1966), p. 13.

18 See Ibid., pp. 56–68.

19 The relationship between modernity and the picturesque is examined in: Caroline Constant, "The Barcelona Pavilion as Landscape Garden: Modernity and the Picturesque," in *The Modern Architectural Landscape* (Minneapolis: University of Minnesota Press, 2012), pp. 45–60.

20 John Summerson, *The Life and Work of John Nash, Architect* (London: George Allen & Unwin, 1980), p. 132.

21 Barnett Newman, "The Sublime Is Now," in Herschel B. Chipp, ed., *Theories of Modern Art* (Berkeley: University of California Press, 1968), p. 552.

22 See Jean-François Lyotard, *The Postmodern Condition: A Report on Knowledge* (Manchester: Manchester University Press, 1984).

SUGGESTED READING

Collins, Peter. *Changing Ideals in Modern Architecture, 1750–1950*. Montreal: MQUP, 1967.

Hitchcock, Henry-Russell and Philip Johnson. *The International Style*. New York: W.W. Norton & Co., 1966.

Hunt, John Dixon and Peter Willis, eds. *The Genius of the Place: The English Landscape Garden 1620–1820*. Cambridge, MA: MIT Press, 1988.

Vidler, Anthony. *The Architectural Uncanny: Essays in the Modern Unhomely*. Cambridge, MA: MIT Press, 1992.

Watkin, David. *The English Vision: Picturesque in Architecture, Landscape and Garden Design*. London: J. Murray, 1982.

4

TECHNOLOGY AND MATERIALS

Beyond the American and French Revolutions, the other great revolution of the late 18th century was the Industrial Revolution (1760–1830), which would radically change the planet by creating expanded mining operations, extensive transportation systems, factory cities, taller buildings, and the destructive by-products of technological innovation. The Industrial Revolution produced new manufacturing processes and materials, including steel, plate glass, and reinforced concrete, that were essential to defining modern architecture. New machines such as the railway locomotive, the steamship, the elevator, the automobile, and the airplane would collapse people's sense of time and space. The 19th century also witnessed the emergence of early forms of "communications" technology, including the telegraph, light bulb, and the telephone, ultimately creating media theorist Marshall McLuhan's concept of the "global village."[1] The heroes of the period were engineers and inventors, such as George Stephenson (1781–1848), Isambard Kingdom Brunel (1806–1859), and Thomas Alva Edison (1847–1931), who created marvels with the new technologies. They essentially married the knowledge of modern science to practical inventions that changed lives around the world.

The effect on architecture would be dramatic as the new materials enabled new forms of expression. Major societal and economic changes led to the design of new types of commercial and industrial buildings: factories, docks and warehouses, railway stations, hotels, markets, department stores, banks, and office buildings. The rapid

DOI: 10.4324/9781003403975-4

change brought on by industrialization and social/political change meant many new types of institutions were established, from hospitals, asylums, and prisons to public museums, concert halls, and libraries. Globally, cities rapidly expanded, drawing millions of people from rural areas. As urban populations dramatically increased and new types of buildings and services appeared, the modern city was born (see Chapter 7).

★ ★ ★

The discipline of engineering, which was so essential for defining the modern architecture of the early 20th century, began with military engineering, particularly in France in the late 17th and early 18th centuries. Military figures such as Sébastien le Prestre de Vauban (1633–1707) and Bernard Forest de Bélidor (1698–1761) systematized the design of military fortifications. This included developing specifications for construction and early efforts to calculate the forces on retaining walls. By the middle of the 18th century, civil engineering, devoted mainly to the design of bridges and roads, emerged as a separate discipline from architecture. The creation of the École des Ponts et Chaussées (School of Bridges and Roads) by Jean-Rodolphe Perronet (1708–1794) in Paris in 1747 was a turning point in the history of civil engineering. Perronet's design for a bridge at Neuilly near Paris, completed in 1772, used early forms of structural calculation. The establishment of the École Polytechnique in Paris in 1795, during the French Revolution, was also a key moment in the history of engineering.[2]

According to historian Hans Straub, Charles Auguste Coulomb (1736–1806) must be considered the founder of structural analysis or building statics.[3] However, it was Louis Marie Henri Navier (1785–1836) who truly established the field, particularly in his lectures to students at the École Polytechnique, first published in 1826. This would lead to further theoretical developments in the field of structural design, something for which the French were famous.[4]

An early example of the new methods modifying traditional practices occurred at St. Peter's Basilica in Rome after cracks appeared in the dome; a controversial report produced in 1748 outlined solutions to the problem that used early forms of analysis. Probably the earliest work of architecture to use an "engineering" or scientific approach in its structural design was the church of Ste. Geneviève in Paris (1790) by the architect Jacques-Germain Soufflot (1713–1780). The design significantly reduced the structural footprint of a typical 18th-century neo-Classical church based on new ideas about the strength of materials. Unfortunately, soon after completion, Ste. Geneviève (now the Panthéon) developed structural cracks due to poor construction. This situation fuelled an intense debate between traditionalists who argued for time-tested approaches to construction and proponents of the new methods of scientific calculation.[5]

★ ★ ★

The Industrial Revolution began in 18th-century Britain and, over the next century, would spread around the world, driven by inventions such as the iron blast furnace, the steam engine, and the spinning jenny.[6] Vital to the development of the Industrial Revolution were advances during the 17th and 18th centuries in the design of steam engines. Large, crude versions were developed for coal mining since coal was an essential energy source. In 1776, the Scottish inventor and engineer James Watt (1736–1819) introduced a set of improvements which would lead to the broad use of steam power for railways, shipping, and manufacturing.

In the early 19th century, the railway locomotive was pioneered by various figures; the first experiment with passenger rail occurred on the Stockton and Darlington line (1825), built by George Stephenson. A significant feat of engineering, the line was designed primarily to transport coal. It launched the railway era, which overtook the world.[7] The design of rails for the new railway industry progressed quickly, resulting first in the use of cast iron and then the stronger wrought iron. Early structural iron beams could now be manufactured in a way similar to rails and were first used in warehouses and factory structures where there was a need for open spaces to accommodate machinery placement.

By the late 18th century, the bridge, as a structure, began to increase in span as new materials and methods drove innovation. Historically, bridges were designed by architects and built of masonry, but by the 19th century, they were the domain of engineers and began to incorporate cast and wrought iron, and eventually steel and reinforced concrete. The Coalbrookdale Bridge (1779), with a span of 30.6 metres (100.5 feet), by Abraham Darby III, T.F. Pritchard, and John Wilkinson, was the first important structure made of cast iron arches. However, the expressive potential inherent in the new material was yet to be realized as the design essentially mimicked a stone bridge.[8]

In the 19th century, the suspension bridge, an old form of bridge construction, was revived as engineers realized how iron chains and steel cables could allow for much longer spans. The Clifton Suspension Bridge in Bristol, completed in 1864, designed by Isambard Kingdom Brunel, William Henry Barlow, and John Hawkshaw, is a striking example of a suspension bridge that used wrought iron chains for a span of 214.0 metres (702 feet). The later Brooklyn Bridge (1873) by the engineer John A. Roebling (1806–1869) used a steel cable for the suspension system; its long span is 486 metres (1595 feet). Other notable 19th-century bridges include the Britannia Bridge (1850) across the Menai Straits, by Robert Stephenson (1803–1859) and William Fairbairn, built using box girders of wrought iron plate. The Firth of Forth Bridge (1890) in Scotland, by engineers Sir John Fowler and Sir Benjamin Baker, dramatically used a tubular steel cantilever structure.[9]

Despite the significant difference in scale between works of engineering infrastructure and architecture, key developments occurred in the structuring of buildings. Iron was first used in a limited way for certain structural elements in industrial buildings and then for entire structural and exterior envelope systems. An important early example was the Library of Ste. Geneviève (1850) in Paris by Henri Labrouste (1801–1875), where iron was used for the columns in the reading room and for the roof structure. A similar approach was employed by Labrouste for the Bibliothèque Nationale, which was completed a few years later. These two buildings demonstrated how much more slender iron columns are than stone ones. Architects throughout the second half of the 19th century struggled with the design challenges associated with the new structural properties and proportions of iron and steel.

Developments in the manufacture of glass, where larger sheets of high-quality glass could be manufactured in quantity, were also essential to creating new types of buildings. Iron and glass were used extensively in the construction of large railway sheds, greenhouses, market halls, and exhibition buildings. The greenhouse designer and landscape architect Joseph Paxton (1801–1865) designed one of the pivotal buildings of the 19th century, the Crystal Palace in London, for the Great Exposition of 1851. The building was 564 metres (1851 feet) long and built of prefabricated cast iron and glass panels on a 2.4 metre module (8 feet). Paxton demonstrated that a very large temporary building could be manufactured and erected in less than eight months. In many ways, the Crystal Palace celebrated the aspirations and innovations of the 19th century.[10] The 300 metre (974 feet) tall Eiffel Tower, completed for the 1889 Paris Exposition by the distinguished engineer Gustave Eiffel (1832–1923), was built of wrought iron and demonstrated how the material performed in a vertical configuration. It would become an iconic symbol of Paris and of the age.

★ ★ ★

In 1855, the English inventor Henry Bessemer (1813–1898) devised a new way of mechanically pushing air through a furnace, resulting in the creation of steel, a material with important tensile properties and the strongest and most versatile form of iron. This innovation resulted in the development of two signature materials of modern architecture: steel and reinforced concrete. In 1857, the American industrialist Elisha Graves Otis (1811–1861) patented a "safe" elevator, guaranteed not to plunge out of control if the cable should break (see Chapter 13). Architects and engineers in Chicago and New York soon employed these innovations to create the tall commercial office building. As Louis H. Sullivan (1856–1924), a pioneering figure in the development of the skyscraper, describes the "modern office building":

> offices are necessary for the transaction of business; the invention and perfection of high-speed elevators make vertical travel, that was once tedious and painful, now easy and comfortable; development of steel manufacture has shown the way to safe, rigid, economical constructions rising to a great height; continued growth of centers and rise in value of ground, stimulate an increase in the number of stories; these successfully piled one upon another, react on ground values.[11]

The Chicago fire of 1871 provided an opportunity for redevelopment. The city was rebuilt as a modern city with a downtown business core defined by tall office buildings, hotels, and department stores. The first skyscraper is attributed to William Le Baron Jenney (1832–1907), a Paris-trained engineer who opened his design practice in Chicago in 1868. He produced a tall fireprotected steel frame building, the Home Insurance building of 1885. The façade was hung from the structure, effectively creating the "curtain" wall and resulting in the building plan and façade operating independently of the structure. Jenney's pioneering concept was then advanced by other architects and engineers. The development of the steel "Chicago Frame" during the 1880s and 1890s was a crucial idea in the progress towards a fully modern architecture.[12]

A series of designs in the next few years by several large Chicago firms advanced the expression of the tall building. The 12-storey Tacoma Building by Holabird & Roche from 1889 emphasized each floor rather than an expression of vertical continuity. Much the same can be said of Burnham & Root's 15-storey Reliance Building (1895). Its modernity comes from other innovations: large expansive windows (known as the "Chicago window"), glazed white tile cladding, and a simple top, creating a light modern feeling.

The firm of Adler & Sullivan combined the talents of engineer Dankmar Adler (1844–1900) with the genius of Sullivan. It would play a crucial role in the Chicago architectural scene, contributing to the refinement of the tall building as a type. Sullivan was a vital figure, influenced by the architecture of Henry Hobson Richardson (1838–1886), the Boston-based architect prolific in a neo-Romanesque style, and the idiosyncratic Philadelphia-based architect Frank Furness (1839–1912) for whom he had worked. Sullivan was also the mentor for a young Frank Lloyd Wright (see Chapter 10). Sullivan, like several 19th century American architects, studied architecture at the famous École des Beaux-Arts in Paris before beginning his employment with Adler in 1879. An iconoclastic poet, he developed a lush and unique approach to ornamentation that employed vegetation in a geometric order inspired by Islamic design and consistent with the Art Nouveau design of the period.

An important early work for the Adler & Sullivan firm was the Auditorium Building (1890) in Chicago, a very large multi-use urban building incorporating a grand performance space, a hotel, and offices. Another breakthrough design for Sullivan was the Wainwright Building (1891) in St. Louis, which was the first tall building to truly express its verticality. It is a robust building executed in red brick and terracotta, employing an extruded order that unifies the middle seven stories and luxurious ornamentation featured on spandrel panels and in the cornice. This emphasis on verticality would inspire many subsequent skyscraper designs, like the neo-Gothic Woolworth Building (1913) in New York by Cass Gilbert (1859–1934). Sullivan's design for the Carson Pirie Scott Store (1904) would consolidate the use of the Chicago window in commercial buildings.

In 1922, the Chicago Tribune newspaper sponsored an international design competition for the design of its new headquarters. It pitted traditionalists proposing neo-Gothic and neo-Classical schemes against modernists such as Walter Gropius (1883–1969).

Figure 4.1 Main Elevation, Adler & Sullivan, Wainwright Building, 1891, St. Louis, Missouri, USA. The elevation is structured by a solid two-storey commercial base which supports seven storeys of office space in a unified expression of verticality; the building is topped off with a highly ornamented cornice. Drawing by Mohammad Moezzi.

The competition signalled the end of traditional design, although the great American Art Deco skyscrapers of the 1930s retained a sense of this along with ornamentation that referenced modern industry.

Ultimately, the tall building, normally devoted to office and residential functions, represents the use of technology to create "the most obvious symbol of capitalistic speculation and private property ownership."[13] The tall building continues to symbolize economic progress for cities across the world. Another result of the developments in Chicago and New York was the creation of the large professional architectural firm, scaled for large commercial buildings. The modern architect Richard Neutra writes of working at Holabird & Roche in the 1920s:

> [T]he firm was surprisingly capable of breeding its own designers, its own engineers, its methodic and technological ideas of procedure. And original procedure begets the original product. Such an office was really a training camp for structural talent and a generator of technical determinants of design.[14]

The drive towards modern architecture in Chicago was briefly interrupted by the World's Columbian Exposition of 1893, which marked a return to traditional principles of composition and style. Based on a plan developed by Daniel H. Burnham (1846–1912) and the important landscape architect Frederick Law Olmstead (1822–1903), the formal design incorporates a number of large white neo-Classical buildings designed by a host of New York and Chicago firms. It would foreshadow Burnham and Edward H. Bennett's later plan for Chicago (1909) and the emergence of the City Beautiful movement (see Chapter 7).

★ ★ ★

The development of reinforced concrete occurred during the 19th century, although concrete, as a naturally occurring material known as *pozzolana*, has been employed since Roman times. In the 18th century, natural concrete or forms of Portland cement were used for industrial applications. Concrete uses a combination of cement and aggregate and is initially a thick liquid that is poured or laid into a formwork. The introduction of steel reinforcing rods into concrete resulted in a material that was strong in compression, with new tensile properties that allowed it to be shaped in complex and unconventional ways.[15] Following a series of experiments by various French and German pioneers, François Hennebique (1843–1921) developed a system of reinforcing concrete. Patented in 1892, it proved ideal for the construction of buildings, and his company erected numerous structures using the new method. An early example of a building employing reinforced concrete is the church of St. Jean de Montmartre (1894) in Paris by Anatole de Baudot. In the early 20th century, bridges of reinforced concrete were constructed with ever-increasing long spans. The Swiss engineer Robert Maillart

(1872–1940) was particularly adept at using reinforced concrete to create striking bridges in the Alps. In the early 20th century, Auguste Perret (1874–1954) and Le Corbusier (1887–1965) pioneered the use of reinforced concrete as an important material for architectural expression (see Chapter 10).

★ ★ ★

The break between architecture and engineering began in the middle of the 18th century and continued through the 19th century. This meant that engineering forged ahead with technological innovation without being hindered by historical styles, while architects became increasingly anxious about how to create the architecture of the Industrial Age.[16] This exploration also underscored the relationship between structure and ornament that would bedevil architects throughout the 19th century. Le Corbusier, in his celebrated text *Toward an Architecture*, published in 1923, noted that engineers were not encumbered by architectural tradition and thus could express the pure function of form in structures like American and Canadian grain elevators. In the 20th century, various architects and architectural movements exploited advanced technologies for conceptualizing buildings, continuing a tradition that had its origins in 19th-century engineering (see Chapter 13).

NOTES

1 See Marshall McLuhan, "The Gutenberg Galaxy," in Eric McLuhan and Frank Zingrone, eds., *Essential McLuhan* (Concord, Ont.: House of Anansi Press, 1995), p. 126.

2 See Peter Collins, *Changing Ideals in in Modern Architecture, 1750–1950* (Montreal: MQUP, 1967), pp. 185–197.

3 Hans Straub, *A History of Civil Engineering* (Cambridge, MA: MIT Press, 1964), p. 151.

4 See Ibid., pp. 152–162.

5 See Collins, *Changing Ideals in in Modern Architecture*, pp. 188–189.

6 See Sigfried Giedion, *Space, Time and Architecture: The Growth of a New Tradition*, 5th edition (Cambridge, MA: Harvard University Press, 1982), pp. 164–290.

7 See Straub, *A History of Civil Engineering*, pp. 163–173.

8 See Ibid., pp. 174–175.

9 See Ibid., pp. 175–177.

10 See L.T.C. Rolt, *Victorian Engineering* (Harmondsworth: Penguin Press, 1970), pp. 148–157.

11 Louis Sullivan, "The Tall Building Artistically Considered," in *Kindergarten Chats and Other Writings* (New York: Dover Publications, 1979), p. 202.

12 See Colin Rowe, "Chicago Frame," in *The Mathematics of the Ideal Villa and Other Essays* (Cambridge, MA: MIT Press, 1982).

13 Joanna Merwood-Salisbury, "The First Chicago School and the Ideology of the Skyscraper," in Peggy Deamer, ed., *Architecture and Capitalism: 1845 to the Present* (New York: Routledge, 2013), p. 37.

14 Richard Neutra, *Life and Shape* (New York: Appleton, Century Crofts, 1962), p. 201.

15 See Peter Collins, *Concrete, The Vision of a New Architecture*, 2nd edition (Montreal: MQUP, 2004).

16 See Collins, *Changing Ideals in in Modern Architecture*, pp. 185–197.

SUGGESTED READING

Braham, William and Jonathan Hale, eds. *Rethinking Technology: A Reader in Architectural Theory*. London: Routledge, 2007.

Condit, Carl W. *The Chicago School of Architecture: A History of Commercial and Public Building in the Chicago Area, 1875–1925*. Chicago: University of Chicago Press, 1964.

Elliot, Cecil D. *Technics and Architecture: The Development of Materials and Systems for Buildings*. Cambridge, MA: MIT Press, 1992.

Forty, Adrian. *Concrete and Culture: A Material History*. London: Reaktion Books, 2012.

Straub, Hans. *A History of Civil Engineering*. Cambridge, MA: MIT Press, 1964.

5

FUNCTIONALISM AND RATIONALISM

The emphasis placed on reason during the 18th-century European Enlightenment would lead to an alignment of architecture with science. This resulted in two key concepts that have been central to the development of modern architecture: functionalism and rationalism. Although both address the form or shape of a building and what this expresses, functionalism places an emphasis on the organization of spaces, while rationalism focuses on the structure of form.

One of the enduring expressions associated with the development of modern architecture, particularly in the 1920s and 1930s, is "form follows function," coined by the American architect Louis H. Sullivan (1856–1924), one of the pioneers of the skyscraper. However, the idea of the function of architecture is a much older concept that can be found in Vitruvius's text, *The Ten Books of Architecture*. Vitruvius (c. 80–15 BC), a Roman architect, states that the three requirements of architecture are durability (*firmitas*), convenience (*utilitas*), and beauty (*venustas*).[1] Describing convenience or utility, Vitruvius writes: "when the arrangement of the apartments is faultless and presents no hindrance to use, and when each class of building is assigned to its suitable and appropriate exposure."[2] The functional organization of buildings has always been important since buildings must respond to practical needs; however, they also respond to cultural, economic, political, technological, and environmental factors.

The word function derives from the Latin word *functio*; however, it was not used commonly in the history of architectural writing before the 20th century. Starting in the 18th century, the concept of

DOI: 10.4324/9781003403975-5

"function" or "purpose" was associated with various fields of science, particularly in biology. For example, 18th-century scientists involved in identifying and classifying plants relied on function and structure as key distinguishing factors.[3] The 18th-century Italian monk Carlo Lodoli was the first person to bring the concept of function into the theory of architecture, along with the idea of "representation."[4]

★ ★ ★

In the early 19th century, the French architectural teacher Jean-Nicholas-Louis Durand (1760–1834) put forward the idea of architecture as largely based on "utility" and "economy." Advocating for the "composition" of standard elements using a planning grid, Durand proposed an architecture devoid of traditional forms, symbolisms, and notions of beauty. Durand writes that a building will be commodious "if the number and size of all its parts, their form, situation, and arrangement, are in the closest possible relation to its purpose."[5] Referencing the work of earlier French theorists, such as Claude Perrault (1613–1688), and the debates between the "ancients" and the "moderns," Durand's theories approximated a modern formulation of architecture.[6]

In the 19th century, key architectural figures, including Gottfried Semper (1803–1879) and Eugène-Emmanuel Viollet-le-Duc (1814–1879), addressed architectural function in their writings, along with concepts associated with rationalism. Louis H. Sullivan's famous statement from 1896 was inspired by various sources, including a reverence for nature,[7] Sullivan writes:

> Whether it be the sweeping eagle in his flight or the open apple-blossom, the toiling work-horse, the blithe swan, the branching oak, the winding stream at its base, the drifting clouds, over all the coursing sun, form ever follows function, and this is the law. Where function does not change form does not change.[8]

This quote is taken from the essay "The Tall Office Building Artistically Considered," in which Sullivan discussed how to appropriately express the new "tall" building (see Chapter 4).[9] Sullivan and Frank Lloyd Wright were particularly inspired by the writings of the English philosopher and biologist Herbert Spencer (1820–1903). Spencer, who derived ideas from Charles Darwin's theory of "evolution," influenced Sullivan's understanding of nature and the "organic," a unifying concept that would also be essential for Wright (see Chapter 10).[10]

The most militant approach to functionalism can be found in the work of Hannes Meyer (1889–1954), the Swiss "objectivist" architect, who was one of the leading proponents of modern architecture during the late 1920s and a key member of the ABC Group. In 1927, he joined the Bauhaus school in Dessau. From 1928–1930, Meyer was its controversial director, the successor to the original founder, Walter Gropius. In his 1925 writings, Meyer unites function and form, often in a manifesto style. He developed a formula for architecture: *function x economics*. Attacking the notion of "composition" in art, Meyer shifted from a technical to a biological definition of purpose or function.[11] Meyer wrote in 1928: "this functional, biological interpretation of architecture as giving shape to the functions of life, logically leads to pure construction: this world of constructive forms knows no native country."[12] According to Meyer, by analyzing the technical requirements, economic factors, and the social and psychological routines of those using a building, a building can be organized.[13] Meyer, along with others, including the Dutch architect Mart Stam (1899–1986), proposed a highly objective concept of functionalism that was understood by many to be the most extreme formulation of modern architecture.

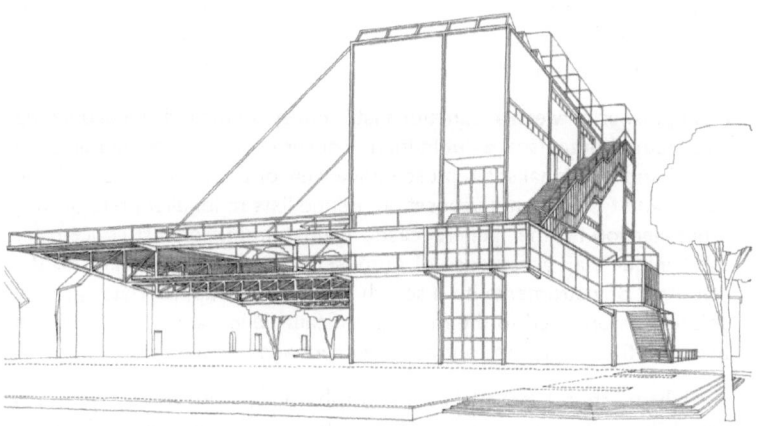

Figure 5.1 Perspective, Hannes Meyer, Petersschule, 1926, Basel, Switzerland. The design features a rectilinear block housing various school spaces from which a large recreational platform and circulation elements are suspended in a clear expression of function. Drawing by Mohammad Moezzi.

By the 1930s, the term "function" had displaced the word "purpose," and the concept of "functionalism" was commonly used in association with modern architecture.[14] However, as curators Henry-Russell Hitchcock and Philip Johnson write in the 1932 catalogue of the International Style exhibition in New York, "functionalists make a particular fetish of planning."[15] In other words, the functional organization of spaces results in a formal solution, where each part is expressed according to its function; this is consistent with Le Corbusier's phrase that the "plan is the generator."[16] This also raises the concept of the building "program," or the list of spaces (and their functions/requirements), the analysis of which is a common part of the design process in modern architecture.[17] While recognizing that function was essential to modern architecture, Hitchcock and Johnson also realized that architecture could not be based on it alone. This foreshadowed the death of functionalism, which was announced by a wide range of architects and critics in the 1960s.[18]

★ ★ ★

The concept of "rationalism" in architecture is often linked to functionalism, as noted previously. However, the two positions are very different, as rationalism addresses form following structure, whereas functionalism emphasizes space and the plan in its focus on form following function. The differences are articulated in German writer Adolf Behne's (1885–1948) book *The Modern Functional Building*, published in 1926, in which he

> distinguishes between a "functionalist" concept of the individual building as a natural organism, a "utilitarian" concern with the "economic principle," and a rationalist's representative view of the virtues of standardization and typification. Purposefully, Behne lists rationalist prerogatives: a predilection for the "general case" against a functionalist concern for the "unique"; an acceptance of purposefulness but a disregard for the "tyranny" of instrumentality; a search for the most "appropriate" general solution as opposed to the most specifically adept, and an assertion of the collective "norm" in contrast to individual particularity.[19]

Rationalism, therefore, places an emphasis on repeatable elements and building solutions or types. It emphasizes the structure of form. Rationalism in architecture is found in the French tradition dating back to the 17th century and has links to the thinking of the French philosopher René Descartes (1596–1650). It gathered momentum in the 18th century with the emergence of biological classification systems and the publication of Marc–Antoine Laugier's text *An Essay on Architecture* in 1753,[20] in which he argues for an essential approach to architecture based on the "primitive hut" and Greek classicism.

The concept of a "type" can be defined "as a concept which describes a group of objects characterized by the same formal structure."[21] It was developed in the late 18th century by architectural theorist A.-C. Quatremère de Quincy (1755–1849), who modified Laugier's concept of the "model" in architecture.[22] The use of type implies that there are consistent, stable, and repeatable forms that endure over time; however, it is also evident from architectural history that types evolve and transform. The use of types also suggests that an architect is less concerned with new and imaginative solutions to problems and is more interested in maintaining continuity with history. In this model, the architect "composes" a building's form using various type elements and solutions, as suggested by Jean-Nicholas-Louis Durand, who proposed a rationalist use of architectural typologies in his books.[23] The contemporary architect Rafael Moneo writes:

> In these terms it can be said that the essence of the architectural object lies in its repeatability. . . . The identification of an architectural element like "column," or of a whole building – "courthouse" – implies an entire class of similar objects with common characteristics.[24]

During the late 18th century and early 19th century, as new social, political, and technological demands arose, a wide range of new building types emerged, each of which needed specific expression. These included museums, art galleries, public libraries, concert halls, legislative buildings, hotels, factories, railway stations, warehouses, housing schemes, prisons, hospitals, etc.

The emphasis on structure made by rationalists in the 19th century overlapped with the Battle of the Styles, or the conflict between Classicism and Gothicism (see Chapter 6). The proponents of the Gothic style argued that it was a language of construction better suited to express structure; this is captured in A.W.N. Pugin's book *True Principles of Pointed or Christian Architecture* (1841), in which he writes: "there should be no features about a building which are not necessary for convenience, construction, or propriety . . . all ornament should consist of enrichment of the essential construction of the building."[25]

The great structural rationalist and theorist of the 19th century was E.-E. Viollet-le-Duc, a figure who would have a wide influence on Art Nouveau architecture; he published various writings on the subject, including his *Lectures on Architecture* (1863 and 1872). Viollet-le-Duc argued for the efficiency of Gothic structures. In his writings, he expressed admiration for both functionalism and rationalism:

> There are two ways of expressing truth in architecture: it must be true according to the programme of requirements, and true according to the methods and means of construction. To be true according to the programme, is to fulfil with scrupulous exactness all the conditions imposed by necessity; to be true according to the methods and means of construction, is to employ materials with a due regard for their qualities and capacities.[26]

Violet-le-Duc's nation of "the nature of materials" would also be an important concept for architects like Frank Lloyd Wright (see Chapter 10). Each material has its own structural properties and should be expressed honestly. Modern architects in the early 20th century largely rejected rationalism and the concept of type and instead emphasized functionalism. However, type can be found in the work of the prominent architect Le Corbusier, with his notion of the "type-objects" which respond to "type-needs" described in his book *The Decorative Art of Today* (1925) which refers to standardized and mass-produced objects.[27]

During the 20th century, Italian Rationalist movements sprang up between 1920–1940 and 1960–1990. In their alternative vision of modern architecture, they resurrected the idea of type. The Italian Rationalists of the 1920s and 1930s were a group of architects, many part of Gruppo 7, aligned closely with the Fascist regime of Benito Mussolini (1883–1945). They developed an architectural approach that fused together modernism and Classicism, often relying on existing typologies or creating new ones (see Chapter 14).

In the 1960s, Italian Neo-Rationalist architects, or the Tendenza, began to analyze the city in terms of types and typologies, looking at the morphological shape of cities. Morphology deals with the internal structure of form. Aldo Rossi (1931–1997), the leading proponent of the "architecture of the city," developed an interpretation of type (and typology and morphology) based on memory and reason. Rossi was one of the most influential architects of the second half of the 20th century, and his book *The Architecture of the City* (1966), remains a key text for architects. Referencing Quatremère de Quincy, Rossi discusses the concept of type: "typology presents itself as the study of types of elements that cannot be further reduced, elements of a city as well as of an architecture."[28] Opposed to what he terms "naïve functionalism," he attacks modernism by stating: "we reject that concept of functionalism dictated by an ingenuous empiricism which holds that *functions bring form together* and in themselves constitute urban artifacts and architecture."[29] Rossi argues that architectural forms should provide a permanent order in the city, within which human events occur. The persistence of an urban artefact also participates in a collective memory. Neo-Rationalism during the 1960s and 1970s also attempted to resurrect urban typologies that had been eliminated from modern cities: the street, the square, the park, the urban block, the quarter or district, and urban monuments.

★ ★ ★

The modern architecture developed in the 1920s strove to break away from historical languages by emphasizing the formal expression of function and structure. In his essay "Form and Figure," Alan Colquhoun suggests that beyond the functional, typological, and structural approaches to architectural form, there is also the "figural." He argues that a form can have a complex set of cultural ideas embedded in it; this invokes the connection of metaphor or "poetic" language to architectural form. Architects such as Aldo Rossi achieved a figural attitude to form by referencing the history of architecture through the use of historical fragments.[30]

NOTES

1 Vitruvius, *The Ten Books on Architecture* (New York: Dover Publications, 1960), p. 17.
2 Ibid.
3 See Ute Poerschke, *Architectural Theory of Modernism: Relating Functions and Forms* (New York: Routledge, 2016), pp. 1–19.
4 See Ibid., pp. 28–43.
5 Jan-Nicholas-Louis Durand, "From *Précis of the Lectures on Architecture* (1802)," in Harry Francis Mallgrave, ed., *Architectural Theory, Volume I* (Malden, MA: Blackwell Publishing, 2006), p. 337.
6 See Alberto Pérez-Gómez, *Architecture and the Crisis of Modern Science* (Cambridge, MA: MIT Press, 1983), pp. 298–314.
7 See Poerschke, *Architectural Theory*, pp. 88–92.
8 Louis H. Sullivan, "The Tall Office Building Artistically Considered," in *Kindergarten Chats and Other Writings* (New York: Dover Publications, 1979), p. 208.

9   Louis H. Sullivan's partner, Dankmar Adler (1844–1900), had a somewhat different approach to the "form follows function" concept; see Thomas Leslie, "Dankmar Adler's Response to Louis Sullivan's 'The Tall Office Building Artistically Considered': Architecture and the 'Four Causes'," *Journal of Architectural Education*, vol. 64, no. 1 (2010), pp. 83–93.

10 See Peter Collins, "The Biological Analogy," in *Changing Ideals in Modern Architecture, 1750–1950* (Montreal: MQUP, 1967), pp. 149–158.

11 See Poerschke, *Architectural Theory*, pp. 104–112.

12 Hannes Meyer, "Building," in Ulrich Conrads, ed., *Programs and Manifestoes of 20th-Century Architecture* (Cambridge, MA: MIT Press, 1971), p. 119.

13 Ibid., p. 120.

14 See Poerschke, *Architectural Theory*, pp. 141–143.

15 Henry-Russell Hitchcock and Philip Johnson, *The International Style* (New York: W.W. Norton & Co., 1966), p. 85.

16 Le Corbusier, *Toward an Architecture* (Los Angeles: Getty Publications, 2007), p. 117.

17 See Collins, *Changing Ideals*, pp. 227–230.

18 See, for example, Reyner Banham, "Conclusion: Functionalism and Technology," in *Theory and Design in the First Machine Age* (London: The Architectural Press, 1960), pp. 320–330; and Stanford Anderson, "The Fiction of Function," *Assemblage*, no. 2 (February 1987), pp. 18–31.

19 Andrew Peckham and Torsten Schmiedeknecht, "The Rationalist Legacy: Complement and Contradiction," Andrew Peckham and Torsten Schmiedeknecht, eds., *The Rationalist Reader: Architecture and Rationalism in Western Europe 1920–1940/1960–1990* (Abingdon: Routledge, 2014), p. 11.

20 See Marc-Antoine Laugier, *An Essay on Architecture* (Los Angeles: Hennessey & Ingalls, 1977).

21 Rafael Moneo, "On Typology," *Oppositions*, no. 13 (Summer 1978), p. 23.

22 See Anthony Vidler, "From the Hut to the Temple: Quatremère de Quincy and the Idea of Type," in *The Writing of the Walls; Architectural Theory in the Late Enlightenment* (New York: Princeton Architectural Press, 1987), pp. 147–164.

23 See Moneo, "On Typology," pp. 23–32.

24 Ibid., p. 23.

25 A.W.N. Pugin, "From *The True Principles of Pointed or Christian Architecture* (1841)," in Mallgrave, *Architectural Theory*, p. 385.

26 E.E. Viollet-le-Duc, "Tenth Discourse," in Elizabeth Gilmore Holt, ed., *A Documentary History of Art, Vol. III* (New York: Anchor Books, 1966), p. 216. See also M.F. Hearn, ed., *The Architectural Theory of Viollet-le-Duc: Readings and Commentary* (Cambridge, MA: MIT Press, 1990).

27 See Le Corbusier, *The Decorative Arts of Today* (Cambridge, MA: MIT Press, 1987), pp. 67–79.

28 Aldo Rossi, *The Architecture of the City* (Cambridge, MA: MIT Press, 1982), p. 41.

29 Ibid., p. 46.

30 See Alan Colquhoun, "Form and Figure," in *Essays in Architectural Criticism: Modern Architecture and Historical Change* (Cambridge, MA: MIT Press, 1981), pp. 190–202.

SUGGESTED READING

Behne, Adolf. *The Modern Functional Building*. Santa Monica, CA: Getty Research Institute, 1996.

Moneo, Rafael. "On Typology." *Oppositions*, no. 13 (Summer 1978).

Peckham, Andrew and Torsten Schmiedeknecht, eds. *The Rationalist Reader: Architecture and Rationalism in Western Europe 192–1940/1960–1990*. Abingdon: Routledge, 2014.

Poerschke, Ute. *Architectural Theory of Modernism: Relating Functions and Forms*. New York: Routledge, 2016.

Rossi, Aldo. *The Architecture of the City*. Cambridge, MA: MIT Press, 1982.

6

STYLE AND NATIONALISM

As influential 19th-century Gothic revivalist architect Augustus Welby Northmore Pugin (1812–1852) writes, "different nations have given birth to so many various styles of Architecture, each suited to their climate, customs, and religion."[1] Here, Pugin links architectural style to nationalism, a phenomenon that was evident in 19th-century architecture at a time when modern nation-states were emerging. The debates around architectural "style" overshadowed the 19th century as architects struggled to create an architecture representative of the modern age. This resulted in what some have described as the "Battle of the Styles," as Classicists (including advocates for Greek, Roman, and Renaissance architecture) fought with Gothicists (including various approaches to Romanesque and Gothic architecture). The word "style" reflects the battle between differing camps, including those advocating for a new architecture. Style typically means a "characteristic . . . manner of expression" or a "manner of living or behaving," often associated with literature, manners, and fashion. It can also mean a "characteristic way, form, or technique of making or producing a thing," which is closer to an architecture where it refers to a recognized architectural language. Style often implies elegance and refinement.[2] First used in literature, style as a concept spread to other disciplines, especially after 1764 with the publication of Johann Joachim Winckelmann's *History of the Art of Antiquity*.[3]

In the mid-18th century, ancient Greek architecture became more accessible to European architects who carried out studies of

DOI: 10.4324/9781003403975-6

ancient temple ruins, particularly at Paestum in Italy and on the Acropolis in Athens. The publication of Marc-Antoine Laugier's book *An Essay on Architecture* in 1753 also created an interest in the subject. Eventually, Greek revival architecture would be important for defining the national aspirations of Scotland, Prussia, and various northern European countries, along with the adoption of it in America in the 19th century. The Greek revival was often used for museums, art galleries, banks, and national monuments, building types that expressed solidity and continuity. In Britain, a noteworthy example is the British Museum by Sir Robert Smirke (1780–1867) and Sydney Smirke (1798–1877), executed during 1823–1846, which adjusted the Greek style to the needs of a modern museum.

Extensive studies of Roman ruins were also undertaken in the 18th century, including the excavation of the site at Pompeii, which began in 1748. Important proponents of Roman architecture included the Italian archaeologist, architect, and visionary Italian architect Giovanni Battista Piranesi (1720–1778) and the Scottish architect Robert Adam (1728–1792). Adam's particular interpretation of Roman architecture was a popular style in the 18th century. The English architect John Soane (1753–1837) produced several important designs in a free interpretation of Roman and English Baroque architecture. Further, Roman architecture inspired the new Republican architecture in America, particularly buildings designed by Thomas Jefferson (see Chapter 2). Roman revivalism would have less impact on the 19th century than the Renaissance revival, which was popular due to its adaptability to the demands of the period and new building types.[4]

Likewise, Romanesque architecture, as an early form of medieval architecture, proved suitable for the demands of the 19th century. An exceptional example of the Romanesque revival is the Natural History Museum (1881) in London by Alfred Waterhouse (1830–1905). The style was particularly popular in America, especially in the hands of Henry Hobson Richardson (1838–1886). Richardson developed a robust interpretation of the Romanesque that he manifested in numerous buildings, including Trinity Church (1877) in Boston and the Allegheny County Courthouse (1888) in Pittsburgh. The Richardsonian style effectively became a national American style in the late 19th century and was copied by many architects; it would inspire architects such as Louis H. Sullivan (see Chapter 4).

The Gothic revivalism of the 19th century was widely adopted for churches and governmental buildings and was employed as a national style. In 18th-century England, experiments with Gothic architecture can be considered novelties, but by the 19th century, Gothic was revived as a serious style, one intended to rival the dominance of Classicism. Gothic architecture provided a range of opportunities for expression because of its association with nationalism, romanticism, rationalism, religion, and social reform.[5] However, as the architectural historian Peter Collins argues, Gothic revivalists often used the style to create affect rather than to solve the problems of planning and function necessary in building types of the period.[6]

The leading proponents of Gothic were the famous art and social commentator John Ruskin (1819–1900), who promoted a Protestant form of Italian Gothic architecture captured in his books *The Seven Lamps of Architecture* (1849) and *The Stones of Venice* (1851–1853), and A.W.N. Pugin, an ardent Catholic and promoter of northern Gothic architecture. Pugin was very active as an architect before his premature death. He managed to publish two key works advocating for Gothic architecture: *Contrasts: Or, a Parallel Between the Noble Edifices of the Middle Ages, and Corresponding Buildings of the Present Day; Shewing the Present Decay of Taste* (1836) and *The True Principles of Pointed or Christian Architecture* (1841). Beyond Pugin, noteworthy and prolific Gothic revivalists included Sir George Gilbert Scott (1811–1878), William Butterfield (1814–1900), and George Edmund Street (1824–1881). In France, Eugène Emmanuel Viollet-le-Duc (1814–1879) believed that Gothic was structurally rational and the logical architecture for the 19th century.

The Battle of the Styles was very evident in the competition for Foreign Office in London in 1857, where proponents of the Renaissance style clashed with Gothic revivalists.[7] In an era of stylistic uncertainty and complexity, where various styles were popular, architects often, for expedient reasons, practised in various styles. These men could be called "indifferent," as opposed to those who championed an orthodox adherence to one style; the architect John Nash (1752–1835) falls into this category. Another result was the emergence of Eclecticism, or the blending together of various styles to create a design.[8] This was evident in the British style known as the Queen Anne revival, which was practised by architects such as Richard Norman Shaw (1831–1912), and the Second Empire style in France exemplified in the Paris Opéra (1875) by Charles Garnier

(1825–1898). The notion of Eclecticism, or a hybrid design, was resurrected in the postmodern era of the 1960s and 1970s.

★ ★ ★

The rise of modern nation-states during the 19th century led to various expressions of nationalism (see Chapter 2), a movement fostered by governing elites and based on notions of citizenship and "the needs of capitalism, the rise of socialism, working-class activism, and the fear of crime."[9] Nationalism can be defined as "the attitude that the members of a nation have when they care about their national identity" and "the actions that the members of a nation take when seeking to achieve (or sustain) self-determination."[10] Nationalism is linked to "national identity," which can evoke notions of ethnicity, shared culture (religion, government, etc.), and land (borders, climate, etc.). Prior to the modern era, territories tended to be ruled by autocratic monarchs, dukes, and princes. Here, we will look at three national situations (Scotland, Prussia, and England) and how specific examples of architecture expressed nationalism. Governmental institutions, such as parliaments, were typically overt expressions of nationalism. Parliaments and congresses were also an emerging building type as nations began to adopt various forms of democracy.

Scotland had retained a form of independence under its own monarchs until the Acts of Union with England in 1707. As early as 1018, Edinburgh has been considered the capital of Scotland. Edinburgh is a distinctive city that takes advantage of its dramatic landscape. Medieval Edinburgh stretches along the sloping "Royal Mile," which begins at Edinburgh Castle and ends at Holyrood Palace (the Abbey). The city features a striking form of medieval architecture that integrates with the topography. In the 18th and 19th centuries, the city expanded greatly with the addition of a large Georgian area made up of streets, squares, circuses, and crescents lined with townhouses (see Chapter 7). Edinburgh was also home to the Scottish Enlightenment of the 18th century, whose heroes included David Hume (1711–1776) and Adam Smith (1723–1790).

After 1810, a series of new Scottish national institutions were built primarily in the Greek revival manner. Calton Hill, one of the high points in the city, became a kind of acropolis for various national monuments, including an unfinished copy of the Parthenon by architects C.R. Cockerell (1788–1863) and W.H. Playfair (1790–1857) known as the National Monument (1829). Playfair, a local architect, went on to design the Royal Scottish Institution (1836) using the Greek Doric order and the National Gallery of Scotland (1854) in the Greek Ionic style. Sited on the south side of Calton Hill is the Royal High School (1829) by Thomas Hamilton (1784–1858), another example of Greek revival architecture.[11] Due to the extensive use of the Greek revival style, Edinburgh is known as the "Athens of the North."

The transformation of Berlin, the capital of Prussia, primarily under the guidance of the architect Karl Friedrich Schinkel (1781–1841), is another important example of a society using architecture to express nationhood. In his early career, Schinkel was primarily involved in painting and designing Romantic theatre sets. A man with diverse abilities and approaches to architecture, Schinkel was appointed State Architect in 1815. This gave him the opportunity to design several public institutions in Berlin. His first project, the small guardhouse called the Neue Wache (1818), signaled his approach.[12] Executed in a precise manner and using the Greek Doric order, it follows on from the design of the Brandenburg Gate (1791) by Carl Gotthard Langhans, a structure that would be a backdrop to many subsequent political events. Friedrich Gilly's project for a monument to Frederick the Great (1797) would also be a source of inspiration for Schinkel.

Schinkel's design for the Berlin Schauspielhaus (1821) is the first of his major neo-Classical public institutions. This would be followed by his most important building and one of the key public institutions of the 19th century: the Altes Museum (1828). With its simple yet dramatic façade, laid out like a Greek stoa and employing the Ionic order, the museum faces a square (the Lustgarten) and the Unter den Linden boulevard beyond. Schinkel also designed a bridge, the Schlossbrücke (1824), to complete the ensemble. Planned in a rational manner that recalls the theories of French architectural theorist J.N.L. Durand, the ensemble of buildings is notable for its clarity. Adapted from a previous building, Schinkel also designed the Berlin Cathedral (1822) adjacent to the Altes Museum.[13]

As architectural historian Hermann G. Pundt has demonstrated, Schinkel carefully sited his buildings to both take advantage of existing opportunities and to correct deficiencies in Berlin's urban fabric. Pundt writes: "Constantly struggling against the realities of financial restrictions and repeated curtailments by a vacillating and reluctant monarch, he [Schinkel] nevertheless succeeded in unifying the core of Prussia's capital city into a comprehensive organism of buildings,

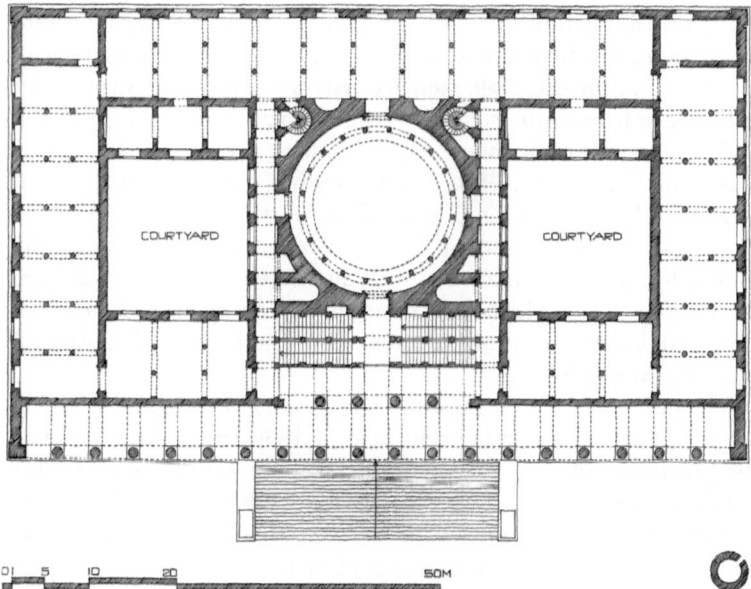

Figure 6.1 Main Floor Plan, Karl Friedrich Schinkel, Altes Museum, 1828, Berlin, Germany. The precise plan for the museum features galleries organized around a circular sculpture rotonda and two courts; a stoa-like colonnade runs across the entry façade. Drawing by Mohammad Moezzi.

spaces, streets, and waterways."[14] Schinkel's reorganization of Berlin gave the city a series of contemporary institutions and expressed Prussian, and later German, nationalism. The architect Leo von Klenze (1784–1864) undertook a similar transformation of Munich in Bavaria, also using the Greek revival style.

Following the creation of the German Empire in 1871, the Reichstag (1894) by Paul Wallot was built near the Brandenberg Gate. Part of the monumental core of Berlin, the original neo-Classical design featured one central legislative chamber for the German parliament, or the Imperial Diet. The Reichstag was badly damaged by fire in 1933 after Adolf Hitler and the National Socialists took control of Germany; it remained unoccupied until after German reunification in 1990.[15]

★ ★ ★

A justifiably famous case of expressing nationalism can be found in the design and construction of the new Houses of Parliament in London. The British parliamentary system is a form of government that descends from the signing of the Magna Carta in 1215. In the 14th century, two chambers emerged, with the formalization of a House of Lords and a House of Commons occurring in the 16th century. The English Civil War of the 17th century, culminating in the Act of Settlement of 1701, redefined the authority of the monarchy and government based on an elected parliament with two houses (the elected House of Commons and the appointed House of Lords) under a "constitutional monarch." The Parliament of Britain was formed in 1707.[16]

The new Palace of Westminster and Houses of Parliament was the subject of a design competition held in 1836 after a fire destroyed the previous building. The rules of the competition stipulated that the design had to be in the Gothic or Elizabethan styles. These were considered to be most suitable for the expression of the British nation. This was in keeping with the concept of a northern nation and the history of architecture during the medieval period and coincided with the emergence of Gothic Revivalism in the 19th century. The competition was won by the team of Sir Charles Barry (1795–1860), known primarily for his Renaissance revival designs, and A.W.N. Pugin. The Houses of Parliament are based on a highly rational plan designed by Barry and organized around a central hall and the two houses. Pugin was responsible for the exterior Gothic detailing and elaborate interiors. For both, he interpreted the language and orna- ment of late English Gothic cathedrals. An older medieval structure, Westminster Hall, was incorporated into the scheme. The whole complex is flanked by Victoria Tower and the clock tower known as "Big Ben," and was completed in 1870. Designed to accommodate all the functions of a parliament, it includes the two primary govern- ing chambers, offices for the Members of Parliament and their staff, and committee rooms.[17]

As befits a large complex, the Houses of Parliament incorporated the latest advances in building technologies for structure, heat- ing, ventilation, and acoustics (see Chapter 13). Some, such as the ventilation theories of the Scottish physician David Boswell Reid (1805–1863), were controversial. The Parliament remains one of the most important buildings of the 19th century, both in terms of the complex technical requirements of a government building and in achieving a lasting expression of British nationalism. As Peter Collins writes:

> Barry created a structure which at least harmonized with the surrounding mediaeval monuments, and expressed, by its ornament at least, the mediaeval origins of the great constitutional principles which it was built to administer and maintain. . . . Indeed, few nineteenth century buildings look so modern as this, with its rectilinear grid of windows and infilling panels stretching nine hundred feet.[18]

The dramatically-sited Canadian parliament in Ottawa follows the British precedent. The Centre Block was originally designed in 1859 by Fuller & Jones (completed in 1866) and re-designed after a major fire destroyed much of the earlier building in 1916. Other noteworthy examples of 19th-century parliamentary complexes include the Hungarian Parliament in Budapest (1902) by Imre Steindl.[19]

★ ★ ★

As architects in the 19th century struggled to define modern architecture, which was consistent with the age, debates over style were waged. The rise of the International Style in the 1920s and 1930s produced a style intended for all cultures and the conquest of modernity over historical revivalism (see Chapter 12). By the 1960s, architects disillusioned with modernity established a plethora of new styles, including Post-Modern Classicism, Regionalism, and Neo-Rationalism that incorporated aspects of revivalism (see Chapter 18).[20] As the American architectural historian Dell Upton argues, beyond the issues discussed previously, style has always been linked to fashion. He notes that styles often "change capriciously and unpredictably" and that "one must keep a close eye on the scene to remain current." And knowledge of popular styles and trends is evidence "of membership in an aesthetic élite."[21]

NOTES

1 A.W.N. Pugin, "From *Contrasts* (1836)," in Harry Francis Mallgrave, ed., *Architectural Theory*, Volume 1 (Malden, MA: Blackwell Publishing, 2006), p. 384.

2 See "Style," in *Shorter Oxford English Dictionary*, Volume 2 (Oxford: Oxford University Press, 2007), p. 3077.

3 Peter Collins, *Changing Ideals in Modern Architecture* (Montreal: MQUP, 1967), pp. 72–73.

4   See Ibid., pp. 96–99.

5   Ibid., p. 100.

6   See Ibid., pp. 104–105.

7   See Ibid., pp. 121–122.

8   See Ibid., pp. 117–123.

9   C.A. Bayly, *The Birth of the Modern World, 1780–1914: Global Connections and Comparisons* (Oxford: Blackwell Publishing, 2004), p. 203.

10   "Nationalism," *Stanford Dictionary of Philosophy*. Accessed January 6, 2022. See: https://plato.stanford.edu/entries/nationalism/

11   The Royal High School was outfitted as the parliament-in-waiting after 1968 prior to the construction of the new Scottish Parliament (2004) designed by the Barcelona-based firm Miralles Tagliabue EMBT. The design was inspired by various Scottish precedents.

12   Located on the Unter den Linden boulevard, the Neue Wache was a royal guard house until 1918. In 1931 the architect Heinrich Tessenow (1876–1950) converted it to a war memorial. In 1960, it became the Memorial to Victims of Fascism and Militarism, and today, it is the Central Memorial of the Federal Republic of Germany for the Victims of War and Tyranny.

13   Schinkel's Berlin Cathedral was demolished in 1893 to make way for the present cathedral.

14   Hermann G. Pundt, *Schinkel's Berlin: A Study in Environmental Planning* (Cambridge, MA: Harvard University Press, 1972), p. 189.

15   During the period when Germany was divided after World War II, the West German parliament was in Bonn. In 1983, the Bundeshaus, a new West German parliament in Bonn, was designed by Behnisch & Partner. Completed in 1992, it features remarkable openness and must be considered a prime example of democratic architecture. Following German reunification, the Reichstag was re-established as the German parliament and was renovated according to a scheme by Norman Foster's firm. Completed in 1999, it is an important reimagining of a historic building.

16   In Britain the monarch is the ceremonial head of state, while the prime minister leads the government (executive) based on the results of an election. The British parliamentary system is used in many former colonies.

17   The monarch, who attends certain events at the parliament in the House of Lords, uses an entrance under Victoria Tower and a series of spaces, including the Royal Staircase and Royal Gallery, during royal processions through the building.

18   Collins, *Changing Ideals in Modern Architecture*, p. 102.

19   More recent buildings include the Parliament Building in Chandigarh, India (1963) by Le Corbusier, the Brazilian Parliament buildings in Brasilia (1960) by Oscar Niemeyer, the National Assembly Building of Bangladesh (1982) by Louis I. Kahn, and the Australian Parliament complex in Canberra (1988) by Romaldo Giurgola.

20 See the chart of styles in Charles Jencks, *The Language of Post-Modern Architecture* (New York: Rizzoli, 1991), pp. 67–68.

21 Dell Upton, *Architecture in the United States* (Oxford: Oxford University Press, 1998), pp. 258–259.

SUGGESTED READING

Bergdoll, Barry. *European Architecture 1750–1890*. Oxford: Oxford University Press, 2000.

Collins, Peter. *Changing Ideals in Modern Architecture*. Montreal: MQUP, 1967.

Lewis, David Frazer. *A. W.N. Pugin*. Liverpool: Liverpool University Press, 2021.

Lewis, Michael J. *The Gothic Revival*. London: Thames & Hudson, 2002.

Snodin, Michael, ed. *Karl Friedrich Schinkel: A Universal Man*. New Haven: Yale University Press, 1991.

7

URBANIZATION AND LANDSCAPE

The relationship between architecture and the city it populates has been radically changing since the late 18th century under new social and political systems, technologies, and infrastructure. The Georgian city in Britain provided a model for reimagining the composition and choreography of urban environments. The Georgian period coincided with the rule of King George I to King George IV (1714–1830s), during which Britain expanded its empire and launched the Industrial Revolution. The era produced a restrained form of Classicism that created elegant and enduring urban environments in cities like London, Bath, and Edinburgh.[1]

Beginning in the late 18th century, the city of London was expanded towards the west on estates held by wealthy aristocratic landowners. Portions of this land were leased to speculative builders, who, together, created the residential squares of London.[2] As architectural historian John Summerson suggests, the use of private speculation resulted in a relative lack of planning. Building on a tradition established by the construction of the Covent Garden Piazza in the 1630s by Inigo Jones (1573–1652), the residential squares of Georgian London were simple classical spaces, typically surrounded by standardized Georgian town-houses and supporting a private garden in the square itself. The first of these new squares was Bloomsbury Square (c. 1661), which would be followed by the construction of many others.[3] The Georgian period was also defined by a standardized housing type for the wealthy: a rowhouse arranged on a long, narrow lot. The residence was separated by a garden from the coach-house and stable at the rear. A timeless

DOI: 10.4324/9781003403975-7

organization of rooms, the Georgian house came in varying sizes and degrees of finish, expressing the relative wealth of the owner.[4]

The city of Bath in West England predates the Roman occupation of Britain. In the early 18th century, it was popular with the wealthy as a spa town famous for its restorative baths. Capitalizing on its fame, various key figures launched an expansion of the city. Beginning in the 1720s, a number of remarkable projects, primarily designed by the father-and-son team of John Wood the Elder (c. 1700–1754) and John Wood the Younger (1728–1782), were developed. The first space was Queen Square (1734) by John Wood the Elder. Using a common façade, individual builders could then build the interiors according to their own designs. Taking advantage of the sloping site, the next stage featured the creation of Gay Street, leading from Queen Square to the north and the Circus (1768), by father and son. John Wood the Younger extended Brock Street to the magnificent Royal Crescent (1774). The square, Circus, and crescent created one of the great urban ensembles of Europe.[5]

A significant example of Georgian urban design can be found in Edinburgh, Scotland. In 1766, following a competition, the city began a series of expansions. The plan established Princes Street, which would become Edinburgh's principal shopping street. Craig's New Town, as the first phase, comprised eight urban blocks stretching between Charlotte Square and St. Andrew's Square along George Street. The first phase was followed by subsequent developments to the west and north that continued Georgian planning themes. The architecture is more diverse than that found in London or Bath; regardless, these extensions of the city provide a consistent structure and scale to a new order of urbanism (see Chapter 6).[6]

John Nash (1752–1835) came from humble origins but rose quickly through British society, largely due to his amusing and ambitious personality.[7] Under the patronage of the Prince Regent (who would become King George IV), his 1811 design for Regent's Park is a significant work of landscape design capping a tradition in London that began in the 17th century when various royal grounds in the city began to be opened to the public. Nash designed a series of scenic residential terraces surrounding Regent's Park that united the city with a landscaped park. He also composed Regent's Street as choreographed sequences of moments which connected the new park to the centre of London.[8] The street thus became a "picturesque" corridor through London inspired by garden design (see Chapter 3).[9] In contrast to the Baroque city, with its emphasis on long axial boulevards and vistas linking locations in space, the Georgian city employed "episodic"[10] spaces within the fabric of the city or along a path.

★ ★ ★

Napoleon Bonaparte (1769–1821) established the First Empire (1804–1815) in France; it ended with his defeat at Waterloo. The French briefly restored the monarchy, which lasted until 1848. The Second Empire (1852–1870), under Napoleon III, would result in a rejuvenation of French architecture. The substantial reconstruction of Paris during this period was one of the greatest urban transformations in history. The result was a carefully ordered city with modern infrastructure. The new plan for Paris was carried out under the prefect Baron Georges-Eugène Haussmann (1809–1891), who oversaw the major demolition of existing buildings and the construction of numerous new projects. The new boulevards, dramatic focal points, public parks, and unified residential architecture created a city of remarkable coherence and beauty. The plan also incorporated new important building types such as railway stations, libraries, markets, department stores, and museums. Nevertheless, the transformation of the city displaced thousands of residents and resulted in a city that was much easier to police. The relatively uninspired French architecture of the 19th century was briefly challenged during the Second Empire by buildings such as the new opera house (1875) by Charles Garnier (1825–1898). This centrepiece of the new city featured an ostentatious and eclectic design. The fabric of the city was supplied by the standardized Parisian apartment building, which framed new streets and accommodated a broad spectrum of residents.[11] In 1900, almost 40 years after the establishment of the London Underground Railway, the Métropolitain subway system opened its first line, rapidly becoming a comprehensive transportation network. In a similar manner to Paris, the expansion of Barcelona, Spain, with the Cerdá plan (1859), also resulted in a consistent urban form, in this case based on a square grid design.

The Austrian Camillo Sitte (1843–1903) published the popular book *City Planning According to Artistic Principles* in 1889. Trained as an architect, he became an educator and writer with an emphasis on Arts and Crafts design. The Ringstrasse, based on a competition scheme (1857), transformed Vienna with new institutions and spaces constructed on the former fortifications. These changes were an impetus for Sitte's study of the history of old European town centres. In his examination of the "relationships between buildings, monuments, and their plazas," he sought to discover artistic and timeless principles of urban design.[12] His theories had a significant impact on German city planning in the early 20th century and on the work of planners outside of Germany.

The City Beautiful movement was an American initiative that influenced urban design in the first decade of the 20th century, with an emphasis on grand schemes and Beaux-Arts civic architecture.[13] It also drew inspiration from the park designs of Frederick Law Olmstead (1822–1903) and Calvert Vaux (1824–1895), particularly their design for Central Park in New York City (1876). Central Park sparked a wave of urban park construction across North America. The urban park would play an evolving role in the development of cities through the 20th century.[14] Another source of inspiration for the City Beautiful was the enormously successful World's Columbian Exposition held in Chicago in 1893. Based on a plan by Olmsted, the "White City" was organized by Daniel Burnham (1846–1912), the energetic Chicago architect, and featured temporary white neo-classical buildings designed by various prominent New York, Boston, and Chicago architectural firms. The City Beautiful was also inspired by the reformist social and political movements of the late 19th century that sought to "improve" the American city.[15] During its brief history, the City Beautiful movement had an impact on the McMillan plan for the National Mall in Washington, D.C. (1902) and numerous urban ensembles across North America. Burnham and Edward H. Bennett's visionary drawings for the *Plan of Chicago* (1909) signaled the end of the movement as more pragmatic and modern ideas took hold.

★ ★ ★

The Industrial Revolution began about 1760. As its impact spread over the next 60 years, large rural populations moved to the new industrial cities looking for work (see Chapter 4). The miserable living and working conditions that resulted were the subject of numerous proposals by reformers, leading to the creation of various utopian models for recalibrating the city. These gained momentum in the second half of the century. The Industrial Revolution led to great migrations of people from rural areas to cities, resulting in overcrowded living conditions and infrastructure ill-equipped to respond to the needs of growing urban populations (see Chapter 4). The notoriously bad living and working conditions in expanding indus-trial cities are described in 1845 by Friedrich Engels (1820–1895), the co-author of the *Communist Manifesto* (1848):

> These slums are pretty equally arranged in all the great towns of England, the worst houses in the worst quarters of the towns; usually one or two-storied cottages in long rows, perhaps with cellars used as dwellings, almost always irregularly built. These houses of three or four rooms and a kitchen form . . . the general dwellings of the working class. The streets are generally unpaved, rough, dirty, filled with vegetable and animal refuse, without sewers or gutters, but supplied with foul, stagnant pools instead.[16]

Reformers and "utopians" emerged with the Industrial Revolu-tion. They sought to influence legislation and create better living and working conditions for the new working classes. Two men of note were Robert Owen (1771–1858) and Charles Fourier (1772–1837). Owen, through his business skills, became a part-owner of spinning mills in New Lanark, Scotland, in 1799. Here, he intro-duced "modern machinery, reasonable working hours, good wages and good living accommodation,"[17] and a school. It was a profitable enterprise that made Owen famous. Later, he attempted to establish model communities in other parts of Britain and America, including a community in New Harmony, Indiana (1825–1827) that was not successful. In contrast to Owen, Fourier developed a community model based on the "phalanstery," which was a large collective hous-ing structure organized around three covered courtyards. Fourier's efforts to build a community failed, but a similar structure was built at Guise (1871) in France by J.B. Godin (1817–1889), using a suc-cessful manufacturing and living arrangement known as a *familistère*.

The Garden City was the brainchild of Ebenezer Howard (1850–1928), who spent much of his career working as a parlia-mentary reporter in London. The publication in 1898 of Howard's *To-Morrow; A Peaceful Path to Real Reform* (republished as *Garden Cities of To-Morrow* in 1902) effectively launched the Garden City, one of the most important concepts in modern urban history. Through text and diagrams, Howard outlined his idea of compact communi-ties that "married"[18] together the best of town and country living. Howard's book describes the management of a town encircled by a "greenbelt" featuring a broad range of greenspaces from the private garden to the public park. In 1899, the Garden City Association was established. Four years later, work began on the first Garden City at

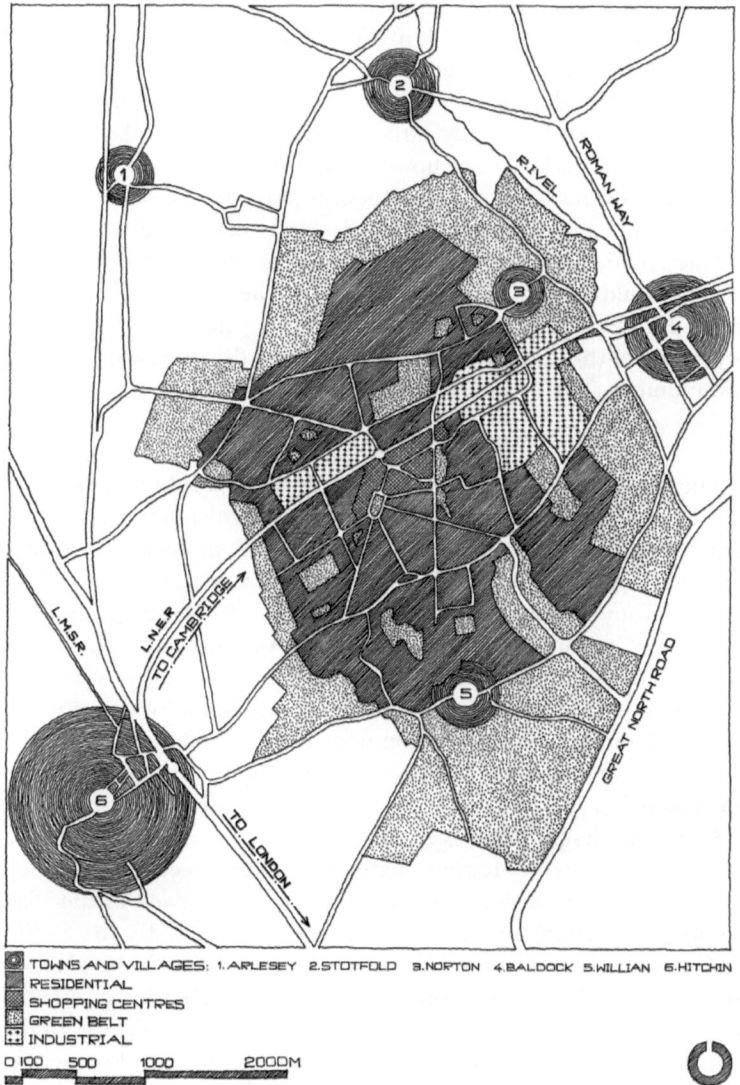

Figure 7.1 Plan, Parker and Unwin, Letchworth Garden City, 1903, England. The plan of the first Garden City shows the organization of the main functional zones, the railway line that bisects the town, the surrounding green belt, and existing towns that were in the area. Drawing by Mohammad Moezzi.

Letchworth, England, based on designs by the architects Barry Parker (1867–1947) and Raymond Unwin (1863–1940). They interpreted Howard's theories in a scheme that placed emphasis on the single-family house and gardens organized in well-designed neighbourhoods. Letchworth initially attracted residents who subscribed to radical and alternative ideas; however, as industry developed, it began to attract working-class families. Incorporating the latest concepts in infrastructure and zoning Letchworth slowly developed over several decades. The Garden City, with its emphasis on low-density healthy living, would have widespread impact.[19] The Garden City movement also helped established city planning as a new discipline at the beginning of the 20th century and influenced the spread of suburban communities after World War II.

★ ★ ★

The modernist city of the 1920s and 1930s was built upon earlier developments with an emphasis on modern transportation systems, commodious housing, green space, and employment centres. Early examples can be found in Arturo Soria y Mata's "Linear City" (1882), Tony Garnier's "Cité Industrielle" (1904–1917), Eugène Hénard's "City of the Future" (1910), and Antonio Sant'Elia's "Citta Nuova" (1914). The modernist city was also a reaction to substandard living and working conditions found throughout cities globally. A pivotal project in the development of the modern city was Le Corbusier's controversial "A Contemporary City for Three Million Inhabitants" (1922). Effectively destroying the traditional structure of the city, the design features 24 skyscrapers at its centre surrounded by highspeed transportation, extensive greenspace, and housing superblocks. The project was subsequently reorganized as the Plan Voisin (1922–1925) and the Ville Radieuse (1930).[20] By the 1930s, Le Corbusier began to modify his urban concepts with the plan for Algiers (1930–1933); he would continue to develop his influential urban schemes, culminating in his design for Chandigarh, India (1950–1965). Other noteworthy modernist urban schemes include Ludwig Hilberseimer's Highrise City (1924), Richard Neutra's Rush City Reformed (1926–1927), and Frank Lloyd Wright's Broadacre City (1932–1935).[21]

The first meeting of the *Congrès Internationaux d'Architecture Moderne* (CIAM) occurred at the Château La Sarraz in Switzerland in 1928. Initiated by Le Corbusier, Siegfried Gideon, and others, the event gathered 24 European architects to promote modernist architecture and urbanism. The group subsequently released the La Sarraz Declaration affirming the concept of the "functionalist" city.[22] The second meeting was held in Frankfurt, Germany, in 1929 with a focus on *Existenzminimum*, or minimum standards for housing design.[23] Frankfurt was chosen because of several housing projects that had been built (1925–1930) under the direction of Ernst May (1886–1970), which united Garden City principles with modern architecture. Walter Gropius, in a lecture at the congress, advocated for parallel rows of tall apartment slabs separated by green space dimensioned according to building heights; this formula had a significant impact on subsequent housing design.[24]

Eventually, CIAM would hold meetings in various locations, along with the work of active groups in various countries. The fourth meeting was held in 1933 on a cruise ship, and in Athens, the sessions concentrated on the functionalist city and resulted in "The Athens Charter," published in 1943.[25] In 95 points, the Athens Charter, written by Le Corbusier, emphasized four functions of the city: housing, work, recreation, and traffic. However, as the eminent American critic and historian Lewis Mumford (1895–1990) pointed out, "what of the political, educational, and cultural functions of the city?"[26] After World War II, the CIAM meetings were progressively taken over by a younger generation who promoted alternative views on the city, culminating in the tenth meeting at Dubrovnik in Yugoslavia in 1956 and the formation of the Team 10 group (see Chapter 18).

Sweden, which remained neutral during World War II, was able to experiment with Garden City and CIAM concepts in housing and urban design. A similar opportunity arose in Britain after the war with the establishment of the New Towns programme in 1946, which resulted in the construction of many new communities also based on modernist principles. The reconstruction of Rotterdam in Holland, after significant war damage, is another example of modern urbanism.

Prominent examples of modernist urban design were Le Corbusier's scheme for Chandigarh as the new capital of the Punjab region of India and Brasília (1956–1960), the new capital of Brazil, designed by Lúcio Costa and Oscar Niemeyer. Le Corbusier (1887–1965) and his primary collaborators (Pierre Jeanneret, Maxwell Fry, and Jane Drew) were appointed by Prime Minister Jawaharlal Nehru in 1950 to design the new city based on a plan by a previous team. The plan features a loose grid of neighbourhoods, or superblocks, with the

Capitol complex located in the northeast sector. Le Corbusier was responsible for the design of the major legislative buildings, including the Legislative Assembly (1963), the High Court (1955), and the Secretariat (1962). The housing areas were designed by other team members.

A decision was made in 1956 by Juscelino Kubitschek (1902–1976), the president of Brazil, to build a new capital city in the centre of the country. While Lúcio Costa (1902–1998) was engaged to develop the plan for Brasília, the architect Oscar Niemeyer (1907–2012) was tasked with designing many of the buildings along the monumental axis, including the National Congress (1960), the Supreme Court (1960), the Presidential Residence (1958), and the Metropolitan Cathedral (1971). The buildings were designed to express the aspirations of the Brazilian nation. However, the scale of the plan opposed tenets of modernism that looked for "democratic" expressions of government.[27] Both Chandigarh and Brasília have been widely criticized, largely as a result of their openness and use of modernist planning principles. There is no doubt there are many shortcomings in the conception of the two cities, especially in terms of providing diverse and vital environments and addressing growth. However, there have been successes as well, especially in standards of living.[28]

★ ★ ★

Widespread discontent with the modernist city emerged in the 1950s and 1960s (see Chapter 18), resulting in a return to the neo-traditional city, which resurrected older forms of urbanism. The publication of Jane Jacobs's popular book *The Death and Life of Great American Cities* in 1961 provided a substantial critique of the modernist city. She fought against it and invasive urban renewal projects by promoting clear distinctions between public and private realms, "eyes upon the street," continuous sidewalks, safe neighbourhoods, diversity, mixed uses, small urban blocks, the preservation of heritage buildings, and other factors that are generally accepted as good urban planning and design today.[29]

Neo-traditionalism manifested itself in Europe with a movement led by Léon and Rob Krier, Aldo Rossi and the Italian Tendenza (see Chapter 5), and Maurice Culot, which advocated for a reconnection with the historic European city.[30] Léon Krier (1946–) is a prominent advocate for the Classical city and has written and taught extensively on the topic. Krier designed the master plan for Poundbury in

England (1993–2025), a traditional community supported by Prince Charles. In America, Peter Calthorpe, Andrés Duany, and Elizabeth Plater-Zyberk are leaders of a movement known as New Urbanism, which also has promoted older urban models. Duany and Plater-Zyberk have designed many neo-traditional communities in North America, including Seaside (1980) in Florida, according to the ideas found in their book *Towns and Town-Planning Principles*.[31]

★ ★ ★

The legacy of the Industrial Revolution resulted in brutal and oppressive urban environments for the working classes. The rise of reformist movements in the 19th century led to the creation of the modernist city of the 1920s with its own set of problems. The resurrection of traditional forms of urban design, beginning in the 1960s, has done much to improve cities around the world. However, in the early 21st century, the city is the focus of widespread study, largely due to global issues such as climate change and the housing crisis. As the architect Thom Mayne states: "The contemporary city is dynamic, unstable, and increasingly difficult to trace as a linear process."[32] In other words, the city has reached a state of complexity that presents significant challenges to planners, architects, politicians, corporations, and citizens.

NOTES

1 See Kerry Downes, *The Georgian Cities of Britain* (Oxford: Phaidon, 1979).

2 A.E.J. Morris, *The History of Urban Form, Before the Industrial Revolutions* (New York: John Wiley & Sons, 1979), p. 263.

3 See John Summerson, *Georgian London* (Harmondsworth: Penguin Books, 1962), pp. 98–112, 191–197.

4 See Ibid., pp. 65–83.

5 See Morris, *The History of Urban Form*, pp. 272–275.

6 See Ibid., pp. 275–279. See also A.J. Youngson, *The Making of Classical Edinburgh, 1750–1840* (Edinburgh: Edinburgh University Press, 1966).

7 See John Summerson, *The Life and Work of John Nash, Architect* (London: George Allen & Unwin, 1980).

8 See Morris, *The History of Urban Form*, pp. 266–272.

9 Summerson, *The Life and Work of John Nash*, p. 132.

10 Ibid., p. 131.

11 See: Leonardo Benevolo, *History of Modern Architecture*, Volume 1 (Cambridge, MA: MIT Press, 1977), pp. 62–95; and Anthony Sutcliffe, *Paris: An Architectural History* (New Haven: Yale University Press, 1993).

12 See George R. Collins and Christine Crasemann Collins, *Camillo Sitte: The Birth of Modern City Planning* (New York: Rizzoli, 1986).

13 See William H. Wilson, *The City Beautiful Movement* (Baltimore: Johns Hopkins University Press, 1989).

14 See Galen Cranz, *The Politics of Park Design: A History of Urban Parks in America* (Cambridge, MA: MIT Press, 1982).

15 See Wilson, *The City Beautiful Movement*, pp. 35–52.

16 Friedrich Engels, *The Conditions of the Working Class in England* (London: Penguin Books, 1987), pp. 70–71.

17 Benevolo, *History of Modern Architecture*, p. 149.

18 Ebenezer Howard, *Garden Cities of To-Morrow* (Cambridge, MA: MIT Press, 1965), p. 48.

19 See Walter L. Creese, *The Search for Environment: The Garden City Before and After* (Baltimore: Johns Hopkins University Press, 1992).

20 See Le Corbusier, *The City of To-Morrow and Its Planning* (New York: Dover Publications, 1987).

21 See Frank Lloyd Wright, *The Living City* (New York: Horizon Press, 1958); and L. Hilberseimer, *The New City: Principles of Planning* (Chicago: Paul Theobald, 1944).

22 See Eric Mumford, *The CIAM Discourse on Urbanism, 1928–1960* (Cambridge, MA: MIT Press, 2000), pp. 9–27.

23 See Karel Teige, *The Minimum Dwelling* (Cambridge, MA: MIT Press, 2002).

24 See Mumford, *The CIAM Discourse on Urbanism*, pp. 27–44.

25 See Ibid., pp. 73–91.

26 Ibid., p. 133.

27 See Styliane Philippou, *Oscar Niemeyer: Curves of Irreverence* (New Haven: Yale University Press, 2008), pp. 211–313.

28 See James Holston, *The Modernist City: An Anthropological Critique of Brasília* (Chicago: University of Chicago Press, 1989).

29 See Jane Jacobs, *The Death and Life of Great American Cities* (New York: Vintage Books, 1961).

30 See Léon Krier, *Rational Architecture* (Brussels: AAM Editions, 1978).

31 See Andrés Duany and Elizabeth Plater-Zyberk, *Towns and Town-Planning Principles* (New York: Rizzoli, 1991).

32 Thom Mayne, *Combinatory Urbanism: The Complex Behavior of Collective Form* (Culver City, CA: Stray Dog Café, 2100), p. 27.

SUGGESTED READING

Cranz, Galen. *The Politics of Park Design: A History of Urban Parks in America.* Cambridge, MA: MIT Press, 1982.

Fishman, Robert. *Urban Utopias in the Twentieth Century.* Cambridge, MA: MIT Press, 1982.

Jacobs, Jane. *The Death and Life of Great American Cities*. New York: Vintage Books, 1961.

Le Corbusier. *The City of to-Morrow and Its Planning*. New York: Dover Publications, 1987.

Sennett, Richard. *The Fall of Public Man*. New York: Vintage Books, 1978.

8

ARTS AND CRAFTS

The Arts and Crafts movement was inspired by A.W.N. Pugin (1812–1852), John Ruskin (1819–1900), and William Morris (1834–1896). Pugin effectively launched the Gothic Revival movement through his work on the new Houses of Parliament (1834–1870); Ruskin was one of the most important writers of the 19th century, dedicated to a wide range of topics, including art, architecture, and society; and Morris, as a devoted follower of Ruskin's ideas, was a primary force behind the Arts and Crafts movement. During the latter part of the 19th century, proponents of the Arts and Crafts reacted against the Industrial Revolution and its inherent mechanization to preserve and promote traditional building construction traditions. Their inspiration was often rooted in ordinary forms of rural building, such as cottages and barns.

Through two of his most influential books on architecture, *The Seven Lamps of Architecture* (1849) and *The Stones of Venice* (1851–1853), John Ruskin advocated for Italian Romanesque and Gothic architecture styles (see Chapter 6). In the first text, he defines the seven "lamps" as Sacrifice, Truth, Power, Beauty, Life, Memory, and Obedience. In the book, Ruskin defines architecture as the "art which disposes and adorns the edifices raised by man, for whatsoever uses, that the sight of them contribute to his mental health, power, and pleasure."[1] In "The Lamp of Truth," Ruskin argues against deceit in buildings by showing structure, honest expression, and "avoiding machine-made ornaments."[2] It is evident that these ideas would directly inspire the Arts and Crafts movement with its emphasis on

DOI: 10.4324/9781003403975-8

hand-crafted construction. Further, in a period where the use of iron as a primary structural material was accelerating, Ruskin argued against its use except in limited applications.[3]

Ruskin writes of the effects created by architecture through the composition of mass and elements, light and shade, ornamentation, material, and colour. Ruskin's ideas about nature had a significant impact on late 19th-century design. In the chapter "The Lamp of Life," he states that beauty depends "on the expression of vital energy in organic things."[4] The life in a building is expressed through the labour of those who built it by hand rather than in the "lifeless" results produced by machines. In "The Lamp of Memory," he proposes that it is the role of architecture and poetry to overcome forgetfulness and preserve the past through enduring construction and the use of ornament that provides historical meaning.[5] In the final section, "The Lamp of Obedience," Ruskin states that "we want no new style of architecture" and that originality is a misunderstood aspiration.[6] Later in his life, Ruskin examined labour and production. In *The Stones of Venice*, Ruskin strongly advocates for creative manual work that challenges the intellect, that is not repetitive, and is not the creation of another; he argues that mechanization divides labour and humans into "small fragments."[7]

Ruskin's theories were put into practice with the design and construction of the Oxford University Museum for Physical Sciences (1860), designed by the Irish architects Thomas Newenham Deane (1828–1899) and Benjamin Woodward (1816–1861).[8] The result captures the notion of "Ruskinian Gothic," inspired by Italian influences. The plan of the Oxford Museum is organized around an exhibition court covered in an iron and glass roof, a feature that did not please Ruskin. Teaching spaces (including lecture rooms and laboratories) dedicated to various scientific disciplines were arranged around it on two levels. Facilities for medicine and chemistry were detached from the main building for safety reasons. The design uses the material of the building and its ornamentation as part of an educational programme that showcases a wide range of British stone (mineralogy and geology), plants (botany and biology), and animals (zoology). Representations of British flora and fauna are carved into the stone column capitals and incorporated into the iron ornamentation. The original group of capitals were carved by James and John O'Shea and Edward Whellan from Ireland, who executed the work with "remarkable and original talent."[9] Richly coloured, the building is an excellent example of 19th-century "polychromy," or the use of colour in architecture.[10]

Despite the success of many buildings inspired by his writings, Ruskin had a "historically inaccurate" view of medieval labour and artistic practices, especially when it came to building the great cathedrals.[11] Ultimately, Ruskin always advocated for a romantic form of medievalism, even in the face of radical social, political, and technological upheaval. Nevertheless, his theories on production (and craft) and nature influenced the Pre-Raphaelite Brotherhood, the Arts and Crafts movement, and the emergence of Art Nouveau design (see Chapter 9).

★ ★ ★

William Morris was a complex figure who grew up in a wealthy family and would turn to Socialism later in life; he was a poet, craftsman, manufacturer, social reformer, and environmentalist.[12] While at Oxford University, Morris discovered Oxford as an ideal city which had retained its medieval history. At Oxford, Morris met important future collaborators, including the artist Edward Burne-Jones (1833–1898), and took to reading Ruskin's works, especially his text "On the Nature of Gothic Architecture" with its emphasis on art and workmanship.[13]

In 1856, Morris entered the office of George Edmund Street as an apprentice. Street was an important Oxford-based Gothic Revival architect. There, he encountered Philip Webb (1831–1915), who would also become a close friend and collaborator. However, it was evident that Morris was not suited for architectural practice and left the firm after a year. Morris moved to London, where he encountered another important figure, the painter Dante Gabriel Rosetti (1828–1882). Rosetti was the leading figure in the Pre-Raphaelite Brotherhood, established in 1848. The Pre-Raphaelites were inspired by medieval and 15th-century Renaissance art and nature. Under Rosetti's influence, Morris decided to concentrate on drawing, painting, and poetry.[14]

In 1859, Morris commissioned Webb to design a house for himself and his wife, Jane Burden, in Upton outside of London. This house, the first independent work by Webb and known as the Red House (1860), would become one of the most important works of 19th-century residential architecture. Inspired by medieval architecture and yet executed in an austere red brick and with simple interiors, the house features a shallow L-shaped plan with internal spaces

GROUND FLOOR PLAN   FIRST FLOOR PLAN

1.ENTRANCE PORCH	6.WAITING ROOM	11.SCULLERY	16.KNIVES	21.DRESSING ROOM
2.HALL	7.BEDROOM	12.HATCH	17.WASHROOM	22.MAID'S BEDROOM
3.PASSAGE	8.STORE	13.LARDER	18.DUST	23.WELL
4.GARDEN PORCH	9.PANTRY	14.KITCHEN YARD	19.DRAWING ROOM	
5.DINING ROOM	10.KITCHEN	15.COALS	20.STUDY ROOM	

0 1 2   5   10   20 M

Figure 8.1 Main and First Floor Plans, Philip Webb, Red House, 1860, Upton, England. The design of the house uses a single-loaded corridor that provides a comfortable organization of spaces, addressing both internal and external factors. Drawing by Mohammad Moezzi.

carefully placed to respond to Morris's lifestyle. Unusually, the main living rooms are on the first floor with the bedrooms, and the servant's areas are generous. In particular, the interiors broke from the conventions of the time and were furnished and decorated according to Morris and Webb's developing approach to design. Hermann Muthesius writes: "It is the first private house of the new artistic culture, the first house to be conceived and built as a unified whole inside and out, the very first example in the history of the modern house."[15]

In 1861, Morris began the company Morris, Marshall, Faulkner & Co. (or the Firm), which would be his major contribution to design and the Arts and Crafts movement. The Firm would become "the best-known decorating business in Victorian Britain, and a byword in good taste amongst the intellectual classes."[16] The mandate of the Firm was to produce better quality products (for decorating the home) and to put into practice the theories of Ruskin. The company produced stained glass, furniture, murals, carvings, metalwork, tapestries, and wallpapers using the talents of its partners and employees. Surprisingly knowledgeable of many hand craft methods, Morris guided much of the work of the enterprise. At this time, Morris also began to design wallpaper, which, along with tapestries and fabrics, would be his most important contributions to design.[17] As its reputation and influence grew, the Firm began to take on important interior commissions, often in collaboration with Philip Webb.

In 1871, the Morris family and Rossetti took on the mainly 17th-century house of Kelmscott Manor, near Oxford. The next decade would be a highly productive one for Morris. Simultaneously, he was becoming more aware of the conditions of the working classes in Great Britain, fuelling his growing interest in Socialism. He also devised the Society for the Protection of Ancient Monuments, an early heritage organization inspired by Ruskin. His growing public presence led to him giving lectures on design and politics. In 1879, Morris and his family moved to a house in Hammersmith on the Thames, which he named Kelmscott House. The redecoration of Kelmscott House is considered the most refined example of Morris's ideas about interior design. Two years later, he acquired Merton Abbey (a former silk-weaving factory) in South London, where he could move all the various production operations.[18]

His most popular book, *News from Nowhere* (1890), was written in the utopian literary tradition (see Chapter 7). Set after 1952, Morris's book describes: "a place of communistic freedom, where men, women and children are equal, beautiful and healthy; money, prisons, formal education and central government have been abolished; the countryside has been reclaimed from industrial squalor and pollution."[19] By the early 1890s, Morris moved away from politics, returning to his love of art and craft. His efforts inspired the establishment of many collective organizations (such as the Century Guild, the Art Worker's Guild, the Arts and Crafts Exhibition Society, and the Central School of Arts and Crafts).[20] He also influenced numerous craft colonies and educational institutions, such as the Darmstadt Artists' Colony, the Wiener Werkstätte, the Deutscher Werkbund, and the foundation of the Bauhaus.

Morris worked tirelessly to preserve a host of craft techniques, and he inspired a generation of architects and designers in Britain and abroad. He advocated for a simpler and more authentic approach to living. His reforming ideas can be summarized as follows:

> [T]he supremacy of utility over luxury; the moral responsibility of design-ers and manufacturers to produce objects of quality; the use of design as a democratic tool for social change. Through the European avant-garde's espousal of these precepts, Morris must be seen as having a funda-mental impact on the early origins of the Modern Movement. But it was Morris's advocacy of a holistic approach to the design and manufacturing processes for aesthetic, social and environmental reasons that was of the most lasting relevance and will remain his greatest legacy.[21]

The Arts and Crafts movement became widespread, inspired by the works of Ruskin and Morris. It placed a particular emphasis on domestic environments and studying local vernacular traditions. In Britain important architects included: Arthur Heygate Mackmurdo (1851–1942), William Richard Lethaby (1857–1931), Charles Francis Annesley Voysey (1857–1941), Charles Robert Ashbee (1863–1942), Mackay Hugh Baillie Scott (1865–1945), Charles Rennie Mackintosh (1868–1928), and Edwin Landseer Lutyens (1869–1944). In America, Gustav Stickley (1857–1942), Bernard Maybeck (1862–1957), Charles Sumner Greene (1868–1957), and Henry Mather Greene (1970–1954) were the leading proponents of the style. Women were also actively involved in the Arts and Crafts movement as designers, makers, and clients.[22] Exceptional examples of Arts and Crafts houses include Munstead Wood (1896) in Surrey, England, designed by Edwin Lutyens for the distinguished garden designer Gertrude Jekyll (1842–1932); Broadleys (1898), overlook-ing Lake Windemere in northern England, by C.F.A. Voysey which represents a "total work of design" (or *Gesamtkunstwerk*) in which all aspects of the house, included the furnishings are designed; and the Gamble House (1909) in Pasadena, California by the Greene Brothers which is constructed primarily in wood.[23]

Hermann Muthesius (1861–1927), a German architect and writer working in the German embassy in London from 1896 to 1904, published his monumental three-volume book entitled *Das englische Haus* in 1904 and 1905. His book essentially celebrates and docu-ments the English house as redefined by the Arts and Crafts move-ment. Muthesius begins his discussion by commenting on British individualism, general dislike of the city, passion for gardening, and love for the private house (or home). Muthesius points out that it was Philip Webb, Eden Nesfield, and Richard Norman Shaw who initiated the reform of the English house.[24] As it evolved, the late 19th-century middle-class English house was developed as modest and comfortable, espousing a certain informality of living, a house that addressed its locale and the climate.[25] As Muthesius writes:

> [T]he genuinely and decisively valuable feature of the English house is its absolute practicality. Whatever it is, it is a house in which people want to live. There is nothing extravagant, no desire to impress upon its conception, no flights of fancy in ornament and jumbles of forms; it does not give itself airs or try to be artistic, there is no pretentiousness, nor even any "architecture."[26]

★ ★ ★

Inspired by the Arts and Crafts movement, the Deutscher Werkbund was established in Munich in 1907 to raise design and manufacturing standards for German industry. The primary figures behind this organization were politician Friedrich Naumann, educator Karl Schmidt, architect Henry van de Velde (1863–1957), and Muthesius. Muthesius was key. He returned to Germany in 1904 to develop his architectural practice and to work in the Prussian Ministry of Trade. He was appointed a professor in 1907 at the Berlin Commercial University.[27] The Werkbund initially expressed itself through its publications and the "encouragement of fruitful cooperation among art, industry, and craft for the enhancement of the quality of work," which concentrated on promoting excellence, education, and the economic benefits of good design.[28] Muthesius provides an overview of the organization's objectives by linking design to cultural expression:

> For its culture is and remains the true index of a nation's culture as a whole. If a nation produces good furniture and good light fittings, but daily erects the worst possible buildings, this can only be a sign of heterogeneous, unclarified conditions, conditions whose very inconsistency is proof of a lack of discipline and organization. Without a total respect for form, culture is unthinkable, and formlessness is synonymous with lack of culture.[29]

The Werkbund spread to Berlin, Dresden, Munich, and Vienna. It attracted a diverse group of proponents to "create a working alliance between art and industry."[30] A group of architects (including Josef Hoffmann, Hans Maria Olbrich, and Peter Behrens (1868–1940)) and various companies were asked to join the initiative to develop and promote good design using mainly machine production. Morris's vision for a return to craft largely failed because he "could only produce high-quality craft objects, for the most part at luxury prices, within a world dominated by the processes of mass production."[31]

Between 1908 and 1914, the Werkbund was involved in a range of activities, including publications and exhibitions, aimed mainly at the German middle class, culminating in the important 1914 Werkbund exhibition held in Cologne. An organization that began with a strong commitment to an Arts and Crafts approach was, by 1914, championing well-designed industrial production. During the Cologne exhibition, a debate raged between those like Muthesius, arguing for standardized architectural "types," and those like Van de Velde, advocating for the role of art and individualism.

The exhibition of 1914 comprised almost 100 buildings filled with a wide range of products and objects. Among the buildings were a small number of important works, including Bruno Taut's Expressionist Glass Pavilion and Walter Gropius's model factory design. Behrens was responsible for the central hall building, which was built in a more conservative style. Overall, the quality of design and production was uneven, demonstrating the monumental challenge the Werkbund had undertaken. However, the exhibition did attract a large audience.[32] After World War I, the foundation of the Bauhaus school in Weimar (1919) under Walter Gropius (1883–1969) was a testimony to Werkbund ideals (see Chapter 16).

Peter Behrens, as the primary interpreter of Werkbund principles, came from a comfortable background in Hamburg, Germany. Initially an artist, he was invited to join the Darmstadt artist's colony in 1899, where he designed a house for his family (1901). Increasingly involved in architecture and design, by 1907, Behrens's work attracted the attention of AEG (*Allgemeine Elektricitäts-Gesellschaft*), the large German manufacturer of electrical equipment. Behrens was hired to design products; as a result, he moved to Berlin and established his studio, which would eventually employ several important future architects, including Gropius, Le Corbusier, and Ludwig Mies van der Rohe. Behrens designed arc lamps, kettles, fans, clocks, and other products for the AEG, overall improving design and manufacturing standards for the company. Behren's design work was not revolutionary; nevertheless, he was a pioneer in German industrial design.[33]

Behrens also designed buildings for AEG, starting with exhibition pavilions. Despite his lack of formal training, he became involved in larger permanent structures for the company. His most famous project is the AEG Turbine Hall (1909) in Berlin, a large manufacturing space serviced by travelling gantries or cranes. Described as a "cathedral" to industry by Le Corbusier, the building is long and precise and constructed mainly in steel and glass, with strong concrete elements defining the corners and the gabled roof form. The building is a landmark in the continuing development towards fully modern architecture because it fuses together architecture and engineering despite its "monumentalizing" references. The Behrens office then designed several large factories and housing schemes for AEG.[34] His later career involved an eclectic range of designs, teaching, and several failed attempts in the 1930s to align himself with the Austrian wing of the Nazi Party.[35]

★ ★ ★

Sociologist Richard Sennett notes that craft "focuses on the intimate connection between hand and head"[36] and materiality. During the 19th century, due to industrialization, there was an effective loss of many hand-crafted building traditions and skills despite the best efforts of the Arts and Crafts movement. The Arts and Crafts movement attempted to demolish the historical divide between "art" and "craft." However, there are examples of craft traditions prevailing during the 20th century in many parts of the world, and the employment of various forms of craft exists today in a wide range of disciplines. Historically, craft in architecture has been associated with workshops, guilds, and traditional methods of construction and training builders. The prevalence of the machine has muddied the waters, but as many architects, like Frank Lloyd Wright, demonstrated in the early 20th century, the machine could be intelligently employed in architectural construction and craft.

NOTES

1 John Ruskin, *The Seven Lamps of Architecture* (London: Cassell and Co. Ltd., 1909), p. 35.
2 Ibid., pp. 69–70.
3 See Ibid., pp. 74–77.
4 Ibid., p. 211.
5 See Ibid., pp. 249–250.
6 See Ibid., pp. 281–283.
7 John Ruskin, "The Stones of Venice II," in E.T. Cook and A. Wedderburn, eds., *The Works of John Ruskin*, Volume 10 (Cambridge: Cambridge University Press, 2011), p. 196.

8 See Eve Blau, *Ruskinian Gothic: The Architecture of Deane and Woodward 1845–1861* (Princeton: Princeton University Press, 1982), pp. 48–81.

9 Ibid., p. 69.

10 See Peter Collins, *Changing Ideals in Modern Architecture* (Montreal: MQUP, 1967), pp. 111–116.

11 See John Unrau, "Ruskin, the Workman and the Savageness of Gothic," in R. Hewison, ed., *New Approaches to Ruskin* (London: Routledge, 1981), pp. 33–50.

12 Fiona MacCarthy, *William Morris: A Life for Our Time* (London: Faber and Faber, 1994), p. vii.

13 See Ibid., pp. 52–81.

14 See Ibid., pp. 110–153.

15 Hermann Muthesius, *The English House* (London: Crosby Lockwood Staples, 1979), p. 17.

16 MacCarthy, *William Morris*, p. 166.

17 See Ibid., pp. 166–196.

18 See Ibid., pp. 391–461.

19 Ibid., p. 585.

20 See Ibid., pp. 589–605.

21 Charlotte and Peter Fiell, *William Morris (1834–1896)* (Köln: Taschen, 1999), p. 52.

22 See, for example, Anthea Callen, *Women in the Arts and Crafts Movement, 1870–1914* (London: Astragal Books, 1979).

23 See Peter Davey, *Arts and Crafts Architecture* (London: Phaidon, 1995).

24 Muthesius, *The English House*, p. 15.

25 See Witold Rybczynski, *Home: A Short History of an Idea* (New York: Viking Penguin Inc., 1986).

26 Muthesius, *The English House*, p. 149.

27 See Joan Campbell, *The German Werkbund: The Politics of Reform in the Applied Arts* (Princeton: Princeton University Press, 1978), pp. 9–32.

28 Reproduced in Stanford Anderson, *Peter Behrens and a New Architecture for the Twentieth Century* (Cambridge, MA: MIT Press, 2000), p. 110.

29 Hermann Muthesius, "Aims of the Werkbund," in Ulrich Conrads, ed., *Programs and Manifestoes of 20th Century Architecture* (Cambridge, MA: MIT Press, 1971), p. 27.

30 Campbell, *The German Werkbund*, p. 28.

31 Anderson, *Peter Behrens*, p. 95.

32 See Campbell, *The German Werkbund*, pp. 57–81.

33 See Anderson, *Peter Behrens*, p. 113–128.

34 See Alan Windsor, *Peter Behrens: Architect and Designer* (New York: Whitney Library of Design, 1981), pp. 77–105.

35 See Ibid., pp. 127–176.

36 Richard Sennett, *The Craftsman* (New Haven: Yale University Press, 2008), p. 9.

SUGGESTED READING

Campbell, Joan. *The German Werkbund: The Politics of Reform in the Applied Arts.* Princeton: Princeton University Press, 1978.

Davey, Peter. *Arts and Crafts Architecture.* London: Phaidon, 1995.

MacCarthy, Fiona. *William Morris: A Life for Our Time.* London: Faber and Faber, 1994.

Ruskin, John. *The Seven Lamps of Architecture.* New York: Dover Publications, 1989.

Rybczynski, Witold. *Home: A Short History of an Idea.* New York: Viking Penguin Inc., 1986.

9

ORNAMENT AND STRUCTURE

The abandonment of traditional forms of ornament was one of the major distinguishing factors in the development of modern architecture in the early 20th century. Historically, the ornamentation of buildings in all traditional cultures served various purposes, primarily to embellish the structure of a building (or an object or the human body), to provide a patterning of surfaces, and to establish a language or style of design. For example, this is evident in Classical, Gothic, and Islamic architecture. As the Gothic Revival architect A.W.N. Pugin wrote in 1841, "all ornament shall consist of enrichment of the essential construction of the building."[1] For Pugin, ornament should be integral to the structure of the building, not merely applied.

According to architectural historian Antoine Picon, ornament traditionally displayed political power through "pleasure and beauty, social rank and prestige, communication and knowledge."[2] Picon also notes that ornament was "connected to enduring visual codes" and was intended to stimulate thought in the spectator.[3] Ornament contributes to the beauty of a design and creates a certain "delight" in the viewer; it expresses wealth and power, signals the purpose of a building, and is essential to an architectural language articulating the elements and the joints and giving an overall coherence that can be "read." In the 19th century, the implementation of machine-made ornamentation challenged the "craft" of architecture and the legitimacy of ornamentation itself, often resulting in the arbitrary and misunderstood use of ornament.

★ ★ ★

DOI: 10.4324/9781003403975-9

The Art Nouveau movement emerged in 1895 with the opening of Samuel Bing's shop in Paris called *Maison de l'Art Nouveau*. In many ways, it pointed forward to the emergence of modernism in the 20th century; however, it also reached a dead end by the time it faded away. And yet, embedded in the several movements (also known as Jugenstil in Germany, Sezessionstil in Vienna, and Modernista in Catalonia) are some of the most unique experiments in the history of architecture. The various Art Nouveau groups sought to preserve craft traditions, often in a spectacular fashion, and looked for new forms of expression based on formal precedents, metaphors, and ornamental systems outside of traditional architectural languages. And while similarities occurred across the various groups, no general approach emerged.

The movement had its origins in the visionary artwork of William Blake (1757–1827), the work of the Pre-Raphaelite Brotherhood painters, Symbolist art, and the ideas of John Ruskin, William Morris, and E.E. Viollet-le-Duc. A sensuous naturalism is evident in Art Nouveau design, inspired by Ruskin's idea that nature should be the source of inspiration but not directly copied. As art historian Robert Schmutzler notes, the "whiplash" line is one of the defining characteristics of Art Nouveau: "[it] had as its main theme a long, sensitive, sinuous line that reminds us of seaweed or of creeping plants. Such a line might also be suggested by the way the spots are scattered in a leopard skin or by the flick of a whiplash, flowing or flaring out."[4]

It was in Belgium that a fully formed Art Nouveau architecture first emerged in the early 1890s. During a decade of dramatic achievement, Victor Horta (1861–1947) developed a "language" of innovative architecture based on his own interpretations of naturalistic form; this presented itself in a series of urban houses for wealthy clients in Brussels. At the time, Brussels was a busy European capital, fully engaged in the latest developments in art and architecture.[5] Horta produced his full-fledged architectural system for the Tassel house (1892) in Brussels, in which he introduced Art Nouveau motifs to the façade. However, it is in the interior where the most innovative aspects of Horta's vision occur. Working within the tight confines of the site, Horta introduced spatial continuities that were also realized in his fluid use of form and sumptuous use of materials. The main floor plan is effectively symmetrical, divided into spatial cells, and naturally lit from the façades and the main staircase. The staircase, as it ascends towards a glass and iron skylight, is one of the most startling and famous examples of Art Nouveau design. One crucial innovation is Horta's integration of exposed iron into his architecture, which is unusual in a domestic setting. An important non-domestic work was Horta's Maison du Peuple, commissioned by the local Socialist organization as a meeting place. It was completed in 1899 and employed a striking use of ironwork and form. The Italian architectural historian Franco Borsi identifies several repeating tendencies in Horta's architecture. These include the whiplash line, tangential structural connections, the curve as optical correction, folding surfaces, complex rhythms, a dialogue of materials, polygonal compositions, the whirling arrangement of space, and transparency.[6] As Borsi notes, Horta was inspired by nature but did not reference specific plants in his elongated, curving, and folding forms. Ultimately, Horta realized Viollet-le-Duc's vision for a new iron, masonry, and glass architecture.

The development of Art Nouveau architecture in Belgium would have a strong connection to what occurred in France, mainly in Paris and Nancy. The dominant French figure was Hector Guimard (1867–1942), known primarily for Parisian apartment buildings, including his Castel Béranger (1898). In 1898, a competition was held to design the entrances to the new Parisian subway system, known as the Métropolitain, or Métro. Guimard was awarded the commission to design three different types of entrances using a modular system of cast iron and glass elements. His novel design used naturalistic elements to introduce a surreal aspect to the streets of Paris.

A third important architect from this period is Antoni Gaudí I Cornet (1852–1926), whose very unusual work is a product of Barcelona and the Catalan region of northern Spain. His career occurred at a time when Barcelona was expanding dramatically and implementing the Cerdà grid plan (1856 and 1859). Gaudí was born in the town of Reus, near Tarragona. In 1873 he moved to Barcelona to study at the new school of architecture. There, he worked for various local practices before qualifying as an architect in 1877.[7] By this time, he had been exposed to a wide range of styles and approaches, including Gothic and Moorish, along with the theories of Viollet-le-Duc. Discussing this period in Gaudí's life, the Catalan architectural historian Ignasi de Solà-Morales writes:

> From the very start of his career, too, we can see Gaudí's encyclopedic taste for using the most varied repertoire of symbols: those of classicism, those of medieval heraldry, those of ecclesiastical symbology, those of nature taken realistically in plant or animal forms. All these cases are accumulated in complex systems of discordant scales, creating a multiple approach to the object designed.[8]

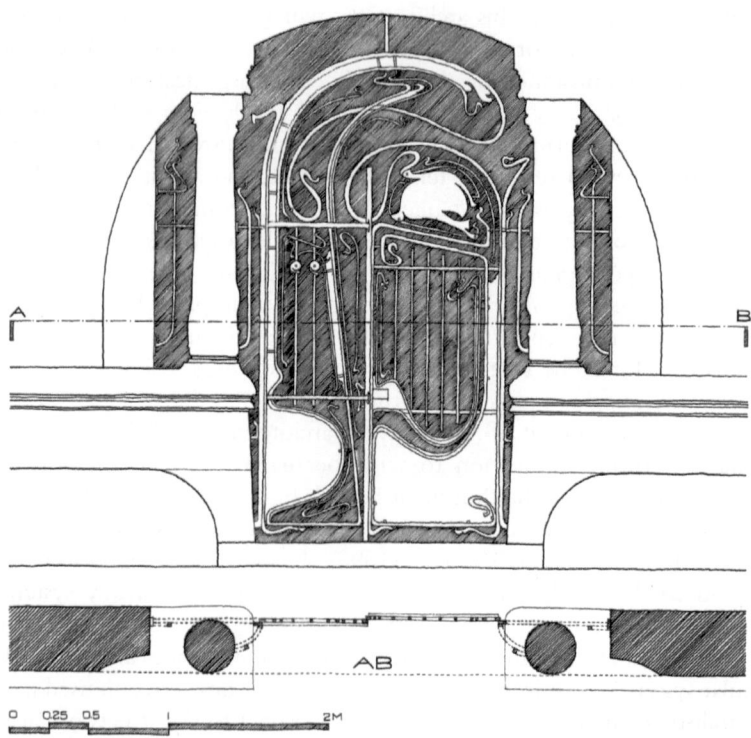

Figure 9.1 Main Entrance, Hector Guimard, Castel Béranger, 1898, Paris, France. The ironwork in the entry gate captures the curvilinear and natural-istic approach characteristic of Art Nouveau design. Drawing by Mohammad Moezzi.

The Palau Güell (1890), a large urban house for a wealthy Barcelona family, represents the best of his early designs. As Gaudí formulated his mature style in relative obscurity, he was involved in an "experi-mental eclecticism."[9] Later, Gaudí designed a small housing develop-ment and the Park Güell (1900–1914), inspired by the Garden City movement, on the western edge of Barcelona. By the early 20th cen-tury, he had refined an approach to an architecture of unprecedented originality. Arguably the most unusual is Gaudí's Casa Battló (1906), a narrow apartment building which features a façade that incorpo-rates a bony structural expression reminiscent of prehistoric animals at lower levels, several storeys that capture an underwater world, and at the top, a dragon-like form that references the Christian story of St. George slaying the dragon. The adjacent Casa Milà (1910) is a larger residential building, which allowed Gaudí more freedom to plan a variety of apartments with fluidity. The stone façade evokes a cliff face, with balcony railings that recall undulating seaweed. The roof is designed as a landscape surveyed by silent figures that encase the numerous chimneys.

After 1908, Gaudí concentrated mainly on designing and constructing the Expiatory Church of the Sagrada Familia (1883–1926), or the main cathedral for Barcelona. Taking over the commission in 1883, Gaudí transformed a more conventional Gothic Revival design into a fantastical one based on his synthesis of sources and his signature use of the repeating catenary arch. Gaudí laboured over an evolving design, which remained unfinished at the time of his accidental death in 1926. For many decades, the construction of the immense cathedral languished. However, in the 21st century, a major effort has been initiated to complete the design using digital fabrication methods.[10]

★ ★ ★

A second school of Art Nouveau design, based on a cooler, more graphic approach, is found in the axis between Glasgow and Vienna, encompassing the work of Charles Rennie Mackintosh (1868–1928) in Scotland, and various architects in central Europe. Early in his career, Mackintosh, who studied at the Glasgow School of Art, established a group called The Four and apprenticed as an architect. The Four comprised Mackintosh, James Herbert MacNair (1868–1955), and the sisters Margaret (1865–1933) and Frances (1874–1921) Macdonald. Together they developed a distinctive graphic style featuring elongated figures, naturalistic lines, and stylized flowers inspired by Pre-Raphaelite artists, Japanese art, and Ruskin.

The Four found some commercial and critical success.[11] Mackintosh was the only member of The Four directly involved in architectural practice; Margaret maintained an important influence on his designs.[12] In 1889, Mackintosh joined the architectural firm Honeyman & Keppie. He became a partner in 1904 before giving up practice in 1914. The 1896 competition for the new Glasgow School of Art was a significant moment in Mackintosh's career.[13] The programme was for a contemporary art school; the designs had to address a challenging site and a very limited budget. The winning scheme was designed by Mackintosh. The first phase of the building opened in 1899; the design demonstrated many novel features, including an asymmetrical main façade with large north-facing windows for the spacious studios and innovative ornamental detailing. The remarkable library wing was completed in a second phase between 1907 and 1909.[14] The West façade for the library wing also incorporates Mackintosh's interest in historic Scottish architecture, particularly "baronial" castles. According to the architectural historian Thomas Howarth the façade,

> is one of the architect's most daring compositions. . . . With its exciting horizontal rhythms and soaring verticals of glass and metal, its large plain surfaces of masonry, and rigid clean-cut angularity of form, this elevation represents not a step forward of a mere decade, but a stride forward of twenty or thirty years in British architectural development.[15]

The Glasgow School of Art has become a much-regarded building of international importance. Other important institutional projects designed by Mackintosh include the Queen's Cross Church (1899) and the Scotland Street School (1906).

Inspired by the Arts and Crafts movement (see Chapter 8), Mackintosh was also committed to interpreting Scottish vernacular architecture, especially in two important houses he designed in the early 1900s: Windyhill at Kilmalcolm (1900) and the Hill House at Helensburgh (1903). Both houses employ functional L-shaped plans, a clear articulation of forms, and plain exteriors finished in grey harled plaster, a traditional Scottish coating. The Hill House is the more developed of the two, with the massing of the house and the arrangement of windows reflecting a comfortable functionalism. The interior features a strong interplay between dark wood panelling and stark white surfaces; stencilled ornamentation is integrated along with carefully designed and located pieces of furniture. The main bedroom is a striking example of one of Mackintosh's "white" spaces.[16] Another important body of work in Mackintosh's oeuvre is a series of popular tearooms that he executed primarily for Miss Catherine Cranston, a successful Glasgow entrepreneur.[17] Committed to a total work of design, Mackintosh designed over 400 pieces of furniture in a wide variety of types; most of his furniture designs were designed for specific spaces.

★ ★ ★

Vienna, Austria, at the beginning of the 20th century, was a fertile and modern city as philosophers, artists, musicians, and architects challenged historical conventions. In particular, the revolutionary psychoanalytical work of Sigmund Freud (1856–1939) captured the *zeitgeist* of the period.[18] It was also a period during which the Austro-Hungarian empire began to decline, coming to an end in 1918. A leading figure in architecture was Otto Wagner (1841–1918), who was born in Vienna and studied architecture at the Technical University and at the Academy of Fine Arts. After graduating in 1863, he established a successful and normative practice. By 1889, Wagner, influenced by younger colleagues known as the "Wagnerschule," embraced an emerging modernity. In 1894, he won the competition to design the infrastructure for Vienna's new commuter train system, the Stadhbahn, a project that would involve 40 stations, bridges, and viaducts. The same year, he was appointed head of one of the architecture programmes at the Academy of Fine Arts.[19]

A trio of younger architects both inspired Wagner and followed in his footsteps: Joseph Maria Olbrich (1867–1908), Josef Hoffmann (1870–1956), and Jože Plečnik (1872–1957). Olbrich was born in Troppau, Silesia (now Opava in Czechia); at the age of 14 he travelled to Vienna to study architecture. In 1897, a group of leading artists and architects, led by the painter Gustav Klimt (1862–1918) and Olbrich, formed a group known as the "Vienna Secession." As the name suggests, the movement was a protest against the establishment art and architecture then in favour. Almost immediately, the group decided it would publish a magazine called *Ver Sacrum* (or Sacred Spring) to disseminate their work and promote the work of key European artists and the Art Nouveau movement. The group secured a site to build a new exhibition building designed by Olbrich. The Secession building instantly announced the presence of a new architecture with its bold one-storey form for the exhibition space, topped by a light gilded dome of laurel leaves supported on four piers.[20] In 1899, after working with Wagner, Olbrich moved to Darmstadt, Germany, to be involved in the creation of a new artist's colony where he designed houses and other facilities in a lyrical and unique interpretation of Art Nouveau.[21]

As Wagner embraced the Secessionist approach of the younger generation, his designs for the Majolica Apartment House (1899), the Karlsplatz station (1899), and the Postal Savings Bank (1906 and 1912) were projects where he came closest to achieving a modern Secessionist architecture. Wagner's book *Moderne Architektur*, first published in 1896, was a radical and influential book; as architectural historian Harry Francis Mallgrave states: "There are three principal themes of *Modern Architecture*: a plea for simplicity in the accommodation of modern needs, the artistic and ethical ruin of eclecticism, and the demand for a new style based on present technologies and methods of construction."[22] Mallgrave argues that Wagner was the first European architect "to state publicly his break with the past."[23]

Josef Hoffmann was born in Pirnitz, Moravia (now Brtnice in Czechia) into a locally important family and studied architecture under Wagner at the Academy of Fine Arts in Vienna (1892–1895). Wagner was one of the co-founders of the Secession group; he was also involved with the Wiener Werkstätte, an organization dedicated to the production of well-designed and crafted products. Hoffmann had a strong interest in the English Arts and Crafts movement, particularly the work of Mackintosh.[24] Hoffmann's most significant building is the large Stoclet House in Brussels (1908), which exists as one of the finest examples of Secession design. Hoffmann continued to practise into the 1940s, experimenting with modernism and executing some work during the National Socialist era in Austria.

Another intriguing architect to emerge from Vienna during the Secession era was the Slovenian architect Jože Plečnik. He first studied at a vocational college in Ljubljana, then in Graz (Austria), before moving to Vienna in 1894 to work for Wagner. He entered the Academy of Fine Arts in 1895, graduating in 1898. Soon after, he started his own practice, experimenting with Art Nouveau, Secession, and even Expressionist influences. Plečnik moved to Prague in 1911 to take a teaching position. In 1920, he was appointed the architect of Prague Castle. Although he would return to Ljubljana in 1922 to take a professorship at the university, he worked diligently on an inventive and sensitive transformation of the Castle until 1935.[25] Plečnik's other major commission in Prague was the Sacred Heart Church (1932). In the mid-1920s, Plečnik began a series of important urban projects in Ljubljana, including various interventions along the city's rivers.

★ ★ ★

The great opponent to the Art Nouveau and Secessionist movement was the Moravian/Austrian architect Adolf Loos (1870–1933). Born in Brno in Moravia (now in Czechia), he studied architecture in Vienna and Dresden before spending several years in the United States. Returning to Vienna in 1896, he established himself as a cultural critic and architect, and a vocal opponent of Art Nouveau design. A champion of English design, Loos's essay "Ornament and Crime" (1908) defined a new attitude to ornament. Loos begins the essay with a racist attack on indigenous cultures by comparing the tattoos of "Papuans" with those of criminals. He categorically states that the evolution of a culture equates to the removal of ornamentation.[26] In the essay, he writes:

> Ornament means squandered manpower and thus squandered health. It has always been so. But today it also means squandered material and both together mean squandered capital. . . . As the ornament is no longer organically connected with our culture, ornament is no longer the expression of our culture.[27]

Loos argues that ornament was not necessary for contemporary design. In his architectural practice, Loos developed a distinctive approach to modern architecture based on abstracted and timeless Classicism. He also developed the *Raumplan* concept for designing houses in which a series of rooms of differing sizes are carefully fitted into a simple volume, creating striking spatial relationships.[28] Noteworthy projects include the Goldman & Salatasch (1911) commercial building in Vienna and a series of houses culminating in the Müller house (1930) in Prague. Loos's impact on modern architecture was complex, based on his challenging of existing ideas and models.[29]

★ ★ ★

The Art Nouveau movement, as expressed differently in various cities and by various architects, was short-lived. Deeply idiosyncratic, the designs often required exceptional craft to execute, and while there are characteristic features, they did not coalesce into a repeatable language of architecture. It quickly became dated as the forces of modernism gained momentum after 1910. As architectural historian Alan Colquhoun observes, it blurred the line between ornament and form (and structure):

> In Art Nouveau, this 'functional' dependency on ornament led to a paradoxical reversal. Instead of merely obeying the form of the object, ornament began to merge with the object, animating it with new life. This had two effects: first, the object became thought of as a single organic entity rather than as an aggregation of separate parts, as in the classical tradition; second, ornament was no longer thought of as "space filling," and a dialogue was set up between two positive values – ornament and empty space. The discovery of what might be called "spatial silence" – probably mainly derived from Japanese prints – was one of Art Nouveau's chief contributions to Western aesthetics.[30]

NOTES

1 A.W.N. Pugin, "From *The True Principles of Pointed or Christian Architecture* (1842)," in Harry Francis Mallgrave, ed., *Architectural Theory*, Volume 1 (Malden, MA: Blackwell Publishing, 2006), p. 385. See also Owen Jones, *The Grammar of Ornament* (London: Day & Son, 1856).

2 Antoine Picon, *Ornament: The Politics of Architecture and Subjectivity* (Chicester: John Wiley & Sons Ltd., 2013), p. 50.

3 Ibid., p. 54.

4 Robert Schmutzler, *Art Nouveau* (London: Thames & Hudson, 1978), p. 7.

5 See Franco Borsi and Paolo Portoghesi, *Victor Horta* (London: Academy Editions, 1991), pp. 37–47.

6 See Ibid., pp. 21–35.

7 See Ignasi de Solà-Morales, *Antoni Gaudí* (New York: Harry N. Abrams, 2003), pp. 7–19.

8 Ibid., p. 18.

9 See Ibid., pp. 20–25.

10 See Joan Norell Núñez, "Gaudí and the Catalan Craftsmen of His Time," in Maria Antonietta Crippa, ed., *Living Gaudí: The Architect's Complete Vision* (New York: Rizzoli, 2002), pp. 85–100.

11 Mackintosh and Margaret Macdonald married in 1900, a year after McNair and Frances Macdonald married.

12 See Roger Billcliffe, *Mackintosh Furniture* (Cambridge: Lutterworth Press, 1984). See also Alan Crawford, *Charles Rennie Mackintosh* (London: Thames & Hudson, 1995), pp. 66–100.

13 See Thomas Howarth, *Charles Rennie Mackintosh and the Modern Movement* (London: Routledge & Kegan Paul, 1977), pp. 53–68.

14 See Ibid., pp. 69–92.

15 Ibid., p. 75.

16 See Ibid., pp. 93–120.

17 See Ibid., pp. 121–147.

18 See Carl E. Schorske, *Fin-de-siècle Vienna: Politics and Culture* (New York: Vintage Books, 1981).

19 Harry F. Mallgrave, "Introduction," in Otto Wagner, ed., *Modern Architecture* (Los Angeles: The Getty Center, 1988), pp. 1–51.

20 See Ian Latham, *Joseph Maria Olbrich* (New York: Rizzoli, 1980), pp. 9–47.

21 See Ibid., pp. 49–119.

22 Mallgrave, "Introduction," p. 29.

23 Ibid., p. 30.

24 See Eduard F. Sekler, *Josef Hoffmann: The Architectural Work* (Princeton: Princeton University Press, 1985).

25 See Damjan Prelovšek, "The Life and Work of Jože Plečnik," in François Burkhardt, Claude Eveno, and Boris Podrecca, eds., *Jože Plečnik, Architect: 1872–1957* (Cambridge, MA: MIT Press, 1989), pp. 26–81.

26 Adolf Loos, "Ornament and Crime," in *Ornament and Crime* (London: Penguin Book, 2019), pp. 187–189.
27 Ibid., p. 195.
28 See Alan Colquhoun, *Modern Architecture* (Oxford: Oxford University Press, 2002), pp. 81–84.
29 In 1928, Loos was charged with the sexual abuse of young girls and possessing child pornography; he was acquitted on the sexual abuse charges but received a suspended sentence for "seduction to indecency." The charges effectively ended his career. See Christopher Long, *Loos on Trial* (Prague: Kant, 2017).
30 Colquhoun, *Modern Architecture*, p. 17.

SUGGESTED READING

Brett, David. *C.R. Mackintosh: The Poetics of Workmanship*. London: Reaktion Books, 2004.

Pevsner, Nikolaus. *Pioneers of Modern Design*. Harmondsworth: Penguin Books, 1960.

Picon, Antoine. *Ornament: The Politics of Architecture and Subjectivity*. Chicester: John Wiley & Sons Ltd., 2013.

Safran, Y., and W. Wang, eds. *The Architecture of Adolf Loos*. London: Arts Council, 1985.

Schmutzler, Robert. *Art Nouveau*. London: Thames & Hudson, 1978.

10

SPACE AND FORM

Architecture has always contained space, space that supports a variety of culturally specific functions, and yet it wasn't until the 19th century that German theorists began to identify space as a distinct aspect of architecture.[1] With the advent of modern architecture in the early 20th century, space, or volume, became a primary feature of architecture along with new concepts of form. As art historian Charles W. Millard writes: "In modernist architecture . . . space is the very substance of the building itself. It penetrates and shapes the structure, and can be said to be neither behind or around it, it is through it and of it, undelimited and re-entrant."[2] In modern architecture, the interconnection between interior and exterior space was also emphasized, along with movement through space. Some of the thinking about modern architectural space was inspired by Albert Einstein's Theory of Special Relativity (1905) and Cubist art that fused space and time together (see Chapter 11).

It was the American architect Frank Lloyd Wright (1867–1959) who first created a new vision of modern architecture. Wright was influenced by architects like Henry Hobson Richardson (1838–1886) and Louis H. Sullivan (1856–1924), his interest in the Arts and Crafts, his love of the mid-Western American landscape, and his passion for Japanese art and design. Wright's distinctive Prairie architecture, developed in the first years of the 20th century, would have an immediate impact on architects, particularly on European architects, after the publication of the Wasmuth portfolio of his drawings in 1910.

DOI: 10.4324/9781003403975-10

Wright grew up in rural Wisconsin in a family with Welsh origins. His mother pushed him to become an architect and introduced him at a young age to the Froebel building block system, a popular German children's toy, which was influential on his later ideas of architectural order. He briefly studied engineering at the University of Wisconsin before moving to Chicago in 1887 to pursue architecture. After apprenticing for the architect Joseph Lyman Silsbee, he joined the well-known firm of Adler & Sullivan in 1888. Sullivan, whom Wright always referred to as his *Leiber Meister* or "dear master," mentored him. Wright was fired from the firm in 1893 due to his "moonlighting" activities, something he did to support his growing family.

After leaving Adler & Sullivan, Wright established his practice. His first project, the Winslow House (1893) in River Forest, Illinois, signalled the beginning of a series of experiments that culminated in the Prairie Style house first published in drawings for the *Ladies' Home Journal* (February and July 1901). Houses such as the Ward Willits House in Highland Park, Illinois (1901) were the first built examples of the new style. This launched a period of immense creative activity that resulted in designs such as the Martin House (1904) in Buffalo, New York, and the Robie House (1907) in Chicago, Illinois. At the same time, he extended his concepts into larger buildings such as the Unity Temple (1905) in Oak Park, Illinois, and the Larkin Company Administration Building (1908) in Buffalo, New York.

Wright described his early accomplishments in a text entitled "Prairie Architecture," published in 1931, in which he wrote about how he defined the Prairie Style. In the text, he describes his reaction in the early 1890s to the contemporary American house; as a result, he eliminated the attic, the basement, and "the room as a box."[3] The Prairie house that Wright developed was horizontally organized to match the prairie, carefully integrated with its site, and employed an open set of interconnected spaces on the main level typically organized around a large fireplace. Wright's emphasis on horizontality was expressed in long overhanging hip roofs and his definition of space through the ordered use of piers and horizontal and vertical planes. Wright's architecture strove for a simple integration of all elements, including heating, lighting, and furniture, creating what he described as an "organic" totality in which every part belongs to the whole. Wright recognized the role of William Morris and the Arts and Crafts movement (see Chapter 8), but unlike them,

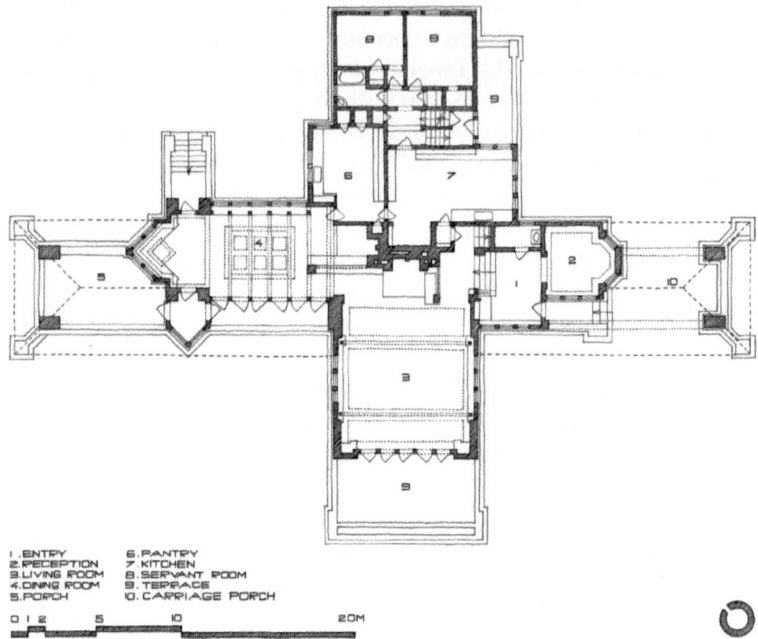

Figure 10.1 Main Floor Plan, Frank Lloyd Wright, Ward Willits House, 1901, Highland Park, Illinois, USA. The cruciform plan, organized around a central fireplace, demonstrates the features typical of the Prairie Style; these include the interpenetration of space and the union of inside and outside. Drawing by Mohammad Moezzi.

he was prepared to employ the machine in building construction.[4] Ultimately, the Prairie house was the breakthrough architects had been seeking during the 19th century.

Architectural historian Robert McCarter provides a comprehensive analysis of the ordering of Wright's buildings, particularly his systemic use of various planning grids and his strict use of geometry. In the early Prairie houses, Wright typically used a pinwheel or a cruciform plan arrangement. McCarter writes that by "disconnecting walls, ceilings, and floors and using them as independent elements, Wright simultaneously *defined* spaces more precisely and *fused* them into larger and more ambiguous compositions."[5] By creating buildings with open plans that broke down the traditional boundaries of space, Wright produced rich spatial systems that were both sheltering and expansive. The spatial organization of a Wright building is related to the way it addresses the site and the choreography of movement through space. His distinctly ordered plans typically used a tartan grid to organize the location of the structure and to create a spatial "weave" that introduced multiple spatial overlaps. Linear shafts, or channels, of space extend through the building and into the landscape; the removal of the corner of rooms and the introduction of corner windows created diagonal movements. The breaking down of the abrupt interface between interior and exterior is usually modulated by covered terraces. The placement of the fireplace at the centre of the house created a condition of movement through the house, consistent with Wright's ideas of living for modern families in suburban Chicago, "to make images of flow a fact, to celebrate continuous space."[6]

As Wright's reputation grew, his personal life became increasingly unconventional and ultimately tragic. As a result of his personal problems and the tumult of World War I, Wright had few commissions until the 1930s, when his reputation revived. Important projects during this difficult period include Taliesin East (1911–1925) in Spring Green, Wisconsin, the Imperial Hotel (1922) in Tokyo, and a series of concrete block houses in California. In 1932, Wright and his third wife, Olgivanna Lazovic, established the Taliesin Fellowship for aspiring architects who wanted to work and learn under Wright. In the 1930s, he developed his sprawling urban scheme known as Broadacre City (1934) and produced designs for low-cost Usonian houses.[7] In a forceful response to the International Style, Wright designed several seminal projects in the last decades of his life, including Fallingwater (1935) in Mill Run, Pennsylvania, the S.C. Johnson and Son Company Buildings (1936) in Racine, Wisconsin, Taliesin West (1937) in Scottsdale, Arizona, and the Solomon R. Guggenheim Museum (1956) in New York.

Wright never fully abandoned the use of ornament and traditional materials, but he used steel and concrete throughout his career. Wright did not produce an "abstract" form of architecture, such as designed by Le Corbusier in the 1920s.[8] One of the most influential architects of the 20th century, Wright's designs would inspire the De Stijl movement in Holland and various European architects. His work would launch regional modernisms in North America, particularly on the West Coast and in the Southwest.

★ ★ ★

Ludwig Mies van der Rohe (1886–1969) acknowledged that the publication of Wright's designs in 1910 had a dramatic impact on him, as it did on other young European architects.[9] Mies was born in Aachen, Germany, where his father worked as a master mason and produced architectural elements. He worked for his father, studied for two years in a local trade school, and was employed in other areas of the building industry. He then took several draughting jobs in local architect's offices before moving to Berlin in 1905. By 1907, he was designing his own houses, and between 1908 and 1911 worked for Peter Behrens (see Chapter 8). In 1911, he established his own practice. His early projects were inspired by Behrens and the classicism of Karl Friedrich Schinkel (see Chapter 6).

During the period 1919–1925, Mies produced drawings for five projects that would have a dramatic impact on his own career and the development of modern architecture. In the drawings he digested the influence of German Expressionism, along with Wright and the De Stijl movement (see Chapter 11). The projects were for two Glass Skyscrapers (1919 and 1921), the Reinforced Concrete Office Building (1922), the Brick Country House (1923), and the Concrete Country House (1924). The drawings for the skyscrapers explored the expressive properties of glass, while the plan for the Brick Country House shows spatial ideas indebted to Wright and the De Stijl group. In 1925, Mies was appointed the director of the Weissenhofseidlung Exhibition held in Stuttgart in 1927, an important display of residential buildings by noteworthy modern architects (see Chapter 12).[10]

In the years 1925–1938, Mies collaborated with the designer Lilly Reich (1885–1947). Together, they designed exhibitions and several important pieces of furniture, including the MR Chair (1927) and the Barcelona Chair (1929).[11] Reich, a self-taught designer, had joined the Deutscher Werkbund in 1912, an organization she was active in throughout her life.[12] In 1930, Mies was appointed the third and last director of the Bauhaus (see Chapter 16). At the Bauhaus, Reich was appointed to head various workshops during 1931–1933. By 1933, the Bauhaus was closed by the National Socialists (Nazis). Reich remained in Germany after Mies moved to Chicago in 1938 to escape Nazism. She would look after his interests in Germany until her death.

Mies's quest for a highly ordered and yet metaphysical architecture was first fully achieved in the Barcelona Pavilion, which was built for an international exposition in 1929. Lacking any real programme the design features a "free plan" of vertical and horizontal planes, often in luxurious materials. As architectural historian David Spaeth writes, "the pavilion exhibits profound structural clarity; simultaneously, it is spatially ambiguous."[13] A significant work of modern architecture, the Barcelona pavilion existed for a year before it was demolished (it was reconstructed in 1986). Abstracting the use of walls and floating roof planes on a raised podium, Mies united a set of influences to create a scheme as architect Philip Johnson describes:

> The design is simultaneously simple and complex: its ingredients are merely steel columns and rectangular planes of various materials placed vertically as walls or horizontally as roofs; but they are disposed in such a way that space is channeled rather than confined – it is never stopped, but is allowed to flow continuously.[14]

The Tugendhat House (1930) in Brno, Moravia (Czechia) was his first functional building in his mature style; it carried on many themes found in the Barcelona Pavilion.

In Chicago, Mies took up the directorship of architecture at the Armour Institute of Technology. Two years later, the Institute merged with another college to become the Illinois Institute of Technology (IIT). Mies was then asked to design the new campus for a site in an existing neighbourhood in Chicago's South Side. Mies devised a formal spatial organization of the campus based on a strict module that governed a simple industrial language of architecture with a palette of steel, brick, and glass. The most significant building on the campus is Crown Hall (1956), designed for the School of Architecture.

In the late phase of his career, Mies developed an austere and precise architecture based on "logic and reason" that was well-suited for corporate clients in America. As Spaeth writes, "It was characteristic of Mies's approach to architecture to reduce every building problem to its clearest most elemental form or state."[15] He invested in the design of the modern skyscraper, devising his signature approach to the curtain wall found in important projects such as the Lake Shore Drive Apartments (1951) in Chicago, the Seagram Building (1958) in New York, and the Federal Center (1973) in Chicago. Among other building typologies, the Farnsworth House (1951) in Plano, Illinois and the New National Gallery (1967) in Berlin stand out. And while his building designs were formal and unyielding in later years, his urban spaces remained subtle and well-considered.

★ ★ ★

The third major figure of modern architecture is Le Corbusier (1887–1965), born Charles-Édouard Jeanneret-Gris in La Chaux-de-Fonds, Switzerland. He is known for focusing on the role of form in architecture. However, Le Corbusier's important architecture, beginning in the early 1920s, has a strong spatial sense. During his formative years, before moving to Paris in 1917, Le Corbusier briefly studied in the local Arts and Crafts school in his hometown, undertook several tours of Europe and Turkey, worked for prominent architects, including Auguste Perret and Peter Behrens, and designed various houses and small buildings in different styles. During this period, he produced the Dom-ino drawing (1915), showing a basic slab and column diagram in concrete that would foreshadow his pioneering work of the 1920s. Later, in 1919, he devised the Maison Monol system and, in 1920, the Maison Citrohan as complementary structural ideas.

Le Corbusier had learned to paint prior to 1917. However, meeting the artist Amédée Ozenfant (1886–1966) later that year would have a transformative impact on his career. Ozenfant instructed him in the avant-garde painting methods of the time. Together, they created Purism, a rationalized interpretation of late Cubism, that featured precise paintings of everyday objects in formal still-life compositions that emphasized the depiction of pure forms. From 1920 to 1925, Le Corbusier and Ozenfant edited a sophisticated journal called *L'Esprit Nouveau*, which allowed them to investigate a wide range of topics and promote their ideas to a wider audience.

Le Corbusier's *Vers une architecture* (*Toward an Architecture*), published in 1923, was a collection of texts from the journal and is arguably the most important book published on modern architecture. He divides the book into sections devoted to mechanical and classical themes.[16] He expresses his admiration for works by engineers, including bridges, grain elevators, and modern machines, an echo of the long debates of the 19th century. In the section "Three Reminders to Architects," he writes: "Volume and surface are the elements through which architecture manifests itself. Volume and surface are determined by the plan. It is the plan that is the generator."[17] Further, he notes: "The architect, through the ordonnance [arrangement] of forms, realizes an order that is a pure creation of mind; through forms, he affects our senses intensely, provoking plastic emotions."[18] By forms, he means pure primary forms, and by "volume," he alludes to space. In the section "Eyes That Do Not See . . ." he discusses ocean liners, airplanes, and automobiles. He states that "the lesson of the airplane is in the logic that governed the statement of the problem and that led to the success of its realization. . . . The problem of the house has not been posed."[19] He goes on to outline his ideas for the modern house, suggesting that a modern house should be as precise as a modern machine. Despite the appearance of being a functionalist, there is a complexity to Le Corbusier's architecture that challenges this interpretation.

As Le Corbusier developed the formal and spatial aspects of Purist painting, he transferred this to his architecture, particularly during the 1920s. Art historian Christopher Green states:

> Le Corbusier approached each Purist building very much as if it were a Purist painting; they were conceived as groupings of smoothly functioning parts composed within the discipline of geometry and a grid of "regulating lines" based on the Golden Section ratio, each functioning part, from light-fitting to radiator, to ramp, an architectural *objet-type* to be placed within an ordered whole. And these buildings are set against their natural surroundings; they are geometric containers, prismatic volumes, each visible façade a frontally composed screen through which light passes to model the surfaces of austere but richly sculptured interiors.[20]

Le Corbusier developed a painting method that typically framed a set of ordinary objects that are viewed frontally in a way that used a plan/elevation method similar to an axonometric. The shallow spaces of the paintings also emphasized the outline of objects, or what the Purists called "a marriage of contours," this informed Le Corbusier's paintings, building plans, and concepts of form and surface.[21] His Purist architecture truly began with a studio house he designed for Ozenfant (1924) in Paris; this was followed by a series of revolutionary designs that gained him international recognition.

Le Corbusier articulated his architectural vision with his architect cousin Pierre Jeanneret (1896–1967) in a text entitled "Five Points of a New Architecture." The five points are: 1) pilotis, 2) roof gardens, 3) *le plan libre*, or the free plan, 4) *la fenêtre en longueur*, or the horizontal strip window, and 5) *la façade libre*, or the free façade. These are a reversal of historical ideas about architecture, supplemented by the "promenade architecturale," which describes the movement through a building's volumes and surfaces. In projects such as the Maison La Roche-Jeanneret (1925) in Paris, the Maison Cook (1927) in Boulogne-sure-Seine, the Villa Stein de Monzie (1928) in Garches, and the Villa Savoye (1931) in Poissy, Le Corbusier presented his fully developed concepts for a modern architecture, particularly his

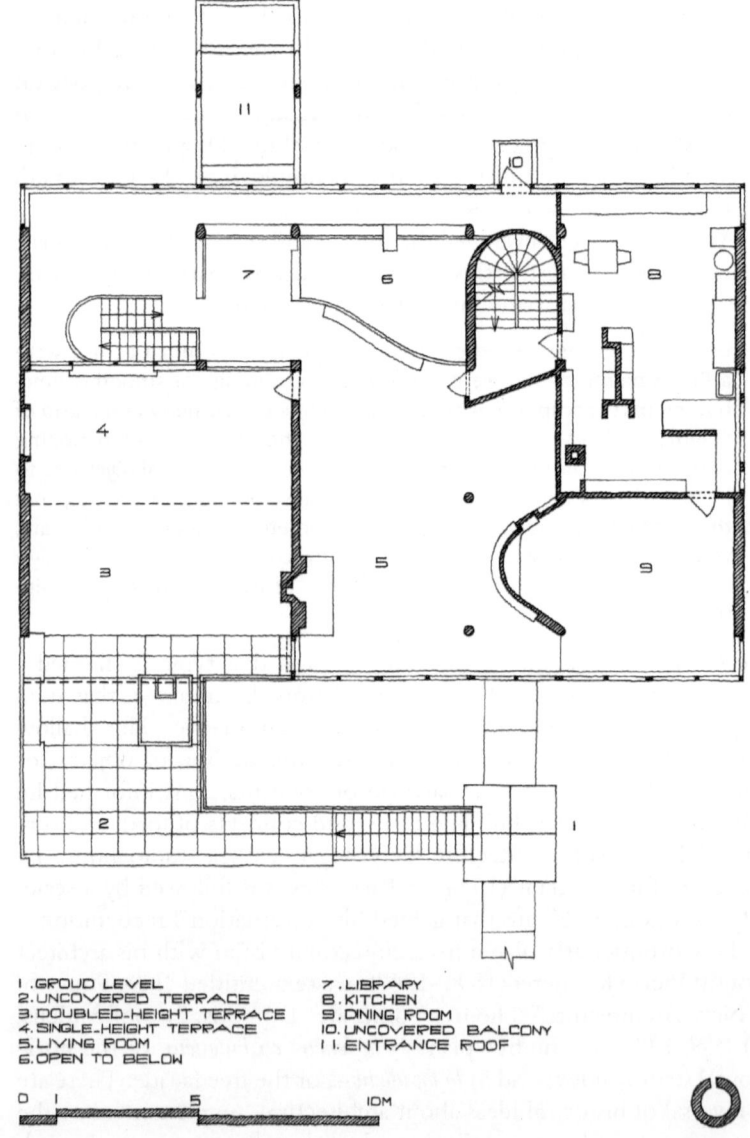

1. GROUD LEVEL
2. UNCOVERED TERRACE
3. DOUBLED-HEIGHT TERRACE
4. SINGLE-HEIGHT TERRACE
5. LIVING ROOM
6. OPEN TO BELOW
7. LIBRARY
8. KITCHEN
9. DINING ROOM
10. UNCOVERED BALCONY
11. ENTRANCE ROOF

0   1   5   10M

Figure 10.2 First Floor Plan, Le Corbusier, Villa Stein-de Monzie, 1928, Garches, Paris, France. The design features an organization of space that is functional, unified by the *promenade architecturale* with its emphasis on movement through space and the careful location of vertical circulation elements such as stairs. Drawing by Mohammad Moezzi.

notion of the free plan. The villas encompassed deep and shallow volumes of space, spaces carved out of defined cubic volumes, and spaces understood through choreographed motion.[22] In the 1920s, he also designed a series of important furniture pieces with Charlotte Perriand (1903–1999)[23] and Pierre Jeanneret. In this period, he also began to produce visionary projects for the city, and his commitment to urban design continued throughout his career (see Chapter 7).

By 1930, Le Corbusier's work took a dramatic shift in direction as he abandoned the strict Purist architecture of the 1920s. As he took on larger projects, he developed an interest in new ways of working with materials, along with a commitment to regional forms of expression. During the 1930s and early 1940s he was involved in wide-ranging exploration, important projects included the Cité de Refuge for the Salvation Army (1933) and the Pavillon Suisse (1933), both in Paris. After World War II, he began a phase distinguished by the use of *béton brut*, or rough poured-in-place concrete, that has become known as the Brutalist style (see Chapter 18). Important late works include the Unité d'Habitation (1952) in Marseilles, the Chapelle Notre-Dame du Haut (1955) at Ronchamp, the Convent of Sainte-Marie de la Tourette (1960) in Eveux-sur-l'Arbresle, and a series of projects in India (1950–1965).

★ ★ ★

The invention of the open or free plan is one of the hallmarks of early 20th-century modern architecture. This ranges from the geometrically ordered space of Frank Lloyd Wright to the Purist space of Le Corbusier. The union of space with movement creates a four-dimensional experience, what the architectural historian Sigfried Giedion termed "space-time" in architecture.[24] Ultimately, as Mies van der Rohe wrote in 1923: "Architecture is the will of the age conceived in spatial terms. Living. Changing. Now."[25]

NOTES

1 See Peter Collins, *Changing Ideals in Modern Architecture* (Montreal: MQUP, 1967), pp. 285–293.

2 Charles W. Millard, "Modernist Architectural Space," *The Hudson Review*, vol. 20, no. 3 (Autumn 1967), p. 450.

3 See Frank Lloyd Wright, "Prairie Architecture," in Edgar Kaufmann and Ben Raeburn, eds., *Frank Lloyd Wright: Writings and Buildings* (New York: Meridian, 1960), pp. 38–47.

4   See Frank Lloyd Wright, "The Art and Craft of the Machine," in Kaufmann and Raeburn, eds., *Frank Lloyd Wright*, pp. 55–73.

5   Robert McCarter, "The Integrated Ideal: Ordering Principles in Wright's Architecture," in Robert McCarter, ed., *On and By Frank Lloyd Wright: A Primer of Architectural Principles* (London: Phaidon, 2005), p. 309.

6   Vincent Scully, *Frank Lloyd Wright* (New York: George Braziller, Inc., 1960), p. 11.

7   See Frank Lloyd Wright, *The Natural House* (New York: Horizon Press, 1954).

8   See Neil Levine, "Abstraction and Representation in Modern Architecture: The International Style of Frank Lloyd Wright," *AA Files*, no. 11 (Spring 1986), pp. 3–21.

9   See Mies van der Rohe, "A Tribute to Frank Lloyd Wright," in H. Allen Brooks, ed., *Writings on Wright* (Cambridge, MA: MIT Press, 1981), pp. 129–130.

10 See Karin Kirsch, *The Weissenhofseidlung: Experimental Housing Built for the Deutscher Werkbund, Stuttgart, 1927* (New York: Rizzoli, 1990).

11 See Christian Lange, *Ludwig Mies van der Rohe & Lilly Reich: Furniture and Interiors* (Ostfildern: Hatje Cantz Verlag, 2006).

12 See Carmen Espegel, *Women Architects in the Modern Movement* (New York: Routledge, 2018), pp. 136–163.

13 David Spaeth, "Ludwig Mies van der Rohe: A Biographical Essay," in Robert V. Sharp, ed., *Mies Reconsidered: His Career, Legacy, and Disciples* (New York: Rizzoli, 1986), p. 18.

14 Philip C. Johnson, *Mies van der Rohe* (New York: Museum of Modern Art, 1975), p. 58.

15 Spaeth, "Ludwig Mies van der Rohe," p. 33.

16 Reyner Banham, *Theory and Design in the First Machine Age* (New York: Praeger Publishing, 1967), pp. 223–224.

17 Le Corbusier, *Toward an Architecture* (Los Angeles: Getty Publications, 2007), p. 102.

18 Ibid., p. 92.

19 Ibid., pp. 161–162.

20 Christopher Green, "The Architect as Artist," in Michael Raeburn and Victoria Wilson, eds., *Le Corbusier: Architect of the Century* (London: Arts Council of Great Britain, 1987), p. 114.

21 See Richard Ingersoll, *Le Corbusier: A Marriage of Contours* (New York: Princeton Architectural Press, 1990).

22 Sigfried Giedion, *Space, Time and Architecture; The Growth of a New Tradition* (Cambridge, MA: Harvard University Press, 1982), p. 529.

23 See Mary McLeod, "Furniture and Femininity," *Architectural Review*, vol. CLXXXI, no. 1079 (January 1987), pp. 43–46.

24 See Giedion, *Space, Time and Architecture*.

25 Ludwig Mies van der Rohe, "Working Theses," in Ulrich Conrads, ed., *Programs and Manifestoes on 20th-Century Architecture* (Cambridge, MA: MIT Press, 1990), p. 74.

SUGGESTED READING

Frampton, Kenneth. *Le Corbusier*. New York: Thames & Hudson, Inc., 2001.

Le Corbusier. *Toward an Architecture*. Los Angeles: Getty Publications, 2007.

McCarter, Robert, ed. *On and By Frank Lloyd Wright: A Primer of Architectural Principles*. London: Phaidon, 2005.

Mertins, Detlef. *Mies*. London: Phaidon, 2014.

Wright, Frank Lloyd. *The Natural House*. New York: Horizon Press, 1954.

11

AVANT-GARDE AND REPRESENTATION

Architects have been employing an evolving set of architectural drawing methods and types for centuries. These can be described as two-dimensional (2D) drawings (such as orthographic drawings: plan, section, and elevation), three-dimensional (3D) drawings (such as perspective and axonometric drawings), and even four-dimensional (4D) approaches which include animations and videos. Architectural drawings include sketches, "presentation" drawings, and construction documents. The word "representation" is often given to a broad range of architectural drawing types and media, which are employed by architects to design and depict buildings.[1] Since the invention of perspective in the 1420s by Filippo Brunelleschi (1377–1446) there have been many transformations in 3D architectural representation. Perspective was initially realized in one-point drawings and paintings, but this would develop into two, three, and multi-point images over time.

Challenges to the conventions of perspective began seriously in the 18th century with Giovanni Battista Piranesi (1720–1778), who produced conventional views of Rome, along with his hallucinogenic and frightening depictions of prison interiors. The prison images, the *Carceri* engravings (1750 and 1761, two editions), broke down the concept of a single viewing position. These suggested a moving observer, something more like the way humans experience the world, as opposed to the static view typically found in perspective compositions.[2] The invention of photography in the 19th century by pioneers such as Louis Daguerre (1787–1851) completely

DOI: 10.4324/9781003403975-11

altered the human perception and representation of the world. This would be augmented by the invention of cinema late in the century. Challenged by these new technologies, painters turned to new subject matters (the Realists) and to new ways of capturing colour, light, and space (the Impressionists).

By the early 20th century, a host of "avant-garde" art movements emerged that were devoted to experimentation and innovation and radically transformed approaches to representation. Some also introduced the concept of abstract art. Avant-garde movements include Cubism, Expressionism, Fauvism, Futurism (see Chapter 13), De Stijl, Surrealism, and Dada. Some of these impacted developments in architecture, and some did not. These new movements invoke the concept of the avant-garde, which dates from the 1850s. The expression comes from French and is a military term that refers to an "advance guard" or "vanguard." The notion of avant-garde is also linked to the concept of the "new" in modernism.

★ ★ ★

Paul Cézanne (1839–1906) was a crucial figure in the development of modern art in the 20th century; his paintings are situated between the atmospheric works of the Impressionists and the development of Cubism. Cézanne's attempts to capture a new approach to painting, "with its brilliant use of colour and its mysterious deformations, which suggested a range of new pictorial concepts,"[3] was immensely influential. In a famous statement, Cézanne writes:

> [T]reat nature by the cylinder, the sphere, the cone, everything in proper perspective so that each side of an object or a plane is directed towards a central point. Lines parallel to the horizon give breadth. . . . Lines perpendicular to this horizon give depth. But nature for us men is more depth than surface, whence the need of introducing into our light vibrations, represented by reds and yellows, a sufficient amount of blue to give the impression of air.[4]

Avoiding the use of perspective, Cézanne painted objects and space as though they were shaped into a perceptual unity. His techniques prefigured the development of Cubism.

The development of Cubism by Pablo Picasso (1881–1973) and Georges Braque (1882–1963), during 1907–1914, produced a new way of depicting a 3D image on a 2D surface. As John Golding states, "Cubism was a completely new pictorial language,"[5] it would have an enormous impact on developments in 20th-century art and design. Picasso already had a well-established reputation and had painted the very important *Les Demoiselles d'Avignon* canvas (1907), a painting representing a group of five prostitutes that foreshadowed the birth of Cubism. Severe, distorted, and angular, the painting captures the figures in a shallow space. While making the painting, Picasso was inspired by traditional African and Polynesian sculpture.[6] Picasso also broke the conventions of perspective by introducing multiple viewpoints. Braque quickly took up the challenge of Picasso's experimentation. By 1908, the two artists were meeting daily, establishing an intense relationship focused on devising new representational techniques.

The two artists achieved a truly Cubist representation in 1909, after which the rate of their invention accelerated. Within months, the complexity of the work had increased, resulting in what is termed "analytical" Cubism. Golding describes this in the following terms:

> These paintings give the sensation that Braque [and Picasso] has felt his way visually around each object and examined its relationships with the other objects around it from several viewpoints. By rendering the areas between the objects in a tactile, material fashion, Braque succeeds in fusing objects and space into a spatial continuum composed of small, fluid, interpenetrating planes [*passage*]. It is this concrete rendering of the space around the highly fragmented objects that gives these paintings a sensation of unprecedented complexity.[7]

During 1910–1911, Braque began to introduce lettering and other devices into his compositions, anticipating later developments, including the invention of collage. The Cubist paintings from this period radically reduced the colour palette to compensate for the complexity of the technique, which involved breaking down the image into planes, incorporating a moving observer, and establishing a fusion of space, time, and object. The subjects of the paintings were typically portraits or still-lifes of ordinary objects. Cubism emphasized the "materialization" of space. By 1910, other artists and patrons had joined the Cubist cause, producing works of great controversy.

A major aspect of Cubism was collage (and/or *papier collé*, as gluing paper to the canvas), a technique pioneered in Picasso's 1912 canvas entitled *Still Life with Chair-caning*. It is "the first painting in which extraneous objects or materials are applied to the picture surface."[8] By adding materials to canvases, such as fragments of newspaper and wallpaper, the Cubists further challenged the established conventions of art.[9]

How did the pictorial inventions of the Cubists translate into architecture? The sculptor Raymond Duchamp-Villon (1876–1918) was one of the first to attempt a Cubist sculpture, which is evident in his *Le Cheval* from 1914. He was also one of the first to propose Cubist architecture in his earlier façade project for the *Maison Cubiste* (1912). Simultaneously, a form of Cubist architecture was also developed by various Czech architects, primarily in Prague.[10] Colin Rowe and Robert Slutzky's seminal essay entitled "Transparency: Literal and Phenomenal," published in 1963, was an effort to link Cubism to architecture through the concept of "transparency," or "overlapping figures."[11] Undoubtedly, the most successful architecture derived from Cubism is found in the Purist work of Le Corbusier from the 1920s (see Chapter 10).

★ ★ ★

German Expressionism emerged as an art movement in 1905 when a group of architecture students established die Brücke (The Bridge) in Dresden. Inspired by the German Art Nouveau, indigenous Non-Western ritual art (from Africa, Oceania, Asia, and the Americas),[12] older Western art, the paintings of Vincent van Gogh (1853–1890) and Paul Gauguin (1848–1903), and the philosophy of Friedrich Nietzsche, the group's name alluded to a "bridge" between the artist and the public.[13] The die Brücke group developed a similar approach to the French Fauvist movement under Henri Matisse (1869–1954). Depictions were angular and often executed in black-and-white woodcuts or highly coloured canvases, often representing urban scenes.

A second group formed in Munich in 1911 around Wassily Kandinsky (1866–1944), known as the Der Blaue Reiter (The Blue Rider) exhibiting society. Deeply committed to spiritualism in art and movements such as Theosophy and Anthroposophy, the group was influenced by sources similar to their Dresden predecessors. In his text *Concerning the Spiritual in Art* (1911), Kandinsky advocates for expressing spirituality through colour, form, and specific shapes (the triangle and pyramid). He writes: "The mutual influence of form and colour now becomes clear. A yellow triangle, a blue circle, a green square, or a green triangle, a yellow circle, a blue square – all these are different and have different spiritual values."[14] There was also a stronger tendency towards abstraction with the Der Blaue Reiter group, particularly in the paintings of Kandinsky, he is often credited with painting the first "abstract" work of art with his *Composition V* painting of 1911.

The relationship between painting and architecture in Expressionism was often tangential, with artists and architects exploring similar themes in their works. A preoccupation with unconventional forms, often angular and jarring, and spiritualism and emotionalism characterized the movement. Expressionism in architecture covers several initiatives, primarily in Holland and Germany. The Amsterdam School is an early manifestation of Expressionism, centring on the work of Michel de Klerk (1884–1923), Piet Kramer (1881–1961), and Johan van der Mey (1878–1949), all of whom worked in the offices of the architect Eduard Cuypers (1859–1927). The first building associated with the Amsterdam movement is the Scheepvaarthuis (1916), designed by Van der May with input from De Klerk and Kramer. Active between 1915 and 1930, the Amsterdam group established its reputation primarily through the design of housing blocks. Inspired by an exalted idea of the architect, the School "stressed the notion of the artist as a prophet, an individual endowed with the gift of special insight and therefore someone capable of recognizing essential truths and transmitting them to society as a whole."[15]

In Germany, the work of an older generation of architects, such as Hans Poelzig (1869–1936), laid the groundwork for the emergence of Expressionist architecture. The figure most associated with German Expressionist architecture was Bruno Taut (1880–1938), who tirelessly promoted the movement until the early 1920s. Taut's own ideas about architecture were inspired by the writings of Paul Scheerbart (1863–1915), who would dedicate his 1914 book *Glasarchitektur* to Taut. In the book, Scheerbart describes the benefits of a glass architecture:

> Our culture is to a certain extent the product of our architecture. If we want our culture to rise to a higher level, we are obliged, for better or worse, to change our architecture. And this is only possible if we take away the closed character from the rooms in which we live. We can only do that by introducing glass architecture, which lets in the light of the sun, the moon, and the stars, not merely through a few windows, but through every possible wall, which will be made entirely of glass – of coloured glass.[16]

Inspired by Gothic cathedrals, this new glass architecture sought to cover the earth in a sparkling array of coloured light. Taut translated Scheerbart's ideas in his most developed Expressionist building, the temporary Glass Pavilion for the Cologne Werkbund exhibition of 1914 (see Chapter 8). The construction featured a kaleidoscopic use of glass and light and included a double skin, coloured glass, and inscriptions devised by Scheerbart.[17] In 1919, Taut published two important books on architecture: *Die Stadtkrone* and *Alpine Architektur*. *Alpine Architektur* features 30 highly evocative drawings executed in pencil and ink, which show a fantastical and colourful crystalline architecture that sits on mountain tops and fills valleys.[18]

Another architect associated with Expressionism was Erich Mendelsohn (1887–1953), a Jewish-German contributor to modernism; his architecture can also be described as "dynamic functionalism" with its emphasis on curvilinear forms.[19] Mendelsohn's most striking building is his early Einstein Tower at the astrophysical observatory in Potsdam, completed in 1921. A laboratory dedicated to the study of Albert Einstein's theories of relativity, the building employs sculptural and organic forms expressing motion. During the 1920s, Mendelsohn established an influential practice in Berlin. He moved to the forefront of modernism with the distinctive use of "sweeping" horizontally banded and curved forms,[20] an expression of the speed of modern life that foreshadowed the development of "streamlining" in design. During the 1920s, many of his clients were Jewish businessmen for whom he designed department stores.[21] The rise of Nazism forced Mendelsohn into exile. After working in England and Palestine, he settled in the United States, where he designed several synagogues.

By 1923, the impact of Expressionism was in decline; however, the movement influenced the formation of the Bauhaus and the early glass skyscraper designs of Mies van der Rohe (see Chapter 10). Beyond the rationalist principles of modern functionalism, Expressionism revealed a spiritual and emotional role in architecture.

★ ★ ★

Space and time. The new architecture takes account not only of space but also the magnitude of *time*. Through the unity of space and time the architectural exterior will acquire a new and completely plastic aspect.[22]

Another vital 20th-century avant-garde movement was the De Stijl group. It arose out of World War I and sought a universalist abstraction by "striving for a precision such as found in the products of the machine" and in the Dutch landscape.[23] Primarily a Dutch movement, it was led by the artist and polemicist Theo van Doesburg (1883–1931), although the formative abstract paintings of

Piet Mondrian (1872–1944) would be the real source of inspiration for the artists, architects, and furniture makers who comprised the loose-knit collective. The De Stijl movement was very effective in integrating "architecture into a universal theory of art" that had widespread appeal, along with an emphasis on rectangular shapes, separated volumes, and asymmetrical compositions (what would become the hallmarks of the International Style, see Chapter 12).[24]

Mondrian, Kandinsky, and the Russian artist Kazimir Malevich (1879–1935) were the first artists to produce abstract or non-figurative paintings (see Chapter 14). Beginning with Fauvist and Symbolist modes of painting, Mondrian discovered Cézanne and Cubism by 1911. From his Cubist phase, he steadily transformed towards what he called "neo-plasticism." He would paint his first truly abstract canvas in 1917 with *Composition in Line*. Striving for harmony and balance, Mondrian developed his famous mature paintings in the 1920s; these were "reduced to a group of "universal," atomic elements: planes of primary color opposing planes of "non-color" – gray, black, white; vertical lines opposing horizontal lines while probing the various planes that delimit the surface of the canvas."[25]

The De Stijl group first met in 1917 and included Van Doesburg, Mondrian, and the architects J.P.P. Oud (1890–1963) and Robert van 't Hoff; Gerrit Reitveld (1888–1964) would join in 1918. The first edition of the *De Stijl* magazine was published in October 1917. Between 1917 and 1931, Van Doesburg tirelessly promoted De Stijl ideas, which included universalism over individualism, and a union of all the arts, especially painting and architecture.

In the early period of De Stijl, Van Doesburg collaborated with various architects; his most important creative collaboration was with the young architect Cornelis van Eesteren (1897–1988). Together, they developed projects such as the *Maison Particulière* (1923) and *Maison d'Artiste* (1923) in drawings and models for an exhibition of De Stijl work held at the Léonce Rosenberg Gallery in Paris in 1923. The models, known as "counterconstructions," described the movement's approach. The art historian Nancy J. Troy writes:

> The sense of floating planes of color is conveyed even more powerfully by van Doesburg's counterconstructions, a series of drawings he made on the basis of van Eesteren's axonometric projections. . . . In the counterconstructions, color itself functions as an architectural material identical to the plane it identifies. In this respect the counterconstructions seem to embody Mondrian's conception of architecture as a multiplicity of planes.[26]

In particular, Van Doesburg's analytical axonometric drawings underscored the planar composition of the design, something implied in Frank Lloyd Wright's Prairie houses designed 20 years earlier.[27] The use of axonometric drawings by Van Doesburg and Van Eesteren was an important innovation in architectural representation, although they did not invent the drawing type.[28]

The Schröder-Schräder house (1924) in Utrecht, by Gerrit Rietveld, remains one of the truly seminal works of modern architecture. Reitveld was trained as a furniture maker and produced a prototype (1917–1918) of what would become the famous red/blue chair. One of the most iconic examples of De Stijl design, the chair possesses a precise structural armature painted black and yellow that supports two planks in red and blue; the design creates a fusion between structure, space, and colour. The Schröder-Schräder house was a collaborative work between the client Mrs. Truus Schröder-Schräder and Rietveld that began in 1923. The design is composed of coloured planes and lines in a 3D realization of De Stijl principles.[29] The lower floor is quite conventional, whereas the upper floor features an open plan subdivided by sliding partitions, fixed elements, and furniture designed by Reitveld. The house is an extraordinary collaboration between client and designer, as Schröder-Schräder lived in the house for 60 years.

★ ★ ★

There were other avant-garde groups from the early 20th century who had some impact on architecture; these include Surrealism and Dada. The Surrealism group, created by the writer André Breton (1896–1966) in 1924, was an impactful movement primarily devoted to writing and painting. Inspired by the theories of Sigmund Freud (1856–1939), the Surrealists examined the subconscious through the analysis of dreams and techniques such as automatic writing. Surrealist painters included Max Ernst (1891–1947), René Magritte (1898–1967), and Salvador Dali (1904–1989). And while there were no architects aligned with Surrealism, various architectural works were identified as having Surrealist qualities.[30] A precursor movement to Surrealism was Dadaism, an international and informal group of artists operating in Zurich, New York, Berlin, Cologne, Hanover, and Paris.[31] Dadaism was renowned for its anarchic and negative approach to art.

Linked to both Surrealism and Dadaism was Marcel Duchamp (1887–1968). After flirting with Cubism (for example, *Nude*

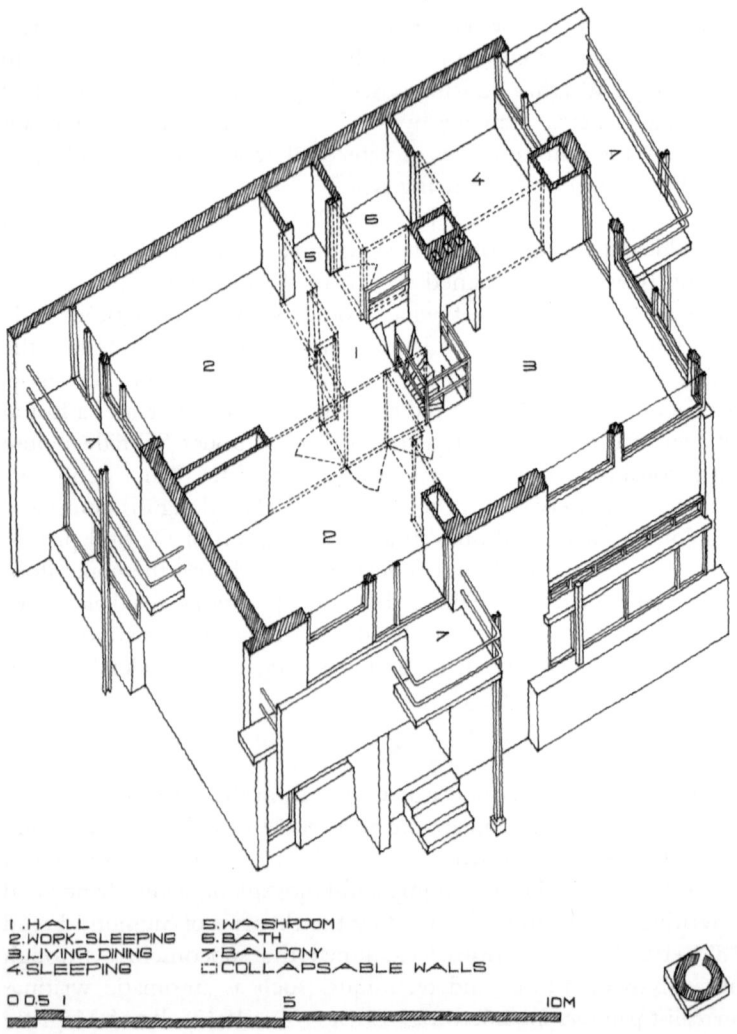

1. HALL
2. WORK-SLEEPING
3. LIVING-DINING
4. SLEEPING
5. WASHROOM
6. BATH
7. BALCONY
☐ COLLAPSABLE WALLS

0 0.5 1   5   10M

Figure 11.1 First Floor Axonometric, Gerrit Rietveld, Schröder-Schräder House, 1924, Utrecht, Netherlands. The plan is divided into four quadrants organized around the stairs. The deployment of sliding partitions and the careful placement of furniture means the space can be organized as either open or closed. Drawing by Mohammad Moezzi.

Descending a Staircase (1912)), Duchamp began to radically question the role of the artist. This was most obvious in his "ready-mades," begun in 1913, in which Duchamp selected industrially produced objects that were objectively recontextualized as works of art. During this period, Duchamp also began a careful study of the history of Western representation, rejecting what he called "retinal" art, pointing toward experiments such as *The Bride Stripped Bare by Her Bachelors, Even* (1915–1923).[32] Ultimately, Duchamp would become one of the most influential artists of the 20th century.

The connections between painting, sculpture, and architecture were unified in the avant-garde movements such as Cubism, Expressionism, and De Stijl. They also challenged the conventions of representation, particularly perspective. The materialization of space and the use of planar elements were also common to Cubism and De Stijl, both vital concepts in the development of modern architecture. Later, there were other important art movements, such as Abstract Expressionism, Pop Art (see Chapter 18), Conceptual Art, Minimalism, and Land Art, that also advanced methods of representation. Finally, the advent of computer-aided design (CAD) since the 1960s has revolutionized architectural representation in significant ways, closing the gaps between conceptualizing a building, drawing it, and having it constructed.

NOTES

1   See Alberto Pérez-Gómez and Louise Pelletier, "Architectural Representation and Perspectivism," *Perspecta*, vol. 27 (1992), pp. 20–39; and Mark Hewitt, "Representational Forms and Modes of Conception: An Approach to the History of Architectural Drawing," *Journal of Architectural Education*, vol. 39, no. 2 (Winter 1985), pp. 2–9.

2   See John Wilton-Ely, *The Mind and Art of Giovanni Battista Piranesi* (London: Thames & Hudson, 1988).

3   John Golding, *Cubism: A History and an Analysis 1907–1914* (London: Faber and Faber, 1988), p. 59.

4   Paul Cézanne, "Letter to Emile Bernard, Aix, 15 April 1904," in Herschel B. Chipp, ed., *Theories of Modern Art: A Source Book of Artists and Critics* (Berkeley: University of California Press, 1968), p. 19.

5   Golding, *Cubism*, p. xv.

6   See Ibid., pp. 33–51.

7   Ibid., p. 82.

8   Ibid., p. 104.

9   See Ibid., pp. 96–108.

10 See Eve Blau and Nancy J. Troy, eds., *Architecture and Cubism* (Cambridge, MA: MIT Press, 1997).

11 See Colin Rowe and Robert Slutzky, "Transparency: Literal and Phenomenal," *Perspecta*, vol. 8 (1963), pp. 45–54.

12 One of the significant issues affecting movements such as Fauvism, Cubism, and Expressionism was the use of non-Western indigenous ritual objects (from Africa, Oceania, Asia, and the Americas) as sources of inspiration. There is also the use of problematic terms such as "primitive" and "tribal" that perpetuate racist and colonial stereotypes. The practice of interpreting works from other traditions raises the issue of "cultural appropriation." See William Rubin, ed., *Primitivism in 20th Century Art: Affinity of the Tribal and the Modern* (New York: Museum of Modern Art, 1984): and Hal Foster, "The 'Primitive' Unconscious of Modern Art," *October*, vol. 34 (Autumn 1985), pp. 50–51.

13 Jill Lloyd, *German Expressionism: Primitivism and Modernity* (New Haven: Yale University Press, 1991), p. 18.

14 Wassily Kandinsky, *Concerning the Spiritual in Art* (New York: Dover Publications, 1977), p. 29.

15 Wim de Wit, "The Amsterdam School: Definition and Delineation," in Wim de Wit, ed., *The Amsterdam School: Dutch Expressionist Architecture, 1915–1930* (Cambridge, MA: MIT Press, 1983), p. 35.

16 Paul Scheerbart, "Glasarchitektur," in Josiah McElheny and Christine Burgin, eds., *Glass! Love!! Perpetual Motion!!! A Paul Scheerbart Reader* (Chicago: University of Chicago Press, 2014), p. 26.

17 Iain Boyd Whyte, *Bruno Taut and the Architecture of Activism* (Cambridge: Cambridge University Press, 1982), p. 35.

18 See Matthias Schirren, ed., *Bruno Taut: Alpine Architektur, A Utopia* (Munich: Prestel, 2004).

19 See Kathleen James, *Erich Mendelsohn and the Architecture of German Modernism* (Cambridge: Cambridge University Press, 1997).

20 Ibid., p. 88.

21 See Ibid., pp. 108–139.

22 Theo van Doesburg, "Towards a Plastic Architecture," in Ulrich Conrads, ed., *Programs and Manifestoes on 20th Century Architecture* (Cambridge, MA: MIT Press, 1971), p. 78.

23 Hans L.C. Jaffé, "Introduction," in Mildred Friedman, ed., *De Stijl, 1917–1931: Visions of Utopia* (New York: Abbeville Press, 1982), p. 12.

24 Philip C. Johnson, "Foreword," in Alfred H. Barr, Jr., ed., *De Stijl* (New York: Museum of Modern Art, 1961), p. 5.

25 Yves-Alain Bois, "The Iconoclast," in Yves-Alain Bois et al., eds., *Piet Mondrian* (Boston: Little, Brown and Company, 1994), p. 315.

26 Nancy J. Troy, "The Abstract Environment of De Stijl," in Friedman, ed., *De Stijl, 1917–1931*, p. 184.

27 See Allan Doig, *Theo van Doesburg: Painting into Architecture, Theory into Practice* (Cambridge: Cambridge University Press, 1986), pp. 152–165.

28 See Yves-Alain Bois, "Metamorphosis of Axonometry," *Daidalos* (September 1981), pp. 41–58.

29 See Ida van Zijl, *Gerrit Rietveld* (London: Phaidon, 2010), pp. 46–71.

30 See Thomas Mical, ed., *Surrealism and Architecture* (Adington: Routledge, 2005); and Jane Allison, ed., *The Surreal House* (New Haven: Yale University Press, 2010).

31 See Hans Richter, *DADA: Art and Anti-Art* (London: Thames and Hudson, 1965).

32 See Octavio Paz, *Marcel Duchamp: Appearance Stripped Bare* (New York: Viking Press, 1978).

SUGGESTED READING

Evans, Robin. *The Projective Cast*. Cambridge, MA: MIT Press, 1995.

Friedman, Mildred, ed. *De Stijl, 1917–1931: Visions of Utopia*. New York: Abbeville Press, 1982.

Golding, John. *Cubism: A History and an Analysis 1907–1914*. London: Faber and Faber, 1988.

Pérez-Gómez, Alberto and Louise Pelletier. *Architectural Representation and the Perspective Hinge*. Cambridge, MA: MIT Press, 1997.

Porter, Tom. *How Architects Visualize*. London: Studio Vista, 1979.

12

INTERNATIONALISM AND UNIVERSALISM

After decades of struggle, various European architects developed modern architecture in the 1920s, building on earlier work by figures like Frank Lloyd Wright (1867–1959), Adolf Loos (1870–1933), and Walter Gropius (1883–1969). For example, Gropius and Adolf Meyer's Fagus Factory (1913), a shoe-last factory in Alfeld-an-der-Leine, Germany, was one of the earliest works of modern architecture in Europe. The arrival of modern architecture was also recognized in two important exhibitions: the Weissenhofseidlung building exhibition (1927) in Stuttgart, Germany, and the "International Style" exhibition held at the Museum of Modern Art (MoMA) in New York in 1932. Despite the Western origins of the new approach, it was proclaimed an "international" style by its proponents, applicable to any place in the world. As Gropius writes:

> In modern architecture the objectivization of what is personal and national is quite clearly noticeable. A modern unifying tendency, conditioned by world communications and world techniques, is making headway in every field of culture, going beyond the national boundaries to which individuals and peoples are still bound. Architecture is always national, but it also always individual, but of the three concentric circles – individual, people, humanity – the third and largest embraces the other two: hence the title: international architecture![1]

The universal aspects of this approach would lead to its downfall. The architectural historian Charles Jencks proclaimed that the death of modern architecture occurred exactly at 3:32 pm on July 15,

DOI: 10.4324/9781003403975-12

1972, in St. Louis, Missouri, when the Pruitt-Igoe Housing scheme (1954) by Minoru Yamasaki was demolished.[2]

★ ★ ★

In 1927, the Weissenhofseidlung building exhibition opened. It featured designs by 16 emerging modernist architects and was organized by the Deutscher Werkbund under the direction of Mies van der Rohe. Projects by Mies, Le Corbusier, Walter Gropius, J.P.P. Oud, and others demonstrated a relatively consistent cubic language that featured flat roofs, light-coloured exterior surfaces, industrial detailing, and no traditional ornament. The designs were "a pure representation of structure, function, and the means of production, taking its form from the fulfillment of these requirements in an entirely "objective" or *sachlich* manner."[3] In signalling the emergence of a modern style, the exhibition of housing projects featuring apartment buildings, single-family houses, and rowhouses received wide attention in the press.

The *Modern Architecture: International Exhibition* at MoMA was organized by Henry-Russell Hitchcock and Philip Johnson at the invitation of Alfred Barr, the museum's director. The work of over 40 architects from 15 countries was chosen based on adherence to three principles:

> [F]irst, a new conception of architecture as volume rather than as mass. Secondly, regularity rather than axial symmetry serves as the chief means of ordering design . . . a third proscribing arbitrary applied decoration.[4]

The exhibition recognized the formative contributions of Frank Lloyd Wright but focused on the leadership of four European architects: Le Corbusier, J.P.P. Oud, Walter Gropius, and Mies van der Rohe (see Chapter 10). Apart from projects by these architects, noteworthy projects that captured the new style included Brinkman & Van der Vlugt's Van Nelle Factory (1930) in Rotterdam; Howe & Lescaze's PSFS Building (1931) in Philadelphia; Ludvik Kysela's Bata Shoe Store (1929) in Prague; and Richard J. Neutra's Lovell House (1929) in Los Angeles. The designs tended to be stark, placing an emphasis on hygiene and employing modern materials of glass, steel, and concrete. The forms and details referenced modern machines, and the "whiteness" of the designs seemed to invoke Mediterranean vernacular construction. This monochromatic impression was underscored by black-and-white photography that eliminated the colours that were often used by early modernists. The book that was published following the exhibition was titled *The International Style: Architecture since 1922.*

Following the exhibition, the International Style would gain widespread adoption throughout the world, particularly in Europe, in the Americas, and in countries colonized by Europeans, particularly in Africa and the Middle East (see Chapter 22). An important case study is the Israeli city of Tel Aviv, which adopted modern architecture, or the "Bauhaus Style," following 1934 and is home to hundreds of modernist buildings.[5] After World War II, the International Style was widely embraced by corporations, particularly for the design of office buildings. A late example of a modernist housing exhibition was the Interbau exhibition in West Berlin which opened in 1957. It featured projects by 48 architects, including Alvar Aalto, Le Corbusier, Walter Gropius, and Oscar Niemeyer.

★ ★ ★

Latin America is an immense area defined in the modern era by its colonial history. Despite the complex differences between the many countries and regions in Latin America, there is also a common history that has created a shared destiny.[6] The development of modern architecture throughout Latin America was impacted by major figures such as Le Corbusier and the emergence of several important regional figures in the post-World War II era.[7] During his first visit to Latin America (1929–1930), Le Corbusier visited Argentina, Paraguay, Uruguay, and Brazil, where he gave lectures and was celebrated as a visionary architect. He experienced the landscape from the air, which gave him a particular perspective on Latin America, and he developed design proposals for several cities.[8]

The earliest modernist house in Latin America was by Gregori Warchavchik in São Paulo, Brazil, and dates from 1927. Shortly afterwards, in 1929, Juan O'Gorman (1905–1982) designed a modernist house for his father in Mexico City. This project caught the attention of the muralist Diego Rivera (1886–1957), who commissioned O'Gorman to design linked house/studios for himself and Frida Kahlo (1907–1954) on an adjacent property. Brightly coloured and inspired by the early Purist architecture of Le Corbusier, the resulting compound (1932) is an important early example of Latin American modernism.[9]

Le Corbusier would make a subsequent trip to Rio de Janeiro in 1936, during which he worked with a local team, under the direction of Lúcio Costa (1902–1998) and with the young Oscar Niemeyer (1907–2012), on a design for the new Ministry of Education and Public Health (MESP). The resulting MESP building, completed in 1945, is a refined 15-story slab building over an auditorium/gallery block employing a brise-soleil on the northern façade, various Corbusian features, references to local traditions, and an early modernist landscape design by Roberto Burle Marx (1909–1994). The project effectively launched the important career of Niemeyer and underscored the influence Le Corbusier would have on Latin American architecture.

Oscar Niemeyer was educated in Rio de Janeiro and eventually found his own unique interpretation of modernism. Niemeyer would also be an ardent leftist for most of his career, which put him in opposition with the ruling military dictatorship during the years it operated in Brazil (1964–1985). In his work, Niemeyer was:

> Deliberately suspending and subtly undermining the rules of Modernist composition, he was able to manipulate and extend its formal possibilities, liberating a much-repressed architectural imagination and demystifying the socialist, rationalist and functionalist rhetoric of doctrinaire Modernism. His architecture of 'liberated . . . sensual curve[s]' and decorated surfaces, privileged the senses over reason.[10]

A crucial project in the development of modern Latin American architecture is the series of buildings that Oscar Niemeyer designed in Belo Horizonte, Brazil (1940–1943). The city's mayor, Juscelino Kubitschek, later the president of Brazil responsible for the new capital city of Brasília, commissioned Niemeyer to design a chapel, casino, dance hall, yacht club, and a hotel for a new development outside the city. Organized around an artificial lake, each of the designs is an experimental essay in modern architecture, particularly the Capela da Pampulha (1942), a small chapel with four thin parabolic vaults clad in painted ceramic tiles. Diverging from a strict adherence to Le Corbusier's tenets, the five buildings signal a more regionally suitable modernism, inflected by local methods.[11]

Brazilian modernism became widely celebrated in the 1940s and 1950s, largely due to Niemeyer's flamboyance as an architect and his focus on employing evocative forms in his designs. Niemeyer was also on the international team assembled to design the United Nations Building (1952) in New York, which included Le Corbusier. The design, mainly attributed to Niemeyer, also includes compromises that resulted from the team's approach to the design. During the 1940s and 1950s modernist housing projects were constructed throughout Latin America, following concepts devised in Europe and North America. A striking example of this is Niemeyer's Edificio COPAN in São Paulo (1953–1966), an enormous curvilinear residential building. Niemeyer was also responsible for most of the major institutional buildings built at Brasília in the late 1950s (see Chapter 7).

Early modern architecture in Argentina was overshadowed by the dramatic output of Brazilian architects. However, an important Argentinian figure was Amancio Williams (1913–1989), who studied both engineering and architecture in his native city of Buenos Aires. He produced an enigmatic and relatively small body of work. He "approached contemporary programs with an innovative attitude, rooting his designs in patient research and elaboration."[12] Williams developed research on typologies and technologies in projects such as Houses in Space (1943), Suspended Office Building (1946), Shells of Minimal Thickness (1951–1966), and High Roofs (1964). Williams's House over the Brook (1945) in Mar del Plata is a well-known design constructed for his father, in which he synthesizes his ideas into a single project.[13]

In the tradition of innovative structural engineering pioneered by figures like the Swiss engineer Robert Maillart (1872–1940), the works of Eladio Dieste (1917–2000) in Uruguay and Félix Candela (1910–1997) in Mexico are important. Dieste was trained as an engineer and spent much of his career working on warehouses that employed long-span brick vaults. Relatively late in his career, he became involved in architecture when he was asked to design the Iglesia de Cristo Obrero (Church of the Christ the Worker, 1960) in a working-class community near Atlántida, Uruguay. Eager to demonstrate his knowledge of brick vaulting, he created a space defined by undulating walls and ceiling to produce a harmonious and inexpensive solution. Dieste would subsequently produce several other works of architecture.[14]

In the late 1930s, a wave of European architects and artists emigrated to different parts of Latin America, some briefly and some for the rest of their careers. One such figure was Candela, who established himself as a pioneer in the use of thin-shelled reinforced concrete structures. Born in Madrid, he studied architecture and fought in the Spanish Civil War before being sent to Mexico in 1939. In the 1940s, he established a design and construction company, and by the early 1950s, important commissions began to appear after he perfected his methods. In his more utilitarian projects, such as warehouses, he often used a repeating thin-shelled concrete inverted umbrella form. In his more remarkable projects, such as the Chapel Lomas de Cuernavaca (1958) and Los Manantiales Restaurant (1958) at Xochimilco, Mexico City, he exploited a hyperbolic paraboloid form.[15]

★ ★ ★

There were several women who contributed significantly to the early Modern Movement and were key figures in the practices of famous male architects. These include Marion Mahony Griffin (1871–1961) who was an instrumental member of Frank Lloyd Wright's office in the early 20th century; Lilly Reich (1885–1947) who worked with Mies van der Rohe in the 1920s and 1930s on furniture and interiors; Aino Maria Marsio-Aalto (1894–1949) who collaborated closely with Alvar Aalto until her untimely death; and Charlotte Perriand (1903–1999) who designed pioneering furniture and interiors while employed with Le Corbusier in the 1920s and 1930s, before launching a successful solo career as a designer (see Chapters 10 and 19). Several other key women also emerged during the formative stages of modern architecture.

Eileen Gray (1878–1976), the Irish-born designer and architect, was an important contributor to the development of modernism in the 1920s. She studied art in London and Paris; early on, she learned the technique of lacquering. After World War I, she was involved in interior and furniture design, mainly in the Art Deco style. During 1922–1930, she operated a store called Jean Désert in Paris to sell her products. After 1921, when she met the architect Jean Badovici, she became involved in architecture and modernist design. Two houses were built according to her designs: the E-1027 house (1929) in Roquebrune-Cap-Martin, France, and the Tempe à Pailla house (1934) in Castellar, France. The two houses by Gray demonstrate that despite appearances of coldness modern architecture can be handled in sensitive and distinctive ways. Several pieces of Gray's furniture remain among the most well-known works of modernist design and are still in production.[16]

Margarete Schütte-Lihotzky (1897–2000) was born in Vienna, where she was trained in both art and architecture. In the early 1920s, she worked with the Viennese Ministry of Housing (under Adolf Loos). During this decade, she began to make a name for herself in housing and furnishing design. In 1926, she was invited to

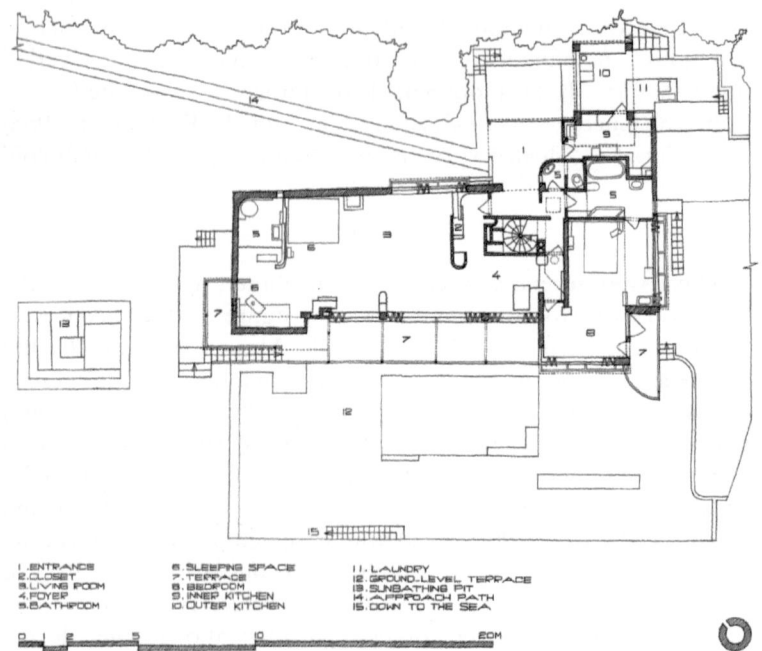

1. ENTRANCE
2. CLOSET
3. LIVING ROOM
4. FOYER
5. BATHROOM

6. SLEEPING SPACE
7. TERRACE
8. BEDROOM
9. INNER KITCHEN
10. OUTER KITCHEN

11. LAUNDRY
12. GROUND-LEVEL TERRACE
13. SUNBATHING PIT
14. APPROACH PATH
15. DOWN TO THE SEA

Figure 12.1 First Floor Plan, Eileen Gray, E-1027 House, 1929, Roquebrun, France. The plan reflects Gray's detailed attention to all aspects of the house as a responsive environment; the precise incorporation of her own furniture designs reinforces this. Drawing by Mohammad Moezzi.

join the team working under Ernst May (1886–1970) on the development of new housing districts for Frankfurt am Main in Germany. During her time in Frankfurt, Schütte-Lihotzky designed the famous "Frankfurt Kitchen," a pioneering design featuring a modern, efficient, ergonomic, and ingenious arrangement of appliances, storage, and counter surfaces. An early example of a standardized design, it was developed as a prefabricated unit and used 6.50 meters (70 square feet) of space (see Chapter 13). The Frankfurt Kitchen was installed in 10,000 homes in Frankfurt. Inspired by compact kitchens found on trains and ships, "the Frankfurt Kitchen was the realization of the kitchen as machine."[17] Schütte-Lihotzky would go on to write articles and lecture on domestic design, adding importantly to the notion of minimum space design, or *Existenzminimum*, a concept popular among modernists in the late 1920s and early 1930s.[18]

Hana Kučerová-Záveská (1902–1944) designed two single-family villas for the Baba Housing estate in Prague: the Villa Suk (1932) and the Villa Balling (1933). Commissioned by a builder, the design of the Villa Suk reflects Kučerová-Záveská's interest in the work of Le Corbusier from the 1920s. The Villa Balling was designed for a composer of popular songs and educator; the building demonstrates a sophisticated handling of its volumes and terraces. These projects are consistent with the modernist functional architecture of the 1920s and 1930s and survive as part of an important modernist housing estate from the period, developed with the Czechoslovak Werkbund. Kučerová-Záveská also designed modernist interiors and furniture and was an important writer on architecture and design.[19]

A distinctive Scandinavian architect was Greta Magnusson-Grossman (1906–1999), who studied in Stockholm. Magnusson-Grossman emigrated to Los Angeles in 1940 after working in Sweden. In Los Angeles, she designed objects, furniture, and interiors for various clients during the 1940s and 1950s, including the Grasshopper floor lamp (1947) and the Cobra desk lamp (1949). She also designed several modernist houses, including the well-known Magnusson-Grossman (Hillside) House (1957) in Beverly Hills, which is structurally expressive as it juts out of its hillside site.[20]

Jane Drew (1911–1996) was born in Thornton Heath on the edge of London and studied architecture at the Architectural Association in London. Following graduation in 1934, she worked for several years, including with her first husband. After that, she worked primarily in partnership with her second husband, Edwin Maxwell Fry (1899–1987), who she met in 1940. During World War II, Drew developed her skills in interior/industrial design, town planning, and post-war reconstruction.[21] In the late 1940s, Drew and Fry were asked to design town housing areas for Harlow New Town as part of the massive drive to develop suitable housing and communities throughout Britain after the war. During the 1940s and 1950s, Drew worked extensively in West Africa, mainly in Nigeria and Ghana, where she and Fry designed buildings for educational institutions and were involved in town planning (see Chapter 23).

Between 1951 and 1954, Drew was part of the team leading the design and construction of Chandigarh, the new capital city of Punjab in India, planned by Le Corbusier (see Chapter 7), based largely on Drew and Fry's experience in Africa.[22] Le Corbusier revised the plan and concentrated on the design of the main government buildings, while Drew, Fry, and Pierre Jeanneret concentrated on the design of housing, neighbourhoods (or sectors), and various other buildings.[23] After working in India, Drew and Fry returned to Britain, where they continued a busy practice. Drew received many honours during her career in recognition of her contributions to architecture globally.[24]

★ ★ ★

Ultimately, the notion of an International Style as a universal language failed. The lack of connection with history and an emphasis on the rational and functional employment of technology resulted in this failure. Ironically, the inability of modern architects to provide acceptable forms of mass housing was crucial, as the architectural historian Spiro Kostof notes:

> When promoted as a forced choice between slum dwellings and the architecture of a new way of life, especially outside Europe, Modernist evangelism bore an uncomfortable resemblance to the colonial mission of "civilizing" subject peoples. The new materials – concrete, steel, glass – were installed universally, but primarily for high-style architecture and the landscape of industry and transportation.[25]

NOTES

1 Walter Gropius, from 1925, quoted in Leonardo Benevolo, *History of Modern Architecture*, Volume 2 (Cambridge, MA: MIT Press, 1977), p. 494.

2 Charles Jencks, *The Language of Post-Modern Architecture* (New York: Rizzoli, 1991), p. 23.

3 Richard Pommer and Christian F. Otto, *Weissenhof 1927 and the Modern Movement in Architecture* (Chicago: University of Chicago Press, 1991), p. 2.

4 Henry-Russell Hitchcock and Philip Johnson, *The International Style* (New York: W.W. Norton & Co., 1966), p. 20.

5 See Michael Levin, *White City: International Style Architecture in Israel* (Tel Aviv: Tel Aviv Museum, 1984).

6 Marina Waisman, "Introduction," in Malcolm Quantrill, ed., *Latin American Architecture: Six Voices* (College Station: Texas A&M University Press, 2000), p. 4.

7 See Patricio del Real and Helen Gyger, eds., *Latin American Modern Architectures: Ambiguous Territories* (New York: Taylor & Francis, 2013), pp. 1–29.

8 See Le Corbusier, *Precisions on the Present State of Architecture and City Planning* (Zurich: Park Books, 2015).

9 See Luis E. Carranza and Fernando Luiz Lara, *Modern Architecture in Latin America: Art, Technology, and Utopia* (Austin: University of Texas Press, 2014), pp. 71–72.

10 Styliane Philippou, *Oscar Niemeyer: Curves of Irreverence* (New Haven: Yale University Press, 2008), p. 12.

11 See Carranza and Lara, *Modern Architecture in Latin America*, pp. 108–112. See Oscar Niemeyer, *The Curves of Time: The Memoirs of Oscar Niemeyer* (London: Phaidon, 2000).

12 Jorge Silvetti, ed., *Amancio Williams* (New York: Rizzoli, 1987), p. 62.

13 See Ibid., pp. 28–43.

14 See Carranza and Lara, *Modern Architecture in Latin America*, pp. 170–171.

15 See Maria E. Moreyra Garlock and David P. Billington, *Félix Candela: Engineer, Builder, Structural Artist* (New Haven: Yale University Press, 2008).

16 See Peter Adam, *Eileen Gray, Architect/Designer* (New York: Henry N. Abrams, Inc., 1987).

17 Susan R. Henderson, "A Revolution in the Woman's Sphere: Grete Lihotzky and the Frankfurt Kitchen," in D. Coleman, E. Danze, and C. Henderson, eds., *Architecture and Feminism* (New York: Princeton Architectural Press, 1996), p. 235.

18 See Carmen Espegel, *Women Architects in the Modern Movement* (London: Routledge, 2018), pp. 164–198.

19 Information on Hana Kučerová-Záveská graciously provided by Dr. Irena Zantovská Murray in a personal communication (December 9, 2021).

20 See Harriet Harriss and Naomi House, "Greta Magnusson Grossman: Living in a Modern Way," *Places* (October 2021).

21 See Iain Jackson and Jessica Holland, *The Architecture of Edwin Maxwell Fry and Jane Drew* (London: Routledge, 2014).

22 See Stanislaus von Moos, ed., *Chandigarh 1956: Le Corbusier, Pierre Jeanneret, Jane B. Drew, Maxwell E. Fry* (Zurich: Scheidegger & Speiss AG, 2010).

23 See Iain Jackson, "Maxwell Fry and Jane Drew's Early Housing and Neighbourhood Planning in Sector-22, Chandigarh," *Planning Perspectives*, vol. 28, no. 1 (2013), pp. 1–26.

24 It is worth noting that while her partner Maxwell Fry received the RIBA Gold Medal in 1964, the same recognition was not accorded to Drew, a discriminatory practice consistent with other major awards programmes, including the Pritzker Prize.

25 Spiro Kostof, *A History of Architecture: Settings and Rituals* (New York: Oxford University Press, 1995), p. 745.

SUGGESTED READING

Carranza, Luis E. and Fernando Luiz Lara. *Modern Architecture in Latin America: Art, Technology, and Utopia.* Austin: University of Texas Press, 2014.

Espegel, Carmen. *Women Architects in the Modern Movement.* London: Routledge, 2018.

Hitchcock, Henry-Russell and Philip Johnson. *The International Style.* New York: W.W. Norton & Co., 1966.

Philippou, Styliane. *Oscar Niemeyer: Curves of Irreverence*. New Haven: Yale University Press, 2008.

Pommer, Richard and Christian F. Otto. *Weissenhof 1927 and the Modern Movement in Architecture*. Chicago: University of Chicago Press, 1991.

13

MACHINES AND SYSTEMS

During the 19th century, architects struggled to adapt new technologies, materials, and processes to create contemporary architecture within existing languages and styles. However, the Crystal Palace (1851), built in London of prefabricated components, demonstrated the possibilities of new building materials and mechanized methods. Conversely, the Arts and Crafts movement which followed largely rejected industrial production (see Chapter 8). Frank Lloyd Wright struck a middle position which advocated for the inclusion of the machine as a necessary part of modern architectural production (see Chapter 10).

The machine has been central to the development of modern architecture. First, mechanized forms of production resulted in new technologies, materials, and processes (see Chapter 4). Second, new kinds of machinery were incorporated into buildings, such as elevators and air conditioners. Third, as a source of design inspiration for modern architects, as machines defined new architecture and new building typologies. Fourth, as a means for those architects who embraced machinist architecture. Ultimately, new mechanical and electrical systems allowed for the creation of new, highly controlled interior environments and faster forms of human movement.

Buildings today are operated by a plethora of machinery and are connected by pipes, cables, and wireless technologies. These mechanical and electrical systems perform many functions and are expensive to install and maintain. The development of modern building systems

DOI: 10.4324/9781003403975-13

was an essential contribution to the evolution of modern architecture. The creation of controlled environments using heating and cooling systems introduced levels of comfort and health unknown previously but also resulted in buildings being significant consumers of energy and contributors to climate change. Traditionally, buildings were heated using fireplaces and stoves that burned fuels such as wood, coal, and gas. By the 19th century, advances occurred in the design of stoves, and heating systems came into use that circulated hot water or steam in pipes with radiators to disperse the heat.

The introduction of ventilation, or the circulation of hot or cool air, was an achievement of modernism that helped create artificial environments. An early example of a building incorporating these technologies was the Houses of Parliament in London which was completed in 1876 (see Chapter 6). Under the architects Charles Barry and A.W.N. Pugin, the Scottish scientist David Boswell Reid (1805–1863) was engaged to design heating and ventilation for the new project. He was let go in 1852 after many disputes and was followed by other engineers who attempted to correct Reid's original design, which resulted in a flawed system that was difficult to manage. Reid was more successful with his subsequent design for St. George's Hall (1854) in Liverpool.[1] Throughout the 19th century, developments occurred in the design of warm air heating systems that used ducts to supply and return heated air throughout a building. Further, advances in the design of thermostats and fans were part of the development of modern heating, ventilation, and air-conditioning (HVAC) systems in the 20th century.

An early example of a building using an integrated heating, ventilation, and cooling system was the Royal Victoria Hospital (1903) in Belfast, Northern Ireland. Architectural historian Reyner Banham argues that Frank Lloyd Wright must be considered "the first master of the architecture of the well-tempered environment."[2] In the Larkin Building (1906) in Buffalo, Wright incorporated vertical shafts that handled the fresh, tempered, and exhaust air in the building. In his Prairie Style houses, Wright integrated "environmental technologies" into his designs in innovative ways and invented concealed lighting. Wright's buildings foreshadowed Louis I. Kahn's development of the concept of "served" and "servant" spaces, the servant spaces incorporating the building systems. This concept can be found in Kahn's Richards Medical Research Building (1961) in Philadelphia, where service towers support the laboratory spaces. At the Salk Institute (1965) in La Jolla, California, Kahn instead used deep service floors to service the research labs (see Chapter 18).

The cooling of indoor environments began with the limited use of ice in conjunction with ventilation systems; this was usually applied in hospitals and places of assembly. The development of mechanical cooling in the 19th century, initially to preserve food, was eventually applied to buildings.[3] The refinement of air-conditioning by Willis H. Carrier (1876–1950) in the early 20th century had a dramatic impact on working and living environments globally after World War II. The first air-conditioned office building and the tallest reinforced concrete building in the world at the time was the 21-storey Milam Building (1928) in San Antonio, Texas. The development of the small domestic air-conditioning unit in the 1950s resulted in "the most sophisticated device for environmental management that mankind has ever possessed."[4] The invention of the suspended ceiling in the 1930s provided a simple means of integrating lighting and acoustic control. As well, the ceiling system hid ductwork and wiring.[5] As Banham points out, the use of mechanical systems meant that architects no longer had to address local climate and context, reinforcing a kind of universal internationalism.[6]

The concept of hoisting is ancient, originally powered by humans, animals, or water. By the early 19th century, steam-powered elevators were used in factories, but they lacked reliability and safety. The improvement of the elevator in the 1850s by the American industrialist Elisha Graves Otis (1811–1861), through his patented safety mechanism, was of critical importance in the development of the tall building. In 1857, Otis's company installed the first passenger elevator in a 5-storey retail building in New York. Various mechanisms were invented over the next few decades, including hydraulic systems; however, the advancement of the electric motor in the 1870s resulted in further improvements to the elevator and widespread adoption after 1887. The introduction of the traction elevator by the Otis Elevator Company in 1903 introduced a modern elevator that was comfortable, fast, safe, and efficient. Further, the need to move large numbers of people up relatively few floors, in places like railway stations and department stores, resulted in the invention and perfection of the escalator in the late 19th and early 20th centuries.[7]

The advent of electricity generation and indoor and outdoor lighting first devised as a system by American inventor Thomas Alva Edison (1847–1931) between 1878 and 1882, transformed how interior and urban spaces functioned. Prior to this, lighting was provided by unreliable and expensive candles, oil and gas amps, and electric arc lamps. The refinement of the incandescent electric light bulb, beginning in the 1840s, was finalized by both Edison and English inventor Joseph Swan (1828–1914) in 1879, simultaneous with the development of methods for generating electricity. The new electric lighting quickly began to replace gas lighting in cities, and indoor electric lighting transformed interior environments. Lighting systems would advance further during the 20th century with inventions in neon gas and mercury vapour methods. An important breakthrough occurred when Westinghouse and GEC launched the "Lumiline" fluorescent tube in 1938. This low-energy, uniform type of lighting immediately impacted the design vocabulary of modern architects. Interior lighting, especially in office buildings, allowed for much larger floor plates, with employees often placed far from daylight. Electricity also provided power for numerous new appliances that, in theory, made living easier.

★ ★ ★

The evolution of the house, particularly in America, during the 19th century involved incorporating new technologies, appliances, and methods. Several prominent women wrote about and promoted the ideals of "domestic management," and the home was the ongoing subject of popular magazines, such as *The Ladies' Home Journal*. Catharine Beecher (1800–1878) was a significant figure in 19th-century American life as she advocated for Christian morality and domestic innovation. Beecher was involved in education before becoming a prolific and successful writer. In 1841, she published her *Treatise on Domestic Economy, For the Use of Young Ladies at Home and at School*, which outlines her notions on the "moral superiority of women" and their capacity for self-sacrifice. With her sister Harriet Beecher Stowe (1811–1896), the author of the popular *Uncle Tom's Cabin*, she co-authored a book entitled *The American Woman's Home* (1869).[8] As architectural historian Dolores Hayden writes:

> She [Beecher] proposes female supremacy in the home, enhanced by two metaphors of female authority: the "minister" and the skilled "professional," harnessing the imagery of religion and business. . . . These metaphors of ministerial and professional activity are supported by a most unusual economic rationalization. Domestic servants are to be replaced by women doing their own housework.[9]

By the time *The American Woman's Home* was published, Beecher's conception of the home had developed into a full "marriage" between a woman and the house.[10] The suburban house design that Beecher and Stowe presented in the book incorporated the latest in equipment and machinery and was carefully planned. Striving for innovation and efficiency, Beecher and Stowe proposed a modern house "to allow the "woman occupant" full visual control over the activities of the home without wasting time and energy walking back and forth."[11] Their ideas were extended into designs for urban tenement buildings. Beecher's publications foreshadowed later developments as the domestic realm continued to transform in the 20th century.

As architect Doris Cole argues, middle-class women in 19th-century America were very invested in the evolving design of the home, embracing numerous technological innovations.[12] By the early 20th century, housekeeping had transformed into "domestic science," as promoted by figures such as Christine Frederick (1883–1970). She developed a school and published books modelled after advances in industrialization by figures like Frederick Taylor (1856–1915), the author of *The Principles of Scientific Management* (1911), and Henry Ford (1863–1947), the founder of the Ford Motor Company. Frederick's most popular book was *Household Engineering: Scientific Management in the Home* (1915), which promoted efficient and organized household management, labour-saving appliances, and concepts such as "standardized operations."[13] Taylorism and Fordism, as methods of "scientific management" applied to industrial production, were also a source of inspiration for many architects at the time.[14]

★ ★ ★

The links between the modern machine and avant-garde art and architecture are very strong, particularly in the work of the Italian Futurists and Le Corbusier (1887–1965). Futurism was an Italian avant-garde art movement involving poets, painters, and architects. The "Founding Manifesto of Futurism," published in early 1909 by the poet Filippo Tommaso Marinetti (1876–1944), signaled the launching of a movement that whole-heartedly embraced modernity, especially machinery, danger, speed, and "universal dynamism." The use of manifestos was favoured by many of the art movements of the early 20th century (see Chapter 11), and the Futurists produced them on a variety of art forms.

Celebrating the modern industrial city, Futurist painting used a "cinematic" approach, where repeated images were used to capture motion along with "force-lines" to strengthen the appearance of speed.[15] The subject matter of many Futurist paintings concentrated on machines and movement. Rapid experimentation occurred between 1909 and 1911. A striking example of the fully developed Futurist approach is found in Giacomo Balla's painting entitled *Abstract Speed + Sound* (1914). Umberto Boccioni brilliantly demonstrated his "plastic" ideas in his *Unique Forms of Continuity in Space* sculpture from 1913, in which a mechanized figure appears to move in and with space.

The only important architect associated with Italian Futurism was Antonio Sant-Elia (1888–1916). Born in Como and talented at drawing, Sant-Elia completed his education by 1911. During a trip to Rome in the same year, he encountered the work of Viennese Secession artists and architects, which had a tremendous impact on his designs. By 1912, Sant'Elia's drawing style had evolved to present dramatic perspectival images of vast monumental structures. Subsequently, a series of sketches, or *dinamismi*, produced in 1913, signaled an emerging interest in simpler modern monumental forms and industrial building typologies. In 1914, Sant-Elia and Marinetti published the "Manifesto of Futurist Architecture," in it, they write:

> We feel that we are no longer the men of the cathedrals, the palaces, the assembly halls; but of big hotels, railway stations, immense roads, colossal ports, covered markets, brilliantly lit galleries, freeways, demolition and rebuilding schemes. . . . We must invent and rebuild the *Futurist* city; it must be like an immense, tumultuous, lively, noble work site, dynamic in all its parts; the *Futurist* house must be like an enormous machine.[16]

In an exhibition held in 1914, Sant'Elia showed drawings of his Città Nuova project. Captivated by the power and modernity of power stations, Sant-Elia paid particular attention to this new type of complex in evocative perspectival images.[17] In the Città Nuova project, black and white drawings depicted tall stepped-back buildings that fuse together architecture and infrastructure. Accentuating new forms of transportation and modern construction materials, the drawings produced a vision of a new industrial city largely devoid of life, nature, or detail.

Throughout the 1920s, the development of a Machine Age style was led by Le Corbusier (see Chapter 10). In *Toward an Architecture,* he praises the designs of engineers and celebrates modern machinery, especially airplanes, automobiles, and ocean liners. Le Corbusier produced several famous statements in the book, one of which is: "A house is a machine for living in."[18] His analogy between architecture and machines has been widely misunderstood. Le Corbusier drew inspiration from modern machinery, stating that the "problem" of the airplane had been posed and solved by aviation designers, whereas the problem of the modern house had not been posed.[19] He then presented the problem of the house and created a "Housing Manual," in which he describes a modern house much like his Purist villas of the 1920s.[20] In his famous statement, Le Corbusier argues for a house that has the precision and responsiveness of a modern machine; however, he did not suggest that the house is literally a machine. An important house from the period that took the mechanization of the house much further was the Maison de Verre (1931) in Paris by Pierre Chareau and Bernard Bijvoet. Designed for a doctor, the house comprehensively expressed a machine-like aesthetic and incorporated a wide range of environmental technologies.

★ ★ ★

Moving beyond the importance of technology and the machine analogy for modern architecture, one group of architects took their commitment to technology to another level. One of the most influential members of this group was the American inventor, engineer, mathematician, and futurist R. Buckminster Fuller (1895–1983). By 1922, following an eclectic education which included stints at Harvard University and in the US Navy, Fuller was engaged in the manufacture of building materials. Interested in universalist theories and efficiency, in 1927, he devised his first major invention, the Dymaxion House. The design featured a metal construction organized around a central service core and mast, from which the rest of the house was suspended. It was a radical experiment in innovative, lightweight design. This led to the Dymaxion car (1933–1934), the prefabricated Dymaxion Bathroom (1937), and the Dymaxion Dwelling Machine (1946). After World War II he began to experiment in the design of lightweight spanning systems, which resulted in tensegrity structures and the invention of the Geodesic dome. The Geodesic dome became Fuller's signature concept, resulting in numerous structures. The most famous realization was the US Pavilion for Expo '67 in Montreal. Fuller fully embraced technology, always seeking optimal solutions that could be widely employed. Concerned about the state of the planet, he also devised the concept of "Spaceship Earth."[21] Another pioneer in the use of technology in buildings, also not trained as an architect, was the French designer Jean Prouvé (1901–1984), who innovated with lightweight uses of metal.

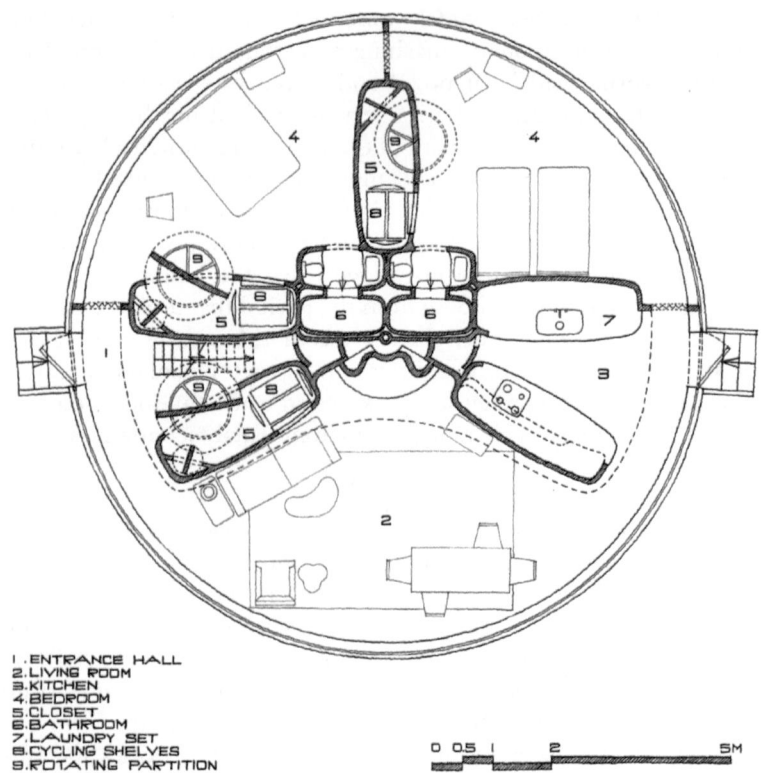

1. ENTRANCE HALL
2. LIVING ROOM
3. KITCHEN
4. BEDROOM
5. CLOSET
6. BATHROOM
7. LAUNDRY SET
8. CYCLING SHELVES
9. ROTATING PARTITION

0   0.5   1   2   5M

Figure 13.1 Main Floor Plan, Buckminster Fuller, Dymaxion Dwelling Machine, 1946. The circular plan is divided into living and sleeping areas using sculptural service and storage elements; these are arrayed around a central structural mast that supports the suspended roof. Drawing by Mohammad Moezzi.

The development of "megastructures" in the 1960s and 1970s resulted in projects that typically involved a large extendable framework or "megaform" into which "discrete, rapidly-changing functional units" can be "plugged-in."[22] In other words, the megastructure employed a sizeable structural system in concrete or steel, into which repeating units were inserted. Groups such as the Metabolists in Japan (see Chapter 20), Archigram in Britain, and the "Urbanisme spatial" movement in France proposed daring and visionary schemes for walking, underground, and floating cities that celebrated technology, machinery, and systems. As Reyner Banham states:

> [A]gainst the International Style's classicizing view of technology and machinery as neat smooth regular solids of anonymous aspect, the younger megastructurists clearly saw technology as a visually wild rich mess of piping and wiring and struts and catwalks and bristling radar antennae and supplementary fuel tanks and landing-pads all carried on exposed lattice frames.[23]

In Britain, the megastructure was conceptualized by people like Cedric Price (1934–2003) and the Archigram group, with a series of unbuilt designs. Price proposed projects like the flexible Fun Palace (1962) as an entertainment facility, which inspired the six members of Archigram, who, in turn, promoted the "experimental" architecture of the early 1960s. Known for their Pop Art-inspired graphics and provocative designs, Archigram produced drawings of visionary schemes, including "Walking City" (1963) by Ron Herron and Brian Harvey and "Plug-In City" (1964) by Peter Cook. The "Plug-In City" drawings captured the vitality of the megastructure idea. The group was particularly interested in expressing technology and exploring new forms of living that included prefabricated capsules, inflatable structures, and nomadic shelters.[24]

The megastructure phenomenon was short-lived; it essentially peaked at Expo '67. In addition to the US Pavilion by Fuller, several key projects were constructed, including the Habitat housing scheme by Moshe Safdie and the Theme Pavilions by ARCOP. Other important Canadian megastructure buildings include Scarborough College (1965) in Toronto by John Andrews, Place Bonaventure (1967) in Montreal by ARCOP, and the McMaster Health Sciences Centre (1972) in Hamilton, Ontario by Craig, Zeidler, and Strong. University campuses, new towns, and housing projects were briefly favoured for megastructure experimentation. The size and machinic approach to the megastructure quickly contributed to its demise. Nevertheless, it spawned the High Tech movement, primarily in Britain, that maintained a commitment to the technological explorations of figures like Fuller.

Richard Rogers (1933–2021), Norman Foster (1935–), and Renzo Piano (1937–) are the pioneering figures in High Tech architecture, an approach that has continued into the 21st century.[25] Each developed a particular take on the role of technology, especially machines and systems, in their building designs. A noteworthy project remains the Centre Georges Pompidou in Paris (1971–1977) by Piano + Rogers, which inverts the traditional relationship between a building and its systems by placing all of its services on the exterior. A literal architectural machine, the building is designed to be highly flexible and adaptable. Despite an initial negative reaction to such a structure in the centre of Paris, it has been a popular facility since it opened.

★ ★ ★

The Canadian media theorist Marshall McLuhan (1911–1980) wrote extensively about technology and media and how these extend the human body. For example, examining the impact of electric light, McLuhan writes:

> Electric light abolished the divisions of night and day, of inner and outer, and of the subterranean and the terrestrial. It altered every consideration of space for work and production as much as the other electric media [telephone, radio, television, etc.] had altered the space-time experience of society.[26]

Developments in heating, ventilation, cooling, lighting, and movement systems continue to impact architectural design. More recently, the adoption of the computer has resulted in the concept of the "smart" building, in which a broad range of building systems are regulated by computers. However, the machinery and systems that have been essential to the development of modern architecture have also dramatically impacted the environment through the widespread exploitation of resources and the production of waste (see Chapter 24).

NOTES

1 See Cecil D. Elliot, *Technics and Architecture: The Development of Materials and Systems for Buildings* (Cambridge, MA: MIT Press, 1992), pp. 285–291.

2 Reyner Banham, *The Architecture of the Well-Tempered Environment* (Chicago: University of Chicago Press, 1969), p. 70. Banham's book is an attempt to correct what he saw as deficiencies in Sigfried Giedion, *Mechanisation Takes Command: A Contribution to Anonymous History* (New York: Oxford University Press, 1948).

3 See Elliot, *Technics and Architecture*, pp. 308–325.

4 See Banham, *The Architecture of the Well-Tempered Environment*, p. 190.

5 Ibid., pp. 213–233.

6 Ibid., p. 239.

7 See Elliot, *Technics and Architecture*, pp. 328–361.

8 See Dolores Hayden, *The Grand Domestic Revolution* (Cambridge, MA: MIT Press, 1981), pp. 55–63.

9 Dolores Hayden, "Catharine Beecher and the Politics of Housework," in Susana Torre, ed., *Women in American Architecture: A Historic and Contemporary Perspective* (New York: Whitney Library of Design, 1977), p. 42.

10 Ibid., p. 44.

11 Leslie Kanes Weisman, *Discrimination by Design: A Feminist Critique of the Man-Made Environment* (Urbana and Chicago: University of Illinois Press, 1994), p. 89.

12 See Doris Cole, *From Tipi to Skyscraper: A History of Women in Architecture* (Boston: i Press Inc., 1973).

13 See Gwendolyn Wright, "The Model Domestic Environment: Icon or Option?" in Torre, ed., *Women in American Architecture*, pp. 20–22.

14 See Mauro F. Guillén, *The Taylorized Beauty of the Mechanical: Scientific Management and the Rise of Modern Architecture* (Princeton: Princeton University Press, 2006).

15 See, Richard Humphreys, *Futurism* (Cambridge: Cambridge University Press, 1999).

16 Antonio Sant'Elia and Filippo Tommaso Marinetti, "Futurist Architecture," in Ulrich Conrads, ed., *Programs and Manifestoes on 20th Century Architecture* (Cambridge, MA: MIT Press, 1971), p. 36.

17 See Esther da Costa Meyer, *The Work of Antonio Sant'Elia: Retreat into the Future* (New Haven: Yale University Press, 1995), pp. 108–110.

18 Le Corbusier, *Toward an Architecture* (Los Angeles: Getty Publications, 2007), p. 150.

19 Ibid., pp. 161–162.

20 See Ibid., pp. 165–176.

21 See R. Buckminster Fuller and Robert Marks, *The Dymaxion World of Buckminster Fuller* (Garden City, NY: Anchor Books, 1973).

22 Reyner Banham, *Megastructure: Urban Futures of the Recent Past* (New York: Harper & Row, 1976), p. 8.

23 Ibid., p. 17.

24 See: Peter Cook, ed., *Archigram* (London: Studio Vista, 1972); and Simon Sadler, *Archigram: Architecture Without Architecture* (Cambridge, MA: MIT Press, 2005).

25 See Colin Davies, *High Tech Architecture* (London: Thames & Hudson, 1999).

26 Marshall McLuhan, *Understanding Media* (New York: McGraw-Hill, 1964), pp. 126–127.

SUGGESTED READING

Banham, Reyner. *The Architecture of the Well-Tempered Environment*. Chicago: University of Chicago Press, 1969.

Banham, Reyner. *Megastructure: Urban Futures of the Recent Past*. New York: Harper & Row, 1976.

da Costa Meyer, Esther. *The Work of Antonio Sant'Elia: Retreat into the Future*. New Haven: Yale University Press, 1995.

Elliot, Cecil D. *Technics and Architecture: The Development of Materials and Systems for Buildings*. Cambridge, MA: MIT Press, 1992.

Hawkes, Dean. *The Environmental Imagination: Technics and Poetics of the Architectural Environment*. Abingdon: Routledge, 2008.

14

AUTHORITARIANISM AND MONUMENTALITY

The 1917 Communist Russian Revolution was one of the major revolutionary events in world history. Communism, as a political system, was originally defined by Karl Marx and Friedrich Engels in *The Communist Manifesto* (1848) and can be defined as a "political and economic doctrine that aims to replace private property and a profit-based economy with public ownership and communal control of at least the major means of production (e.g., mines, mills, and factories) and the natural resources of a society. Communism is thus a form of socialism."[1] Communism proposes a classless system, where each performs according to their abilities and needs, and differences between manual and intellectual labour, and rural and urban living are downplayed. Through the design of governmental institutions and infrastructure, architecture can express the power of a leader or the aspirations of a people.[2]

A year of civil unrest in Russia led to the February 1917 revolution, which resulted in the abdication of Tsar Nicholas II, the supreme ruler, the following month. Vladimir Lenin (1870–1924), the leader of the revolution, returned from exile two months later. During the October 1917 revolution, the Bolsheviks (or Communists) seized control of the city of Saint Petersburg. A civil war followed between the Red Army (Bolshevik) and the White Army (anti-Bolshevik) forces. Ultimately, the Union of Soviet Socialist Republics (USSR) was established in December 1922. The death of Lenin in 1924 resulted in a power struggle, with Joseph Stalin (1878–1953) emerging as the Communist Party leader by 1927. Under Stalin, the Soviet

DOI: 10.4324/9781003403975-14

Union would become a one-party state that became increasingly authoritarian, resulting in the deaths of millions of Soviet citizens. The Soviet Union ended officially in 1990.

In architectural terms, the first decade following the Russian Revolution has been described as a "heroic" period. The revolution allowed the artists and architects to escape the rigidity of the tsarist era. It was during this period that various new architectural movements (Constructivist, Rationalist, and Formalist) emerged, each attempting to define the institutions of a new Communist system. They were typically avant-gardist, influenced by European art movements such as Cubism and Futurism (see Chapter 11). This included the Suprematist movement founded in 1913 and led by the painter Kasimir Malevich (1879–1935), which produced abstract geometric works in vivid colours.

The younger generation of Soviet artists was inspired to forge strong alliances between painting, sculpture, and architecture. An impressive example of this is found in the work of Vladimir Tatlin (1885–1953). Inspired by avant-garde modern art, he produced "counter-relief" constructions or small abstract sculptures made from various materials. A particularly important post-revolutionary work was Tatlin's design for a 400-metre (1,310-foot) high monument to the Third International (1920). A distinctive conical spiraling form, the open structure was intended to support four revolving geometric volumes (two cylinders, a pyramid, and a hemisphere) to accommodate a legislative function, reading rooms, gymnasia, flexible space, and an "agitation centre."

Many of the designs for new Soviet building types were the subject of design competitions. This is the case of the Palace of Labour competition held in 1922. A watershed moment in Russian architecture, the third-place entry by the Vesnin brothers remains one of the most compelling examples of a design for a new Soviet institution and received high praise from the architect Moisei Ginzburg (1892–1946) as "the first demonstration of our new approach."[3] The Vesnin brothers (Alexandr (1883–1959), Leonid (1880–1933), and Viktor (1882–1950))[4] also produced a striking design for the Moscow Bureau of the Newspaper Leningrad Pravda competition of 1924, which is described as:

> The design of the building represents a characteristic solution in a period yearning for glass, steel, and concrete. All accessories – which on a typical city street are usually tacked onto the building – such as signs, advertising, clocks, loudspeakers, and even the elevator inside, have been

incorporated as integral elements of the design and combined into a unified whole. This is the aesthetic of constructivism.[5]

Constructivism was the most recognizable form of Russian architecture during the 1920s as an exuberant expression of a new society. Other striking examples include El Lissitzky's (1890–1941) design for a Tribune for Lenin (1920) and his horizontal skyscrapers or "Sky-hooks" (1924) that expressed a new architectural language. Involved in numerous collaborations and exhibitions, El Lissitzky was an envoy for avant-garde design between Russia and Europe.

Ginzburg absorbed a wide range of influences, resulting in his book *Style and Epoch* in 1924, in part as a response to Le Corbusier's book *Toward an Architecture* (1923). In the book, Ginzburg advocates for "constructive" architecture, which includes concepts of movement and mechanization;[6] he writes:

> Constructivism, as one of the facets of a modern aesthetic, born of clamorous life, steeped in the odors of the street, its maddening tempo, its practicality and everyday concerns, and its aesthetic . . . is unquestionably one of the characteristic aspects of the new style, avidly accepting modernity in all of its positive and negative aspects.[7]

Housing was a special area of interest for a communist society.[8] Ginzburg's Narkomfin Communal House project (1930) remains the most famous and the most developed of all the residential experiments. It was a housing prototype, combining bourgeois and communist living units, along with communal facilities, that echoed contemporary designs by Le Corbusier and famously employed the "skip-stop" section where corridors are located on alternate floors.[9]

Konstantin Melnikov (1890–1974) made his early reputation with his scheme for the dynamic Soviet pavilion for the 1925 Exposition des Arts Décoratifs in Paris. Melnikov later designed his own idiosyncratic house in Moscow (1927) based on a cylinder. Creating a position between the avant-garde and traditionalists, Melnikov produced designs for workers' clubs built by various trade unions, including the famous Rusakov Worker's Club (1928) in Moscow for the Union of Municipal Workers. Defined by "the searing angles of the cantilevered forms,"[10] or the protruding auditoria, the Rusakov Worker's Club is expressive and dynamic, with a single large hall capable of being subdivided into six smaller spaces.

An important hotbed of Constructivist design thinking was found in the architecture schools in Moscow. Ivan Leonidov (1902–1959) demonstrated this with his diploma project for the Lenin Institute of Librarianship (1927) as a "visionary" architecture, like much of the unbuilt work of the 1920s. The other young visionary architect of note was Iakov Chernikov (1889–1951), who produced several books of drawings between 1927 and 1933.

In the 1920s, Soviet architects took on the challenges of designing buildings for a Communist society. Eventually, conservative forces prevailed as the avant-garde architects were seen as too aligned with the West and modern technology. Echoing this opposition Lenin states, "Proletarian culture is not something dreamed up out of nowhere; nor is it the invention of people who call themselves specialists in proletarian culture."[11] The Palace of Soviets competition (1931–1932) ultimately signalled the end of the avant-garde phase. The competition called for the design of two large congress halls and various smaller auditoria. The competition winner was Boris Iofan, a conservative architect who established the eclectic and bombastic Stalinist "wedding cake" approach that became the official Socialist Realist style.

Beginning in the 1930s, this new style was used for numerous buildings that would transform Moscow and other cities. Projects for academies, administrative complexes, enormous public spaces, and hotels were favoured by Social Realist architects. In the executed buildings, monumentality is evident, combined with a richness of materials and details. The enormous Red Army Theatre project (1940) in Moscow by Karo Alabyan and Vasily Simbirtsev, based on the five-pointed Communist star, is a good example of Socialist Realism.[12]

In 1931, Moscow, as the capital of the Soviet Union, "was granted extraordinary political and economic advantages."[13] Stalin backed a plan to transform Moscow the following year. In 1935, a General Plan for the city was issued, which accommodated growth, greenspace, a monumental organization of key institutions, and new infrastructure, including the celebrated Moscow underground metro system with its luxurious stations. Following the aftermath of World War II a taller type of building began to populate the Moscow skyline, such as the Moscow State University complex (1949–1953) by Lev Rudnev. The death of Stalin resulted in the demise of Socialist Realism. However, Communist monumentalism was adopted in countries like the Democratic People's Republic of Korea, various Soviet satellite countries, and the People's Republic of China.

★ ★ ★

The rise of Fascism in Europe in the 1920s, particularly in Italy and Germany, resulted in one of the darkest periods in human history. The dictatorships of Benito Mussolini (1883–1945) and Adolf Hitler (1889–1945) established "authoritarian" or "totalitarian" control in their respective countries. Both employed architecture to express the characteristics of their regimes. Fascists exploited the idea of a crisis where a group or nation perceives it is victimized or under attack, resulting in the group taking action against its identified enemies. Typically led by a charismatic leader, the group or nation resorts to trusting the leader's rhetoric, often employing violent means in its creation of an authority over personal freedoms. The group, or nation, tends to be unified by race, religion, and a nation-state, and acts in righteous belief.[14]

Fascism has been an insidious force since it was born on March 23, 1919, in Milan by a diverse group under the direction of Benito Mussolini, a disaffected former Socialist journalist.[15] Following this, the movement spread rapidly in Italy, with Mussolini being appointed prime minister in October 1922. By removing the opposition, Mussolini established a one-party state. Under the Fascists, Italy moved to expand its colonial control and aligned itself with Germany and Japan at the start of World War II. After an armistice with the Allies was agreed on by Italy in September 1943, Mussolini was imprisoned. Briefly reinstalled in power by Germany, Mussolini was executed by Communists on April 28, 1945. During Mussolini's two decades of tumultuous rule, the state commissioned numerous works of architecture, often referencing the glorious past of the Roman Empire. Ambitious projects included a new plan for Rome (1925–1938) and a new Città Universitaria (1932–1935) in Rome, both under the direction of the leading Fascist architect Marcello Piacentini (1881–1960).

A state-sponsored Fascist style emerged that was a fusion of modernism, Rationalism, and classicism, particularly evident in the work of a group of architects known as Gruppo 7, who emerged in late 1926. The most well-known member of Gruppo 7 was Giuseppe Terragni (1904–1943), who was from the Como region and joined the Fascist Party in 1928. He is known for designing a series of apartment buildings in Como and Milan. The most important commission of his career was the Casa del Fascio in Como (1932–1936), the local headquarters of the Fascist party, or as he described it, the "glass house of Fascism."[16] Cubic in form and following the typology of the Renaissance palazzo, the Casa del Fascio supported offices, meeting

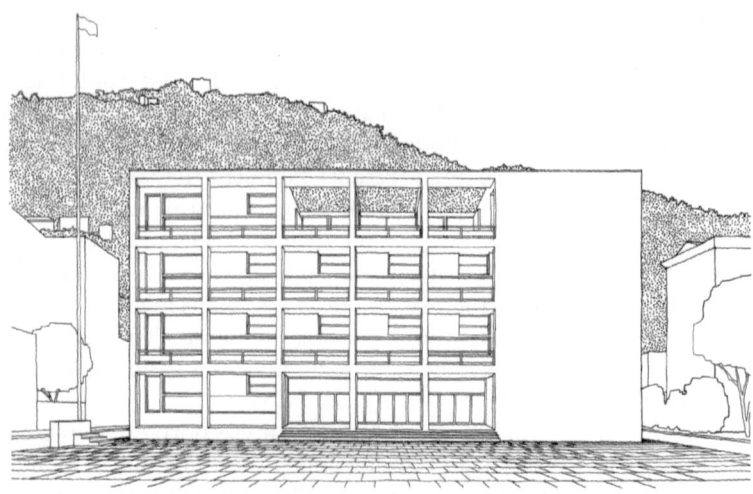

Figure 14.1 Perspective, Giuseppe Terragni, Casa del Fascio, 1936, Como, Italy. The simple rectangular four-storey façade features five open colonnaded bays to the left and two closed bays to the right; the building supported displays of Italian Fascist authority. Drawing by Mohammad Moezzi.

rooms, and a central atrium. The four differing facades and material qualities of the building are described as follows: "There is a curious ambiguity about the overall composition of the Casa del Fascio. . . . It is simultaneously more solid and more transparent."[17] Clad in marble, the primary façade supports a shallow balcony space across much of its length. During rallies, key members of the Fascist party were arrayed across the façade in a military and nationalistic spectacle. Terragni's unbuilt Danteum project (1938) for Rome was intended to be a national centre for the study of Dante Alighieri (1265–1321), the great Italian poet. Terragni has developed a reputation in recent years for his sophisticated handling of volume, form, and surface.[18]

Of all the institutional projects built during the period, the Esposizione Universale di Roma (EUR) is the clearest expression of Italian Fascist architecture. Laid out by Piacentini to emulate Roman town planning, the site was intended for a failed 1942 World's Fair to celebrate Fascist accomplishments. Ultimately developed as an economic centre, the complex was completed when facilities were added for the 1960 Summer Olympic Games. The most iconic of the buildings remains the Palazzo della Civiltà Italiana (1942) by

Giovanni Guerini, Ernesto La Padula, and Mario Romano. A simple six-storey block clad in Travertine marble, the Palazzo occupies the most prominent location in the EUR and features the use of a repeating arch motif. Adalberto Libera's (1903–1963) Palazzo dei Congressi (1942) at the EUR remains one of the most important examples of the state style applied to a large congress hall. Libera was also a member of Gruppo 7 and another of the primary Italian architects of the era.[19] Influenced by modernist developments elsewhere in Europe and yet retaining a certain formalism or traditionalism, Italian Fascist architecture remains controversial and enigmatic.

★ ★ ★

The rise of Adolf Hitler and the formation of the Nazi Party would unleash tremendous forces, particularly after Germany invaded Poland on September 1, 1939, triggering World War II. In 1921 Hitler became the leader of the German Workers' Party, later the National Socialist (or Nazi) Party. Incarcerated from 1923–1924 after a failed coup in Munich, Germany, he wrote his notorious autobiography *Mein Kampf* while in prison. By late 1932 the Nazi Party held the most seats in the German Reichstag, and on January 30, 1933 Hitler was appointed chancellor. This began the systematic transformation of Germany into a one-party totalitarian state with the help of the secret police or SS (Gestapo) and the subsequent elimination of "enemies," especially Jews, intellectuals, and other opponents of the regime. Hitler's mission was to establish the Third Reich, following the German Empire (1871–1918) and the Weimar Republic (1918–1933). By the end of 1941, Hitler had invaded the Soviet Union and controlled much of Europe and North Africa. Eventually, the Allied Forces defeated the German war machine in 1945.

Hitler was a failed architect and painter who devoted much time during his rule to Nazi architectural projects. Under Hitler's control, National Socialist architecture was developed both for institutional buildings and for more ordinary structures which were either based on a monumental neo-classicism or on German vernacular architecture; modern architecture was rejected outright as left-wing and "foreign." Hitler's first architectural advisor was Paul Ludwig Troost (1878–1934); they both admired the work of Karl Friedrich Schinkel (see Chapter 6). Together they produced the early House of German Art (1936) in Munich, which, with its austere Doric order and precise lines, became a blueprint for Nazi public architecture.

After his death, Troost was replaced by Albert Speer (1905–1981), who had studied with and worked for the German traditionalist architect Heinrich Tessenow (1876–1950). Speer's impact was immediate, beginning with his designs for the Zeppelinfeld grounds (1934) at Nuremberg, the location of enormous Nazi party rallies (up to 100,000 people). The design employed an austere and monumental classicism; at rallies, this was supported by searchlights, flags, and insignia, which created frenzied displays of force. By 1938, Speer devised the New Chancellery in Berlin as Hitler's office and salon. Carefully choreographed to enhance the persona of the leader, Speer's design used rich materials, monumental classicism, and Nazi paraphernalia to create an intimidating experience for visitors. Together with Hitler, Speer devised a plan for Berlin, inspired by ancient Rome, to be the grandiose capital of the Third Reich. It terminated on an immense domed Great Hall (a pantheon of German heroes). According to architectural historian Barbara Miller Lane:

> To Hitler, architecture was thus better suited than any other art to express national greatness . . . architecture not only "expressed" the unity and power of the nation but could also help to create it. Great buildings, he [Hitler] told the assembled party members in 1937, could create the kind of common "will" which he had earlier called their necessary prerequisite . . . it was the function of architecture to impress the ideas of its creators upon other nations and, even more important, upon posterity.[20]

Along with their military machine, the Nazis developed an enormous system of transit camps, concentration camps (such as Dachau, Bergen-Belsen, and Buchenwald), labour camps, and extermination camps (including the most notorious and largest camp Auschwitz-Birkenau, located in Poland) throughout the territories they controlled.[21] Established as early as 1933, concentration (or labour) camps were used to house "undesirables" as the Nazis took control of Germany. Early inmates were incarcerated as slave labour devoted to realizing Nazi projects.[22] The design of concentration and extermination camps employed architects as part of the process.

The "Turn to the East," launched by the Nazis with the invasion of Poland in 1939, had much to do with the history of Germany and Eastern Europe.[23] The Germanification of the Polish territories by the Nazis consumed enormous amounts of building material which was manufactured by slave labour in the concentration camps.[24] The largest camp was Auschwitz-Birkenau, which was originally established in 1940 as a work camp for producing construction materials.

It was abandoned early in 1945 with the arrival of Soviet troops. By the summer of 1942, following the Nazi command's decision to implement the "Final Solution," or the elimination of all Jews in Europe, it was converted to an extermination camp where over one million people were eventually murdered. Heinrich Himmler (1900–1945), a leading member of the Nazi party, is often described as the "architect" of the Holocaust.[25]

The initial Auschwitz camp had 22 brick barracks and a further 22 wooden horse stable barracks, along with various other structures (including a crematorium), all surrounded by barbed wire. In the early phase of Auschwitz, Poles and prisoners of war were systematically executed, but horrendous living conditions also produced numerous deaths. As the camp grew, its development was overseen by an architectural office under the direction of August Schlachter (1901–1996). In 1941, a major expansion of the camp was designed by SS architects in Berlin under Hans Kammler (1901–1945). Karl Bischoff (1897–1950) became the new head architect at Auschwitz, where he oversaw further expansions of the camp and directed the on-site architects.[26]

In late 1941 the Nazis began to experiment with gassing Soviet prisoners using Zyklon B gas. The processing, housing, and extermination of prisoners were carefully designed, and in 1942, the adjoining camp at Birkenau was opened, planned to house up to 100,000 prisoners. Eventually, at Auschwitz-Birkenau, buildings were developed that incorporated gas chambers, morgues, and crematoria in innocuous-looking structures. Prisoners, mainly Jews, were separated upon arrival at Auschwitz-Birkenau, either to join the workforce or to be murdered immediately. The atrocities of the Holocaust, in which millions died, were the result of a political system based on extreme nationalism and racism and, by a regime that depended on architects and architecture to support its programs.[27]

★ ★ ★

Both Communist and Fascist authoritarian regimes were opposed to the use of modern architecture, instead promoting monumental forms of architecture. In the case of the Soviet Union, the following objections to modern architecture were articulated in 1932 by Swiss architect Hans Schmidt:

1. The ideas of modern architecture, known in the West under the labels of "constructivism," "functionalism," and "mechanism,"

are an outgrowth of contemporary capitalism and its rationalized and standardized technology.

2. Modern architecture's renunciation of monumentality and symbolic expression, its disavowal of absolute beauty, and its inability to carry out the artistic and ideological mission of architecture, are an expression of the decline of bourgeois culture.[28]

NOTES

1   "Communism," *Encyclopedia Britannica*. https://www.britannica.com/topic/communism. Accessed January 6, 2022.

2   See Cecil D. Elliott, "Monuments and Monumentality," *Journal of Architectural Education*, vol. 18, no. 4 (March 1964), pp. 51–53.

3   Quoted in Catherine Cooke, "Images in Context," in *Architectural Drawings of the Russian Avant-Garde* (New York: Museum of Modern Art, 1990), p. 23.

4   See S.O. Khan-Magomedov, *Alexandr Vesnin and Russian Constructivism* (New York: Rizzoli, 1986).

5   El Lissitzky, *Russia: An Architecture for World Revolution* (Cambridge, MA: MIT Press, 1984), p. 32.

6   See Anatole Senkeviotch, Jr., "Moisei Ginzburg and the Emergence of a Constructivist Theory of Architecture," in Moisei Ginzburg, *Style and Epoch* (Cambridge, MA: MIT Press, 1982).

7   Ginzburg, *Style and Epoch*, p. 102.

8   El Lissitzky, *Russia*, p. 35.

9   See Victor Buchli, "Moisei Ginzburg's Narkomfin Communal House in Moscow: Contesting the Social and Material World," *JSAH*, vol. 57, no. 2 (June 1998), pp. 160–181.

10   S. Frederick Starr, *Melnikov: Solo Architect in a Mass Society* (Princeton: Princeton University Press, 1978), p. 136.

11   Quoted in Cooke, "Images in Context," p. 27.

12   See Alexei Tarkhanov and Sergei Kavtaradze, *Stalinist Architecture* (London: Laurence King, 1992).

13   Ibid., p. 80.

14   Robert O. Paxton, *The Anatomy of Fascism* (New York: Vintage Books, 2004), pp. 219–220.

15   Ibid., p. 5.

16   Thomas L. Schumacher, *Surface and Symbol: Giuseppe Terragni and the Architecture of Italian Rationalism* (New York: Princeton Architectural Press, 1991), p. 166.

17   Ibid., p. 168.

18   See Peter Eisenman, *Giuseppe Terragni: Transformations, Decompositions, Critiques* (New York: Monacelli Press, 2003).

19 See Francesco Garofalo and Luca Veresani, *Adalberto Libera* (New York: Princeton Architectural Press, 1992).

20 Barbara Miller Lane, *Architecture and Politics in Germany 1918–1945* (Cambridge, MA: Harvard University Press, 1985), p. 188.

21 See Paul B. Jaskot, *The Architecture of Oppression* (London: Routledge, 2000).

22 See Deborah Dwork and Robert Jan Van Pelt, *Auschwitz, 1270 to the Present* (New York: W.W. Norton & Co., 2002), pp. 98–104.

23 See Ibid., pp. 38–91.

24 See Ibid., pp. 172–173.

25 See Ibid., pp. 276–283.

26 See Ibid., pp. 197–235.

27 See Ibid., pp. 307–353.

28 Hans Schmidt, "The Soviet Union and Modern Architecture," in El Lissitzky, *Russia*, p. 220.

SUGGESTED READING

Cooke, Catherine. *Russian Avant-Garde: Theories of Art, Architecture and the City.* London: Academy Editions, 1995.

Dwork, Deborah and Robert Jan Van Pelt. *Auschwitz, 1270 to the Present.* New York: W.W. Norton & Co., 2002.

Jones, Kay Bea and Stephanie Pilat, eds. *The Routledge Companion to Italian Fascist Architecture: Reception and Legacy.* Abingdon: Routledge, 2021.

Lane, Barbara Miller. *Architecture and Politics in Germany 1918–1945.* Cambridge, MA: Harvard University Press, 1985.

Tarkhanov, Alexei and Sergei Kavtaradze. *Stalinist Architecture.* London: Laurence King, 1992.

15

VERNACULAR AND TRADITION

Vernacular architecture is generally understood to encompass ordinary buildings built using anonymous local knowledge and materials, precisely developed over time to meet the needs of a local culture and climate. Vernacular buildings comprise the majority of the world's architecture.[1] This tradition does not place emphasis on innovation or authorship; instead, it concentrates on appropriateness and continuity. There are spatial, environmental, material, technological, formal, and cultural aspects of vernacular architecture that locally evolved over long periods of time. As architectural historian Paul Oliver writes about vernacular architecture:

> [I]t embraces what is known and what is inherited about the dwelling, building or settlement; it includes the collective wisdom and experience of the society concerned, and the norms that have become accepted by the group as being appropriate to their built environment. It is also to do with the inherited knowledge of the natural environment of climate, topography, seasonal variation, natural hazard, suitability of site. Inevitably this spills over into the values of the society and how they may affect, through belief, observance, ritual, and respect for ancestors or deities, what might be seen as more practical considerations to those outside the group.[2]

Historically, architects tended to focus on designing buildings for the powerful and wealthy, including monarchs, religious organizations, and rich merchants, in established styles, such as Classicism or Gothic. Ordinary types of buildings, such as urban and rural houses, agricultural structures, and industrial buildings, were not considered architecture and did not involve architects. In the 19th century,

DOI: 10.4324/9781003403975-15

the Arts and Crafts movement in Europe and America introduced the radical idea that ordinary vernacular buildings could be studied and interpreted by architects. For example, the "cottage," as a simple rural building type, was the basis for many houses designed by Arts and Crafts architects. In places like England, where there was a long history of local building traditions, this meant drawing and recording the use of local materials and techniques, much as Richard Norman Shaw and Eden Nesfield did in the 1850s when they were young architects.[3] Likewise, in America in the late 19th century, the "Shingle Style" was popular in New England, where architects, including prominent figures like Henry Hobson Richardson and his Stoughton House (1883) in Cambridge, Massachusetts, drew inspiration from ordinary local buildings.

The architect Adolf Loos famously described in his essay "Architecture" (1910) how a villa by an architect in a rural setting was like "an unnecessary scream" that shatters the peaceful environment that seemed as though it had been created by God.[4] In the text, Loos underscores the distinction between architecture as a professional act and architecture as a vernacular act. Vernacular architecture was a source of inspiration for various nationalist movements, including German Nazism (see Chapter 14), and it provided a basis for challenging the ubiquity of modern architecture in many cultures. Mediterranean traditional culture, which evolved typologies such as the courtyard house, the Italian hill town, and the North African casbah, also provided a continuing source of inspiration for architects in the 20th century.[5]

The advent of modernism, with its focus on progress, innovation, and individual creativity, seemingly moved away from vernacular models. However, relatively soon after the development of the International Style in the 1920s and 1930s, architects in many countries, disillusioned with modernity, turned back to vernacular traditions to create regionally and culturally specific architecture. This effort to blend modernism and vernacular tradition could fall into what historian Eric Hobsbawm calls "invented tradition."[6]

In the 1930s, Le Corbusier (1887–1965) shifted his architectural approach quite dramatically towards a "monumentalization of the vernacular,"[7] abandoning the Purist architecture of the 1920s that had made him the leader of the modern movement (see Chapter 10). Disillusioned with the Machine Age, Le Corbusier took inspiration from simple ordinary structures, such as those he encountered on his famous travels early in his career, especially in the Balkan region in 1911.[8] This would remain vital to his work for the remainder of his life and can be found in designs beginning with the de Mandrot house (1931) near Toulon, France, which interpreted the farmhouses of the region and was built of local stone. The vernacular was also evident in his work in Algeria in the 1930s and in his later Maisons Jaoul (1955) in Paris. These projects involved the use of natural materials and simple construction methods, what can be described as an "expressive *bricolage*"[9] that also employed a distinctive approach to form. Le Corbusier, rather than directly imitating vernacular traditions, derived a more fundamental inspiration from it. Other modern architects, including Alvar Aalto, also incorporated the vernacular into their designs (see Chapter 19).

Postmodernist architects, including Charles Moore (1925–1993) and Robert Venturi (1925–2018), drew inspiration from vernacular building traditions (see Chapter 18). This is evident in the widely influential Sea Ranch Condominium (1965) by Moore Lyndon Turnbull Whitaker north of San Francisco, with its use of simple forms and wood as a material that inspired many like-minded projects.[10] Venturi and Rauch's Trubek and Wislocki houses (1971) in Nantucket, Massachusetts, interpreted the colonial vernacular wooden buildings of New England.[11] A student of Moore's, the Canadian architect Brian MacKay-Lyons (1954–), has embedded his practice in the local building traditions of Nova Scotia and its coastal fishing communities. MacKay-Lyons writes:

> Vernacular is not a style or an image. It is a process or cultural view, connected to material culture and the culture of building. By taking up new technologies and materials the vernacular is always contemporary and forward-looking rather than sentimental or backward-looking. For the architect, to embrace the vernacular is by definition to accept the idea of convention.[12]

★ ★ ★

The study of vernacular traditions intersected with modernism in Egypt, Turkey, and Iran; the three countries are predominantly Islamic, and each has a long cultural history. The Islamic world is, to a large extent, shaped by continuing traditions. Modern architects in the region have often interpreted traditional technologies (tents, wind towers, masonry methods, etc.) and typologies (souks, mosques, minarets, etc.) in innovative ways. This applies to Islamic architects practicing in their own countries and international firms who have been commissioned to undertake projects in the region.[13]

For 5,000 years, Egypt has been home to various important cultures and remains a vital centre in the Arab and Islamic world. It is a desert country dominated by the Nile River and the cities of Cairo and Alexandria. With a well-established architectural profession, Egypt relies somewhat less than other countries on outside architectural firms. The most well-known and influential Egyptian architect was Hassan Fathy (1900–1989), who attacked modernism and advocated for the use of simple traditional construction methods and architectural forms. Despite a relatively modest body of work, his thinking has been inspirational to architects throughout the region. Early in his career, he learned about traditional mud brick construction, particularly the vault and arch methods used by Nubian builders. He advocated for maintaining craft traditions in poor communities and using their skills to build their settlements. His practice began in the 1930s. An early and critically important project was the village of New Gourna (1953) near Luxor. The village included housing and public facilities and was only partially completed due to various administrative problems. He also designed the unfinished village of New Bariz (1970), and several houses in Cairo. Integrating courtyards and natural ventilation principles, he sought an architecture that was modest, suitable, locally built, and inspired by vernacular practices. Outside of Egypt, he designed projects in Iraq, Kuwait, and the United States.[14] In his important book *Architecture for the Poor*, Fathy outlines his theories, experiences, and early projects. He writes about tradition in developing societies:

> Tradition among the peasants is the only safeguard of their culture. They cannot discriminate between unfamiliar styles, and if they run off the rails of tradition they will inevitably meet disaster. Willfully to break a tradition in a basically traditional society like a peasant one is a kind of cultural murder, and the architect must respect the tradition he is invading.[15]

Concerned with the inappropriateness of modern techniques in poor rural communities in Egypt, Fathy argues that maintaining traditions "is not necessarily old-fashioned or synonymous with stagnation."[16] Traditions exist in cycles that can be long or short, old or new; the architect must override personal expression for the betterment of the community.

★ ★ ★

The secular modern Turkish republic was established in 1923 following a War of Independence (1919–1923) and the end of the centuries-old Ottoman Empire. Mustafa Kemal Atatürk (1881–1938) led the founding of a republic which resulted in many changes in Turkish society and the adoption of a programme of modernization. This eventually resulted in a turning away from traditional styles of architecture and embracing the International Style. The construction of the new capital city of Ankara, beginning in 1923, was an important project in Turkey's modernizing movement.[17]

The initial buildings in Ankara were built in a more traditional style known as the First National Style. However, by the 1930s, the impact of designs by European émigré modernist planners and architects, mainly from Germany and Austria, was widely evident. An international competition held in 1927 for the design of the new city was won by the German planner Herman Jansen, based on a Garden City-inspired scheme that encircled the existing city with planned neighbourhoods and wide streets. A series of "grand projects," including a major dam, parks, and a model farm, supported the development of the new capital. Model villages were developed to improve the agricultural system, and new factory towns were built to promote industry.[18] A new generation of Turkish architects, many trained in Europe, also began to emerge in the 1930s. A classical tendency was evident in many projects as well, exemplified in Atatürk's Mausoleum (1942) in Ankara by Emin Onat and Orhan Arda, underscoring the close relations between Germany and Turkey during this era.

In reaction to the colonizing influence of European modernism, Turkish architects, such as Sedad Hakki Eldem (1926–1986), began to look carefully at Turkish traditional architecture. Eldem studied the traditional Turkish house as a specific set of spaces, evolving a modern version as a result. His Taslik Coffee House (1948) in Istanbul is an example of his approach.[19] This resulted in a successful career designing houses in the 1950s and 1960s.

In 1950, Turkey moved from a secular authoritarian government to a populist democratic one. The modernization programme continued with great success, concentrating on the refurbishment of Istanbul as a cultural centre with new boulevards, parks, and institutions. The dominance of the International Style was on full display in the Istanbul Hilton Hotel (1955) designed by Skidmore, Owings & Merrill with Sedad Eldem. A representation of American culture and the theories of Le Corbusier, the hotel has come to symbolize the inappropriateness of imposing modern architecture on non-Western cultures.[20]

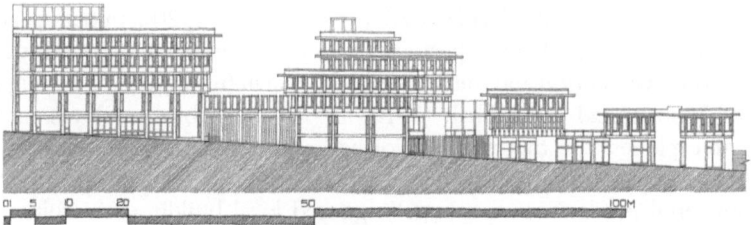

Figure 15.1 East Elevation, Sedad Eldem, Zeyrek Social Security Agency, 1964, Istanbul, Turkey. The design features articulated pavilions grouped along a major boulevard showcasing the inspiration derived from traditional Turkish houses; the scheme is designed to fit the context, acting as an interface between the building and surrounding neighbourhoods. Drawing by Mohammad Moezzi.

From 1946 to 1980, Turkish cities grew significantly, triggering housing shortages and the emergence of informal settlements.[21] After 1960, instability marred the political situation in Turkey. At the same time, Turkish architects, like their colleagues in the Islamic world, became increasingly disillusioned with the International Style. Sedad Eldem's Zeyrek Social Security Agency (1964) in Istanbul is a well-known example of integrating local and international influences. By referencing the traditional Turkish house in a modern office building, Eldem broke down the mass into smaller pavilions interwoven with public spaces and pathways (the design won an Aga Khan award in 1986). The use of the "fragmented block," or a collection of pavilions of varying sizes, became a common plan diagram in the 1960s.[22] Turkish architects and clients also embraced a variety of modern construction systems in industrial and commercial projects.

Despite Turkey being constitutionally a secular state, it is still a strongly Islamic country. The mosque remains a vital aspect of Turkish society. The Parliament Mosque Complex (1989) in Ankara by Behruz and Can Cincini is an example of contemporary mosque design. The architect Turgut Cansever (1920–2009) was widely respected for his ability to balance his religious values with the design of regionally sensitive secular buildings. As elsewhere, postmodernism impacted Turkish architecture in the 1980s, primarily in the design of buildings for the tourism industry. More recently, architects like Han Tümertekin and Nevzat Sayin have again been involved in developing regionally appropriate modern architecture.

★ ★ ★

Iran began a "modernization" project in the 1920s, initiating an era known as the Pahlavi period (1925–1979), which ended with the Islamic Revolution and the removal of the Shah from power. The reign of Mohammad Reza Shah (1919–1980) can be broken down into three phases: the first phase involved a continuation of architectural traditions, the second phase during the 1960s saw the introduction of universal modernism that largely ignored local building and cultural practices and a third phase in the 1970s that saw the development of Iranian regional architecture.[23] In the 1950s, Houshang Seyhoun (1920–2014) emerged as a transformative architect who designed several key works, including the Omar Khayyam Mausoleum (1963) in Nishabur and the Ferdowsi Mausoleum Teahouse/Museum (1968) in Tus. Seyhoun also took on an important role as an educator. He left Iran after the Islamic Revolution and died in exile.

During the 1970s, projects such as the Iran Center for Management Studies in Tehran (1975) by Nader Ardalan, the Shustar New Town (1977), and the Tehran Museum of Contemporary Art (1977) by Kamran Diba (1937–) were among the most accomplished and important projects built.[24] In the 1980s, the architect Hadi Mirmiran (1945–2006) had a significant impact on Iranian architecture. He graduated from Tehran University in 1968. He worked for various companies before becoming the principal architect for a large engineering firm. An educator and the winner of several important competitions, he is particularly remembered for his National Academies of the Islamic Republic of Iran competition entry (1994) and his Rafsanjan Sports Complex (2002). Mirmiran provided a model that blended international and Iranian influences in his designs.[25]

The Aga Khan Award for Architecture, sponsored by Prince Karim Aga Khan IV (Imam of the Nizari Ismaili community of Shia Muslims), was launched in 1977 and has raised the global profile of modern Islamic architecture. The programme brings together, every three years, a distinguished jury to select projects built for Islamic communities (architecture, planning, historic preservation, and landscape architecture) around the world. The Aga Kahn Awards have raised the profile of Islamic architecture globally. The *Mimar: Architecture in Development* journal was established in 1981 (and operated until 1992) for the study and dissemination of Islamic architecture. The programme places a particular emphasis on how architects interpret local conditions.

★ ★ ★

The relationship between vernacular and modern architecture has often been overlooked. In examining Le Corbusier's connection to vernacular architecture, Francesco Passanti argues that he wanted to establish modern architecture as a widely practised form of the vernacular. Passanti writes:

> Its [the vernacular] principal role . . . was not as a source of architectural motifs but as a conceptual model for a natural relationship between society and its artifacts, hence society and architecture; specifically, a conceptual model for the notion of a *modern vernacular* – one as naturally issuing from modern industrial society, and as representative of it, as the traditional vernacular of common parlance had been of earlier societies.[26]

NOTES

1 See Sibyl Moholy-Nagy, *Native Genius in Anonymous Architecture* (New York: Horizon Press, 1957); Mete Turan, ed., *Vernacular Architecture: Paradigms of Environmental Response* (Aldershot: Avebury, 1990); and D. Upton and J.M. Vlach, eds., *Common Places: Readings in American Vernacular Architecture* (Athens: University of Georgia Press, 1986).

2 Paul Oliver, *Built to Meet Needs: Cultural Issues in Vernacular Architecture* (London: Routledge, 2006), p. 110.

3 See Andrew Saint, *Richard Norman Shaw* (New Haven: Yale University Press, 1976); and R.W. Brunskill, *Illustrated Handbook of Vernacular Architecture* (London: Faber and Faber, 1987).

4 See Adolf Loos, "Architecture," in Y. Safran and W. Wang, eds., *The Architecture of Adolf Loos* (London: Arts Council, 1985), p. 104.

5 See Michelangelo Sabatino, "Toward a Regionalist Modernism: Italian Architecture and the Vernacular," in Leen Meganck et al., eds., *Regionalism and Modernity: Architecture in Western Europe, 1914–1940* (Leuven: Leuven University Press, 2013), pp. 197–217.

6 Eric Hobsbawm, "Introduction: Inventing Traditions," in E. Hobsbawm and T. Ranger, eds., *The Invention of Tradition* (Cambridge: Cambridge University Press, 2012), p. 1.

7 Kenneth Frampton, *Modern Architecture: A Critical History* (London: Thames & Hudson, 2020), p. 255.

8 See Francesco Passanti, "The Vernacular, Modernism, and Le Corbusier," *JSAH*, vol. 56, no. 4 (December 1997), pp. 438–451.

9 Frampton, *Modern Architecture*, p. 257.

10 See Gerald Allen, *Charles Moore* (New York: Whitney Library of Design, 1980).

11 See Thomas Beeby, "Association and Dissociation: The Trubek and Wislocki Houses," in Christopher Mead, ed., *The Architecture of Robert Venturi* (Albuquerque: University of New Mexico Press, 1989), pp. 68–84.

12 Brian MacKay-Lyons, "Seven Stories from a Village Architect," *Design Quarterly*, no. 165 (Summer 1995), p. 9.

13 See Udo Kultermann, *Contemporary Architecture in the Arab States* (New York: McGraw-Hill, 1999), pp. 1–18.

14 See Ibid., pp. 19–30. See also James Steele, *An Architecture for People: The Complete Works of Hassan Fathy* (London: Thames & Hudson, 1997); and Ahmad Hamid, *Hassan Fathy and Continuity in Islamic Architecture: The Birth of a New Modern* (Cairo: American University of Cairo Press, 2010).

15 Hasan Fathy, *Architecture for the Poor: An Experiment in Rural Egypt* (Chicago: University of Chicago Press, 1973), p. 25.

16 Ibid., p. 24.

17 See Sibel Bozdogan and Esra Akcan, *Turkey: Modern Architectures in History* (London: Reaktion Books, 2012), pp. 17–20.

18 See Ibid., pp. 26–47.

19 See Ibid., pp. 96–103.

20 See Annabel Wharton, *Building the Cold War: Hilton International Hotels and Modern Architecture* (Chicago: University of Chicago Press, 2001). See also Bozdogan and Akcan, *Turkey*, pp. 114–130.

21 See Bozdogan and Akcan, *Turkey*, pp. 139–169.

22 See Ibid., pp. 175–185.

23 See Farshad Farahi, "World of Similitude: The Metamorphosis of Iranian Architecture," *Architectural Design*, vol. 82, no. 3 (2012), p. 59. See also: Pamela Karimi, "Old Sites, New Frontiers: Modern and Contemporary Architecture in Iran," in E.G. Haddad and D. Rifkind, eds., *A Critical History of Contemporary Architecture, 1960–2010* (London: Routledge, 2014), pp. 339–358; and M. Reza Shirazi, *Contemporary Architecture and Urbanism in Iran* (Cham, Switzerland: Springer, 2018). Mohammad Moezzi also provided information on modern Iranian architecture.

24 See Darah Diba, "Contemporary Architecture of Iran," *Architectural Design*, vol. 82, no. 3 (2012), pp. 70–79.

25 See Saman Sayar, "Assimilating the Authentic with the Contemporary: The Work of Hadi Mirmiran 1945–2006," *Architectural Design*, vol. 82, no. 3 (2012), pp. 80–87.

26 Passanti, "The Vernacular, Modernism, and Le Corbusier," p. 447.

SUGGESTED READING

Bozdogan, Sibel and Esra Akcan. *Turkey: Modern Architectures in History*. London: Reaktion Books, 2012.

Fathy, Hasan. *Architecture for the Poor: An Experiment in Rural Egypt*. Chicago: University of Chicago Press, 1973.

Kultermann, Udo. *Contemporary Architecture in the Arab States*. New York: McGraw-Hill, 1999.

Lejeune, Jean-François and Michelangelo Sabatino. *Modern Architecture and the Mediterranean: Vernacular Dialogues and Contested Identities*. Abingdon: Routledge, 2010.

Rudofsky, Bernard. *Architecture Without Architects*. Garden City, NY: Doubleday & Co., 1964.

EDUCATION AND PROFESSIONALISM

The Roman architect Vitruvius (c. 80–15 BC) addresses the education and necessary skills of an architect in the opening book of his famous *Ten Books of Architecture*; he writes the architect "should be equipped with knowledge of many branches of study and varied kinds of learning."[1] The medieval figure of the master mason combined both design and construction abilities as he directed the construction of the great Gothic cathedrals. During the Renaissance, it was often those trained as artisans or artists, such as Brunelleschi (1377–1446), Michelangelo (1475–1564), and Raphael (1483–1520) who became architects. Later, men such as Claude Perrault (1613–1688) and Sir Christopher Wren (1632–1723) entered architecture with scientific backgrounds. In the 17th and 18th centuries, it was not uncommon to join the discipline with training in masonry construction or military engineering. The formal education of architects began in France in the 18th century; it has evolved significantly since then. As the discipline evolved, aspiring architects could train through apprenticeships or by studying in schools of architecture.[2] It is worth noting that both Frank Lloyd Wright and Le Corbusier had little academic training; instead, they learned in various architectural offices before starting their own practices (see Chapter 10).

Architectural education in France descended from the establishment of the Académie Royale d'Architecture in 1671, an elite institution which provided lectures to architects. The first comprehensive school of architecture was a full-time private school established by Jacques-François Blondel in Paris in 1743. Blondel

DOI: 10.4324/9781003403975-16

became a professor in the school of the Académie Royale d'Architecture in 1762.[3] After the French Revolution (1789–1799), the educational system in France was reorganized. It was only in 1819 that the celebrated École des Beaux-Arts was created as a strict educational system. Its curricula focussed on the three prominent "fine arts": architecture, painting, and sculpture.

Architecture students of the École des Beaux-Arts experienced a unique educational approach. They had to belong to an *atelier* run by a respected architect, or "master," in Paris, either in the school or externally. The *atelier*, comprising 50–100 students, was a home base where students undertook their design exercises, prepared for the qualifying exams, which included drawing, geometry, and history tests, and learned the discipline of architecture. Students admitted to the École des Beaux-Arts followed a rigourous programme of design exercises and competitions. They took courses on statics and strength of materials, descriptive geometry, stereotomy (the cutting of three-dimensional solids into shapes, such as in masonry construction), perspective, construction, and history.

Eighteen design exercises of varying types were offered each year; these could be short sketch competitions or longer rendered ones. Students followed their studies at their own pace rather than following a set curriculum. After completing the second (lower) class and the first (upper) class, students then undertook the final thesis exercise, which involved a design and lengthy examination. Selected senior students then completed the prestigious Prix de Rome, which allowed the winner to study in Rome and usually guaranteed a successful career.[4] The École des Beaux-Arts was famous for its large and abstract design problems that focused on public institutions, the results of which were typically formally composed and beautifully drawn (plans, sections, elevations, and perspectives). The École tended to promote a classical approach to design; however, as the 19th century progressed, the stylistic influences became more elaborate and eclectic. Various well-known architectural concepts were developed at the École including the *esquisse*, or short 12-hour "sketch" exercise; the *parti*, or fundamental plan organization for the design; the architectural "program"; and the *charrette*, or quick design exercise.

The École des Beaux-Arts architectural education was very influential, particularly in America, where the German polytechnical system was also important.[5] Several well-known American architects studied at the École, including Richard Morris Hunt (1827–1895), Henry Hobson Richardson (1838–1886), and Louis H. Sullivan (1856–1924). Many American schools of architecture adopted its methods. By the 1930s, the influence of the École had declined, and in 1968 it was closed.

★ ★ ★

The rise of modern architecture in the early 20th century resulted in dramatic changes to architectural education. The most influential modern design school was the Bauhaus, established by Walter Gropius (1883–1969) in Weimar, Germany, in 1919. Before World War I, in which he served, he had made a name for himself as a young architect. He designed, with Adolf Meyer, the Fagus Factory in Alfeld an der Leine (1911–1912) the first important work of European modern architecture (see Chapter 12).

To create the Bauhaus, Gropius amalgamated two existing schools. His vision for the school sought to unite the Arts and Crafts tradition with modern art, especially Expressionist art (see Chapter 11). As Gropius writes in the initial programme: "Architects, sculptors, painters, we all must return to the crafts! For art is not a 'profession.' There is no essential difference between the artist and the craftsman."[6] The role of learning crafts in a workshop was central to the Bauhaus pedagogy, an idea that was also consistent with the earlier Deutscher Werkbund (see Chapter 8).

Initially focusing on the training of painters, sculptors, and architects the school's curriculum quickly evolved into the model that made it famous. Gropius hired several significant artists during the early phase to be "masters," including painters Paul Klee (1879–1940) and Wassily Kandinsky (1866–1944). Studies began with a six-month basic design course known as the *Vorkurs*, initially developed by the Swiss artist Johannes Itten (1888–1967). Students who completed this then selected a three-year workshop course in stone, wood, metal, clay, glass, colour, or textiles leading to a Journeyman's Diploma. This, in theory, was to be followed by training in building design and construction. Less an architecture school than a design and art school, the students and teachers at the Bauhaus created in the 1920s an influential range of work in graphic design, furniture, art, industrial design, theatre design, and textiles.

The first few years in Weimar were difficult, given the German economy and political differences between the school and the local government. In 1925, Gropius was required to relocate the Bauhaus

Figure 16.1 Second Floor Plan, Walter Gropius, Bauhaus, 1926, Dessau, Germany. Dynamically and functionally composed, the design of the Bauhaus locates the student accommodations at the top, classrooms to the left, and workshops at the lower right. Drawing by Mohammad Moezzi.

to Dessau in 1925, where he found more sympathetic support. In Dessau, Gropius had the opportunity to design the most important building of his career, the new facilities for the school. A landmark work of modern architecture (1926), the design clearly articulates the various functions of the school in a dynamic pinwheel composition that is articulated by large amounts of glass and industrial detailing.

The building was a prime example of the emerging International Style (see Chapter 12).

The introductory basic design course was the most important legacy of the Bauhaus educational system. After it was initially developed by Itten, it was taken over in 1923 by the Hungarian artist László Moholy-Nagy (1895–1946). A rational artist influenced by Russian Constructivism, Moholy-Nagy's appointment signalled a change in direction towards a more objective and technological approach to design. A third key teacher involved in the introductory course was Josef Albers (1888–1976), an early graduate of the Bauhaus who worked with Moholy-Nagy. The course is famous for its emphasis on fundamental skill building in form, space, materials, and colour, and it was widely copied.

In Dessau, further changes were made to the curriculum, and new teachers joined the school, including the Austrian graphic designer Herbert Bayer (1900–1985) and the Hungarian-German furniture designer/architect Marcel Breuer (1902–1981). Both graduates of the Bauhaus, each contributed significantly to modernist design in the 1920s. In 1927, the controversial Swiss architect Hannes Meyer (1889–1954) was appointed to run the new architecture department. In January 1928, Gropius resigned from the institution he had founded, appointing Meyer as his successor. Meyer was less sympathetic to art and was strongly left-wing. His directorship led to a stronger focus on architecture and introduced new areas such as town planning and photography. Many of the teachers left or were disillusioned with the new practical approach. By 1930, Meyer was forced to resign and was replaced by Ludwig Mies van der Rohe (1886–1969). Under Mies, the designer Lilly Reich (1885–1947) ran the interior design and textiles workshops. Until her arrival, Greta Stölzl (1897–1983) was the only woman to run a Bauhaus workshop. Women comprised a significant portion of the student body throughout the school's history. The early 1930s were a time of political instability, marked by the rise of the Nazi party. In 1932, the Bauhaus was again forced to move, this time to temporary facilities in Berlin. By the next year, the Bauhaus was permanently closed.[7]

In the aftermath of the Bauhaus, and with the rise of Nazism, many leading German architects left Germany. Gropius moved to Boston, where he chaired the Department of Architecture in the Graduate School of Design at Harvard University (1937–1952), and Mies van der Rohe moved to Chicago, where he chaired the Department of Architecture at the Illinois Institute of Technology

(1938–1959). Both men also had successful careers in private practice. Schools of design aligned with Bauhaus principles included the Vkhutemas school in Moscow (1920–1930), Black Mountain College in North Carolina (1933–1957), and the Hochschule für Gestaltung in Ulm, Germany (1952–1968).

★ ★ ★

The third important educational system is the American "environmental design" model, which originated in the 1930s. Influential figures included historian Lewis Mumford, housing expert Catherine Bauer, and architect Vernon DeMars. The concept of environmental design placed an emphasis on collaborative design involving diverse teams of experts, an approach that concentrated more on social and environmental factors and less on design as an author-driven process. This also involved uniting the design disciplines involved in the environment, which placed architecture, landscape architecture, and urban planning together in one academic unit. This occurred first in the 1940s and 1950s at Harvard University, the Massachusetts Institute of Technology, and the University of Pennsylvania. However, it was in 1959 at the College of Environmental Design at the University of California in Berkeley under Dean William W. Wurster (1895–1973) that the most comprehensive approach to environmental design was developed.[8] After a career in practice, Wurster married Catherine Bauer (1905–1964) in 1940 and was the Dean at MIT before going to Berkeley in 1950.[9] In the 1960s, the Berkeley programme was driven by important thinkers and educators, including Christopher Alexander (1936–2022) and his seminal work on "pattern language" and Horst Rittel (1930–1990) and his concept of the "wicked problem." With its emphasis on research, ecology, social behaviour, systems analysis, organizational structures, and unifying a wide range of disciplines, the environmental design paradigm was adopted by many design schools in North America during the 1960s and 1970s.

The School of Architecture at the Catholic University of Valparaíso in Chile began a radical experiment in 1952 under the architect Alberto Cruz and the poet Godofredo Iommi. Based on a collaborative approach that united poetry and architecture, the programme involved working on architectural commissions, poetic journeys (*travesias*), and eventually, the creation of the Open City (*Ciudad Abierta*) in Ritoque in 1970.[10] The Open City is an experimental community that comprises unusual structures built over time by the students working with contractors. The use of a "design-build," or hands-on learning, has a long tradition in architectural education and has been used in programmes such as the Taliesin Fellowship, founded by Frank Lloyd Wright in 1932. More recently, the design-build approach was made famous in the Rural Studio at Auburn University in Alabama, originally established in 1993 under the direction of the architects Samuel Mockbee and Dennis K. Ruth.

Other noteworthy schools of architecture include the schools associated with historically black colleges and universities in the USA, including the Tuskegee Institute and Howard University (see Chapter 23).[11] The Cambridge School of Architecture and Landscape Architecture, associated with Smith College in Massachusetts, operated as a school for women from 1915 until 1942. More recently, the Cooper Union in New York under John Hejduk (1929–2000) and in London the Architectural Association under Alvin Boyarsky (1928–1990)[12] created influential architectural programmes.

★ ★ ★

The birth of the modern profession of architecture, as opposed to architecture as an "art," began at the beginning of the 19th century. The British architect Sir John Soane (1753–1837) can be regarded as "the father of the modern profession."[13] Soane writes:

> The business of the architect is to make the designs and estimates, to direct the works and to measure and value the different parts; he is the intermediate agent between the employer, whose honour and interest he is to study, and the mechanic, whose rights he is to defend. His situation implies great trust; he is responsible for mistakes, negligences, and ignorances of those he employs; and above all, he is to take care that the workmen's bills do need exceed his own estimates.[14]

Professionalism implied a more organized approach to the design and construction of buildings, with architects having defined training and roles. Furthermore, there was a defined relationship with clients, builders, and others involved in the process. It also meant public, legal, and ethical responsibilities and led to the establishment of new oversight organizations such as the Royal Institute for British Architects (RIBA), established in 1834, and the American Institute of Architects (AIA), created in 1857.[15] Typically, governments allowed, through legislative acts, the power for the profession to self-govern. Professional architectural organizations can regulate the profession and advocate for the discipline of architecture. Many countries, especially those that operated under colonial regimes, adopted Western forms of professional organization. For example, the Indian Institute of Architects, initially aligned with the RIBA, was created in 1929, and the Nigerian Institute of Architects was created in 1960. In Latin America, the Instituto Brasileiro de Arquitetos (Brazil) was established in 1921, and the Colegio de Arquitectos de Chile in 1942. Elsewhere, the Architectural Institute of Japan was established in 1887, and the Chamber of Architects of Turkey in 1954.

In America, Henry Hobson Richardson, who had studied at the École des Beaux-Arts, established his office in Boston in 1866. He instituted many ideas imported from his French experience to direct his practice and train his staff. In the last quarter of the 19th century, Chicago underwent a significant building boom (see Chapter 4). The many large-scale firms led to the creation of the modern commercially oriented architectural office. These firms, such as Burnham and Root (1873–1891), Holabird and Roche (1880-present), and Adler & Sullivan (1883–1896), were highly organized and specialized; in these offices, architecture was treated as a business. In New York, a similar phenomenon occurred, with practices like McKim, Mead, and White (1872–1961) dominating the scene. Eventually, in the post-World War II era, firms of international impact emerged. These included the Chicago-based Skidmore, Owings, and Merrill firm (SOM, 1936-present) with multiple offices and hundreds of employees. SOM divided its office structure into administration, design, production, and construction, a model used by many large firms today. This model is based on team-oriented practice, where the role of the individual designer is downplayed.[16]

Architecture firms range in size from small to large and focus on a wide range of building types; they approach the design of the built environment in many ways depending upon culture and experience, ideology and regulation, and economic and material situations. However, by the 21st century, the educational and professional standards for the architecture profession globally are largely standardized.

* * *

Educational and professional models for architects responded to the eras in which they exist; however, as environmental theorist David Orr points out, current practices will need to change moving forward:

> We have good reason to believe that humankind will build more buildings in the next fifty years than in the past 5,000. Done by prevailing design

standards, we will cast a long shadow on the prospects of all subsequent generations. No longer can be substitute cheap fossil energy for design intelligence or good judgement. The implications for the education of architects and the design professions generally are striking.[17]

NOTES

1 Vitruvius, *The Ten Books of Architecture* (New York: Dover Publications, 1960), p. 5.

2 See Mark Crinson and Jules Lubbock, *Architecture – Art or Profession? Three Hundred Years of Architectural Education in Britain* (Manchester: Manchester University Press, 1994).

3 See Peter Collins, "The Eighteenth Century Origins of Our System of Full-time Architectural Schooling," *Journal of Architectural Education*, vol. xxxiii, no. 2 (November 1979), pp. 2–6.

4 See Jean Paul Carlhian, "The École des Beaux-Arts: Modes and Manners," *Journal of Architectural Education*, vol. xxxiii, no. 2 (November 1979), pp. 7–10. See also Arthur Drexler, ed., *The Architecture of the École des Beaux-Arts* (New York: Museum of Modern Art, 1977).

5 See Michael J. Lewis, "The Battle Between Polytechnic and Beaux-Arts in the American University," in Joan Ockman, ed., *Architecture School: Three Centuries of Educating Architects in North America* (Cambridge, MA: MIT Press, 2012), pp. 66–89.

6 Walter Gropius, "Programme of the Staatliches Bauhaus in Weimar," in Ulrich Conrads, ed., *Programs and Manifestoes on 20th Century Architecture* (Cambridge, MA: MIT Press, 1971), p. 49.

7 See Frank Whitford, *Bauhaus* (London: Thames & Hudson, 1984), pp. 166–196.

8 See Avigail Sachs, *Environmental Design: Architecture, Politics, and Science in Postwar America* (Charlottesville: University of Virginia Press, 2018), pp. 9–42.

9 See Richard C. Peters, "W.W. Wurster," *Journal of Architectural Education*, vol. xxxiii, no. 2 (November 1979), pp. 36–41.

10 See Raúl Rispa, ed., *Valparaíso School: Open City Group* (Montreal: MQUP, 2003).

11 See Craig L. Wilkins, "Race and Diversity: African Americans in Architecture Education," in Ockman, ed., *Architecture School*, pp. 374–379.

12 See Igor Marjanovic and Jan Howard, *Drawing Ambience: Alvin Boyarsky and the Architectural Association* (St. Louis: Mildred Lane Kemper Art Museum, 2014).

13 John Wilton-Ely, "The Rise of the Professional Architect in England," in Spiro Kostof, ed., *The Architect, Chapters in the History of the Profession* (Berkeley: University of California Press, 2000), p. 194. See also Barrington

Kaye, *The Development of the Architectural Profession in Britain* (London: George Allen & Unwin Ltd., 1960).

14 Wilton-Ely, "The Rise of the Professional Architect in England," p. 194.

15 See Dell Upton, "Defining the Profession," in Ockman, ed., *Architecture School*, pp. 36–65.

16 See Bernard Michael Boyle, "Architectural Practice in America 1865–1965–Ideal and Reality," in Kostof, ed., *The Architect*, pp. 309–344; Andrew Saint, *The Image of the Architect* (New Haven: Yale University Press, 1983); and Mary N. Woods, *From Craft to Profession: The Practice of Architecture in Nineteenth-Century America* (Berkeley: University of California Press, 1999).

17 David Orr, "Architecture, Ecological Design, and Human Ecology," in K. Tanzer and R. Longorio, eds., *The Green Braid: Towards an Architecture of Ecology, Economy, and Equity* (Abingdon: Routledge, 2007), p. 15.

SUGGESTED READING

Bergdoll, Barry and Leah Dickerman, eds. *Bauhaus 1919–1933: Workshops for Modernity*. New York: Museum of Modern Art, 2009.

Colomina, Beatriz et al., eds. *Radical Pedagogies*. Cambridge, MA: MIT Press, 2022.

Drexler, Arthur, ed. *The Architecture of the École des Beaux-Arts*. New York: Museum of Modern Art, 1977.

Kostof, Spiro, ed. *The Architect, Chapters in the History of the Profession*. Berkeley: University of California Press, 2000.

Sachs, Avigail. *Environmental Design: Architecture, Politics, and Science in Postwar America*. Charlottesville: University of Virginia Press, 2018.

17

GENDER AND DISCRIMINATION

For the most part, women have been excluded from practicing architecture until relatively recently due to sexist discriminatory practices
perpetuated by men and male-dominated institutions. Despite this
history, women have performed various roles in the conception and
construction of architecture throughout history.[1] First, according to
architect Susana Torre, in many cultures, "women were the original
builders, [although] they were only passive, marginal actors in the
intellectual process that resulted in the differentiation of "building"
as a function of shelter and survival from "architecture" as a function of culture."[2] Second, women were often accorded the role of
the muse as objects of beauty or the source of inspiration for the
male architect; this notion is captured in Greek mythology. Third,
a significant number of women worked in partnership with their
husbands or partners (occasionally same-sex partners), often overlooked for their contributions to the field; notable figures include
Margaret Macdonald, Aino Maria Marsio-Aalto, and Denise Scott
Brown. Fourth, there were those "exceptional" women, beginning in the 19th century, who had isolated opportunities and the
strong character to become architects and, in some cases, to run their
own practices; this was the case with figures like Julia Morgan and
Eileen Gray.[3] Fifth, many women in the profession of architecture
were effectively anonymous workers, unrecognized for their contributions, or relegated to the "domestic" aspects of the discipline.
Sixth, there were women immersed in architecture who contributed through communal organizations or by writing on the subject.

DOI: 10.4324/9781003403975-17

Seventh, women also acted as clients for important works of architecture, such as Dr. Edith Farnsworth commissioning Mies van der Rohe to design her house in the 1940s.

Historically, women who practiced architecture faced many obstacles. Those women who were able to work as amateurs, trained as apprentices, or studied in the new schools of architecture were pioneers. Early women who worked in the field of architecture were typically well-to-do "amateurs," such as Lady Wilbraham (1632–1705), a British aristocrat who reputedly designed the Palladian-style Weston Park country house in 1671. It has been suggested that she may have designed hundreds of projects by directing male colleagues.[4] Working-class women in the 19th century were often involved in the manufacturing of building materials. Women who did enter architectural firms were typically assigned more menial tasks and were prevented from active involvement in designing anything but domestic interiors. And while Arts and Crafts architects in Europe and America were often willing to hire women as employees, they usually restricted their advancement in the profession.[5]

★ ★ ★

The US supported the formal education and training of women in architecture earlier than most countries. Pioneering women in American architecture have been relatively numerous, including Minerva Parker Nichols (1861–1948), Theodate Pope Riddle (1868–1946), Isabel Roberts (1871–1955), Lilian J. Rice (1889–1938), and Jean Bodman Fletcher (1915–1965). Many women trained in the field tended to end up in domestic or interior design or landscape architecture, areas that were generally considered more suitable for women by men. In 1958, there were 320 women registered architects in the country, about 1% of the profession; of these, about 24% had their own practices, shared practices with their husbands, or were partners in firms.[6] In 2020, approximately 20% of licenced American architects were women.[7]

Prior to 1900, despite numerous obstacles, there were a small number of women architects working in America.[8] These women took various paths to become successful in architecture. Mother Joseph of the Sacred Heart (1823–1902) was born Esther Pariseau near Montreal, Quebec. In 1845, she entered the Sisters of Providence, an order of nuns, taking her name from her father, who was a carriage maker and taught her practical skills. In 1856, she was sent to the Pacific Northwest (Washington and Oregon states). There, she designed, built, and maintained hospitals, schools, and orphanages for the Sisters throughout the region over many years, including Providence Academy (1873) in Vancouver, Washington. Although not formally trained, Mother Joseph performed all the functions of an architect.[9]

Louise Blanchard Bethune (1856–1913) was the first woman to be voted an associate member of the American Institute of Architects (AIA) in 1888. She was also the first woman to be made a Fellow of the AIA in the following year. After apprenticing at a firm in Buffalo, New York, at the age of 25 she decided to open an office with her husband, eventually known as Bethune, Bethune & Fuchs. The best-known work authored by Bethune is the large Hotel Lafayette (1904) in Buffalo. Active in the local architectural community, she was a pioneering figure in the profession.[10]

Sophia Hayden (1868–1953), the first woman to graduate from MIT in architecture in 1890, won a national competition for women only to design the Woman's Building for the 1893 World's Columbian Exposition in Chicago. One of 13 entrants, Hayden's Italian Renaissance scheme was relatively simple, befitting a temporary exhibition building. Hayden contributed little to architecture after the Exposition.

Mary E.J. Colter (1869–1958) was devoted to the study of desert landscapes of the American Southwest, including learning about local indigenous cultures. As a result, she developed a regionally suitable architecture mainly for the tourism and hospitality industry. Colter never became a registered architect; instead, her drawings were transformed into working drawings by company architects. She designed hotels, railway stations, and restaurants along the Santa Fe Railroad in the American Southeast from 1902 to 1942, working mainly for the Fred Harvey Company. In 1913, she embarked on a series of designs for the Grand Canyon site, which was emerging as a major tourist destination.[11] Through her work, she helped establish standards for buildings in the national parks.

Eleanor Raymond (1887–1989) graduated from the Cambridge School of Architecture and Landscape Architecture for women in 1919. Raymond opened an office in partnership in the same year and, by 1928, was on her own, focusing mainly on the design of houses. Although she was trained in the classical style, she gravitated towards modernism. Often working with and for women, Raymond designed several noteworthy buildings, including the Rachel Raymond House (1931) in Belmont, Massachusetts, and a Sculptor's Studio (1934) in Dover, Massachusetts. Always interested in new technologies, she designed a series of innovative model houses for her client, Amelia Peabody. These included the Plywood House (1940), the Masonite House (1944), and the Sun House (1948).[12] In 1938, Raymond obtained a Master of Architecture from Smith College, and in 1961, she was elected a Fellow of the AIA.

Lutah Maria Riggs (1896–1984) won a scholarship to the University of California at Berkeley in 1917, where she studied architecture and graduated in 1919. After a brief internship, she joined the architectural office of George Washington Smith in Santa Barbara, California. By 1924 she was a partner in the practice, earning her licence in 1928. In 1931, Riggs launched her own firm. Despite the Depression, she continued to work on residential projects, including the Baron Maximilian von Romberg Villa and Estate (1938) in Montecito, California, and a series of houses (1940) in Rolling Hills, California. During World War II she worked on film sets for MGM and Warner Brothers. Known for her house designs in both the Spanish colonial and modernist styles, Riggs continued to practice actively into the late 1970s.[13]

More recently, Beverly Willis (1928–2023) has been an important role model and an advocate for women in architecture through both her practice and the Beverly Willis Architecture Foundation (BWAF), which she established in 2002. She initially studied aeronautical engineering and fine arts. Willis established an interior design practice in San Francisco in 1958 before opening Beverly Willis Architect in 1966. Concentrating on housing and buildings for the performing arts, Willis's firm gained a reputation for well-designed projects such as the Nob Hill Court Condominiums (1972) in San Francisco and the San Francisco Ballet Building (1983). A pioneer in developing software for site analysis and the adaptive reuse of older buildings, Willis designed over 800 projects during her long career.[14]

In America, women have also been important contributors to architectural history, theory, and criticism. These have included Louisa Caroline Tuthill (1798–1879), who wrote the first book on the history of American architecture. Published in 1848, it was titled *History of Architecture from the Earliest Times; its Present Condition in Europe and the United States; With a Biography of Eminent Architects and a Glossary of Architectural Terms by Mrs. L.C. Tuthill. With Numerous*

Illustrations.[15] Other early architectural writers included Mariana Van Rensselaer (1851–1934), a well-known architectural critic and historian who published an important biography on Henry Hobson Richardson in 1888.[16] The influential architectural critic Ada Louise Huxtable (1921–2013) first honed her writing skills working at the Museum of Modern Art. In 1963, she was hired as the architectural critic for *The New York Times* newspaper, where she made a reputation for being tough and astute. She was awarded a Pulitzer Prize for Criticism in 1970 and published several books, including *Frank Lloyd Wright: A Life* (2008).[17] In recent decades, many American women have contributed to architectural scholarship, particularly the history of women in architecture; these include Diana Agrest, Jennifer Bloomer, Beatriz Colomina, Diane Ghirardo, Dolores Hayden, Leslie Kanes-Weisman, Mary McLeod, Joan Ockman, Daphne Spain, Susana Torre, and Gwendolyn Wright.

★ ★ ★

The career of Julia Morgan (1872–1957) remains largely an anomaly in American architecture. Morgan, who was born and practiced in San Francisco, was the first woman to enter the prestigious École des Beaux-Arts in Paris, graduating in 1902. Returning to San Francisco, she briefly worked for California Crafts architect Bernard Maybeck (1862–1957) before establishing her own practice in 1904. During almost five decades, Morgan designed over 700 projects. She was adept at a wide range of styles (Beaux-Arts, California Crafts, Mediterranean, Mission, etc.) and building types (hotels, houses, churches, schools, etc.). Her most famous work is the William Randolph Hearst estate at San Simeon in central California, a project she worked on for 20 years. Upon closing her office in 1951, Morgan destroyed the records from her years of practice.[18]

Morgan's practice operated typically with about 10 employees, many of them women. One former employee wrote of Morgan: "Not only was she one of the most talented of West Coast architects; she was also far more accomplished in the area of building technology than any of the men I have known."[19] An early commission was for a Mission-style bell tower in concrete at Mills College, known as El Campanil (1906). Subsequent projects for the college included the Margaret Carnegie Library (1906) and a gymnasium (1916). Schools were also an important part of Morgan's portfolio, including the Ming Quong Chinese Girls School (1925) in Oakland.[20]

Churches were a typology that Morgan designed in a range of styles, primarily for Baptist and Presbyterian congregations. One of her finest works of architecture was the Saint John's Presbyterian Church and Sunday School (1910) in Berkeley. Executed largely in wood in the California Crafts style, the design incorporates both horizontality and banks of vertically proportioned windows. The interior employs a striking use of a redwood structure that modulates the light entering the space.[21] Throughout her career, Morgan also designed numerous houses in an eclectic range of styles varying in size from cottages to mansions.[22]

Many of Morgan's clients were influential women and women's organizations. During the first decades of the 20th century, there was significant growth in organizations dedicated to the betterment of women in society; these included women's clubs, community groups, and the progressive Young Women's Christian Association (YWCA). Morgan designed most of the YWCA facilities in California and the surrounding states, including centres in Oakland (1915), Salt Lake City (1920), Honolulu (1927), and San Francisco (1930).[23]

Morgan designed many projects for the influential Hearst family, starting with projects for the energetic mother of William Randolph Hearst (1863–1951).[24] A 25-year alliance between Morgan and Hearst, who amassed a fortune in newspapers and other media, began when he commissioned her to design the Examiner Building in Los Angeles in 1915. In 1919, Hearst first discussed the development of a new home on a hilltop at San Simeon in central California. Designing for an informed client inspired Morgan to integrate many references and historical elements into the enormous complex. The project, mainly completed by 1939, comprised 127 rooms, all supporting pieces from Hearst's substantial collection of art and objects.[25]

Morgan's reputation has grown in recent years. She practiced "academic eclecticism," an approach widely used by American architects between the 1880s and 1930s. As Richard Longstreth writes:

> Architects of this period sought to foster a gradual evolution in their art by drawing from a wide range of historical precedents, modifying and combining them according to contemporary needs. In the process, they rejected the nineteenth-century conception of style. They believed in an all-encompassing order, unconfined by traditional stylistic parameters and based on broad, abstract principles.[26]

In 2014, Morgan was awarded the AIA Gold Medal posthumously, the first woman to receive the medal.

★ ★ ★

Several women were key figures in the development of modern architecture (see Chapter 12). Following the collapse of modern architecture in the 1960s, a younger generation of women brought new visions to architecture globally, of which the following are representative.

Lina Bo Bardi (1914–1992) and her husband emigrated to Brazil from Italy in 1946, where she had worked with Gio Ponti and Bruno Zevi. Her early Casa de Vidro (1951) in São Paulo is a carefully planned example of a lightweight modernist house on a sloping site.[27] In 1957, she was commissioned to design a new facility for the São Paulo Museum of Art (MASP), which was completed in 1968. Adjacent to a park, Bardi's iconic solution was to place the main gallery in a glass box lifted above a public plaza to protect views. The gallery is supported by a long-span reinforced concrete structure later painted red; below the plaza is the auditorium and support functions.[28] Bardi was particularly interested in expressing local cultures; this is evident in SSEC Pompeia Leisure Center in São Paulo (1986), which involved the transformation of several existing factory sheds into a facility for leisure, recreation, and culture. Designed for a working-class community, she described her approach as an *architettura povera*, or a "poor architecture."[29] She also wrote about architecture, designed furniture, and worked in theatre throughout her career.[30]

One of the most prominent Italian architects of the post-Second World War II period was Gae Aulenti (1927–2012). Educated at the Milan Polytechnic, she graduated in 1954 and went on to a very diverse career in Milan, designing architecture, interiors, exhibitions, furniture, and stage sets. Aulenti initially worked for the Italian journals *Casabella* and *Lotus International*. Her designs tend to employ a strict formalism, consistent with the Italian architecture of the period. Her work became increasingly postmodern during her career. She was internationally renowned for her museum work, her most significant project being the Musée d'Orsay (1986) in Paris, in which she transformed a former railway station into a set of galleries dedicated to Impressionist art. Aulenti was also commissioned to design the National Museum of Art at the Georges Pompidou Centre in Paris (1985) and major museums in Barcelona, San Francisco, and Genoa.[31]

In Ireland, there is a vital architectural community, primarily in Dublin. Grafton Architects is a partnership established in 1978 by Yvonne Farrell (1951–) and Shelley McNamara (1952–), named after a prominent street in Dublin.[32] Both partners were educated at University College Dublin. Early projects were relatively modest and included Temple Bar Square (1996) and The Long House (2001) in Dublin. Featuring a sensitive modernist approach that integrates into contexts and employs a precise use of materials, these early projects laid the groundwork for larger international commissions. The breakthrough occurred when Grafton Architects won a limited competition to design an extension to the Economics Faculty (2008) at Bocconi University in Milan. A difficult programme and site led Grafton Architects to a daring and celebrated solution that suspends numerous offices above a major auditorium and other teaching spaces. Much of the building is below grade, organized around numerous courtyards, and clad in a unifying local stone.[33] Other significant projects include the University Campus UTEC (2015) in Lima, Peru, and the Toulouse School of Economics (2019). In 2020, the two partners were awarded the RIBA Gold Medal and the Pritzker Architecture Prize.

Canadian-born Alison Brooks (1962–) was educated at the University of Waterloo, Ontario, prior to moving to London in 1988.

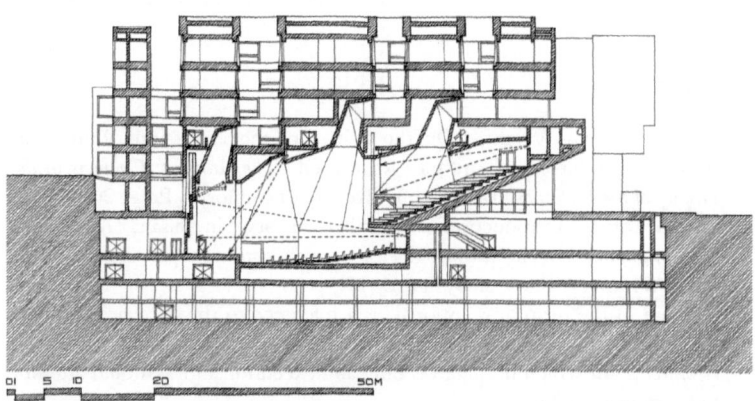

Figure 17.1 Section, Grafton Architects, Economics Faculty, Bocconi University, 2008, Bologna, Italy. The scheme features blocks of offices and classrooms located over a major auditorium; light wells are carefully shaped to bring natural illumination into the auditorium. Drawing by Mohammad Moezzi.

She opened the award-winning Alison Brooks Architects in 1996. Disenchanted with the state of housing design in Britain, she made innovative housing design a cornerstone of her practice. An early commission, the Atoll Spa Hotel (2000) in Helgoland, Germany, launched her reputation for careful and thoughtful design. Brooks has expanded into university residences, cultural buildings, and large housing projects. Her award-winning Newhall Be Housing scheme (2012) for Harlow New Town demonstrates that dense and innovative housing can be produced for a developer. The design features townhouses and apartments that strategically use courtyards and are clad in black siding and beige brick.

★ ★ ★

Opportunities for women in architecture have expanded significantly since the 1980s, with figures such as Kazuyo Sejima and Zaha Hadid gaining international attention (see Chapters 20 and 21) and many women contributing to the profession globally. Nevertheless, women and minorities still face significant barriers to their success in architecture. As Leslie Kanes Weisman reminds us:

> Space, like language, is socially constructed; and like the syntax of language, the spatial arrangements of our buildings and communities reflect and reinforce the nature of gender, race, and class relations in society. The uses of both language and space contribute to the power of some groups over others and the maintenance of human inequality.[34]

NOTES

1 See Gwendolyn Wright, "On the Fringe of the Profession: Women in American Architecture," in Spiro Kostof, ed., *The Architect: Chapters in the History of the Profession* (Berkeley: University of California Press, 2000).

2 Susana Torre, "Introduction: A Parallel History," in Susana Torre, ed., *Women in American Architecture: A Historic and Contemporary Perspective* (New York: Whitney Library of Design, 1977), p. 11.

3 The use of the term "exceptional" is a reference to the derogatory use of the word by Pietro Belluschi in a 1955 article entitled "Should You Be an Architect?" in which he suggests only an "exceptional girl" should attempt to become an architect.

4 Lynne Walker, "Women in Architecture," in J. Attfield and P. Kirkham, eds., *A View from the Interior: Feminism, Women and Design* (London: Women's Press, 1989), p. 92.

5 See Ibid., pp. 96–98.

6 Mary Otis Stevens, "Struggle for Place: Women in Architecture: 1920–1960," in Torre, ed., *Women in American Architecture*, p. 90.

7 See https://www.acsa-arch.org/resource/where-are-the-women-measuring-progress-on-gender-in-architecture-2/. Accessed February 6, 2024.

8 See Judith Paine, "Pioneer Women Architects," in Torre, ed., *Women in American Architecture*, pp. 54–69.

9 See Carla Blank and Tania Martin, *Storming the Old Boys' Citadel: Two Pioneer Women Architects in Nineteenth Century North America* (Montreal: Baraka Books, 2014), pp. 43–57.

10 See Adriana Barbasch, "Louise Blanchard Bethune, The AIA Accepts Its First Woman Member," in Ellen P. Berkeley and Matilda McQuaid, eds., *Architecture, A Place for Women* (Washington, DC: Smithsonian Institution Press, 1989), pp. 15–25.

11 Matilda McQuaid, "Educating for the Future: A Growing Archive on Women in Architecture," in Berkeley and McQuaid, eds., *Architecture, A Place for Women*, p. 254. See also Arnold Berke, *Mary Colter, Architect of the Southwest* (New York: Princeton Architectural Press, 2002).

12 See Doris Cole, "Eleanor Raymond," in Torre, ed., *Women in American Architecture*, pp. 103–107.

13 See Sarah Allaback, *The First American Women Architects* (Chicago: University of Illinois Press, 2008), pp. 193–204.

14 See K.H. Anthony and S. Dave, "Leaving a Lasting Legacy: Beverly Willis: Groundbreaking Architect, Artist, Designer, Filmmaker, and Philanthropist," in Anna Sokolina, ed., *The Routledge Companion to Women in Architecture* (Milton: Taylor & Francis, 2021), pp. 357–369.

15 See Lamia Doumato, "Louisa Tuthill's Unique Achievement: First History of Architecture in the U.S.," in Berkeley and McQuaid, eds., *Architecture, A Place for Women*, pp. 5–13.

16 See Lisa Koenigsberg, "Mariana Van Rensselaer, An Architecture Critic in Context," in Berkeley and McQuaid, eds., *Architecture, A Place for Women*, pp. 41–54.

17 See Suzanne Stephens, "Obituary: Ada Louise Huxtable, 1921–2013," *Architectural Record* (January 18, 2013), https://www.architecturalrecord.com/articles/2780-obituary-ada-louise-huxtable-1921-2013. Accessed December 8, 2021.

18 See Sara Holmes Boutelle, *Julia Morgan, Architect* (New York: Abbeville Press, 1995), pp. 7–39.

19 Walter Steilberg, quoted in Ibid., p. 45.

20 See Ibid., pp. 51–66.

21 See Ibid., pp. 69–75.

22 See Ibid., pp. 129–166.

23 See Ibid., pp. 83–95.

24 See Ibid., pp. 169–173.

25 See Ibid., pp. 174–215.

26 Richard Longstreth, *On the Edge of the World: Four Architects in San Francisco at the Turn of the Century* (Cambridge, MA: MIT Press, 1983), p. 9.

27 See Luis E. Carranza and Fernando Luiz Lara, *Modern Architecture in Latin America: Art, Technology, and Utopia* (Austin: University of Texas Press, 2014), pp. 160–161.

28 See Ibid., pp. 208–209.

29 Lina Bo Bardi, "The Architectural Project," in Ibid., p. 98.

30 See Zeuler R.M. de A. Lima, *Lina Bo Bardi* (New Haven: Yale University Press, 2013).

31 See Margherita Petranzan, *Gae Aulenti* (New York: Universe, 2002).

32 See Robert McCarter, *Grafton Architects* (London: Phaidon, 2018).

33 Yvonne Farrell and Shelley McNamara, "In Dialogue with Gravity," in Grafton Architects, ed., *Dialogue and Translation* (New York: GSAPP Books, 2014).

34 Leslie Kanes Weisman, *Discrimination by Design: A Feminist Critique of the Man-Made Environment* (Urbana and Chicago: University of Illinois Press, 1994), p. 2.

SUGGESTED READING

Berkeley, Ellen P. and Matilda McQuaid, eds. *Architecture: A Place for Women*. Washington, DC: Smithsonian Institution Press, 1989.

Rendell, Jane, Barbara Penner, and Iain Borden, eds. *Gender Space Architecture: An Interdisciplinary Introduction*. London: Routledge, 2000.

Sokolina, Anna, ed. *The Routledge Companion to Women in Architecture*. Milton: Taylor & Francis, 2021.

Spain, Daphne. *Gendered Spaces*. Chapel Hill: University of North Carolina Press, 1992.

Torre, Susana, ed. *Women in Architecture: A Historic and Contemporary Perspective*. New York: Whitney Library of Design, 1977.

18

HISTORY AND ORDER

In the 1950s and 1960s, several movements arose that challenged the orthodoxy of modern architecture. Many of these advocated for contextualism and a renewed connection to the history of architecture. These movements can be described as postmodernist because they are consistent with the tendencies of the period (see Chapter 1). An important essay, "Nine Points on Monumentality," published in 1943 by Josep Lluís Sert, Fernand Léger, and Siegfried Giedion, suggested the possibility of including monumentality in modern architecture, something that had been missing. Further, the Torre Velasca (1960) in Milan, Italy, by Belgiojoso, Perressutti, and Rogers, with its overt references to medieval architecture, generated debates at the time as to how history should be interpreted. Discussing the limitations of modern architecture, the Italian architect and historian Paolo Portoghesi writes:

> [T]he Modern Movement, beginning in the twenties, tended to translate into a set of constraining rules, into a real orthodoxy, three fundamental dogmas: *the functionalist analysis* as a starting point for architectural research; *the annihilation of the traditional grammar of architecture* with all its differences corresponding to places and civilizations; *the identification between architectural progress and the use of new technologies* understood as potential generators of language.[1]

The modern architecture that emerged in the 1920s and 1930s proved to be relatively short-lived, as disillusionment with the new architecture set in after World War II. This history is evident in the

DOI: 10.4324/9781003403975-18

meetings held by the *Congrès Internationaux d'Architecture Moderne* (CIAM), which was established in 1928 by a group of prominent modern architects led by Le Corbusier. During the tenth CIAM meeting, held in 1956 in Dubrovnik, a younger group emerged, announcing themselves as Team 10 (CIAM officially ended in 1959 at the eleventh meeting in Otterloo, Holland). The younger generation considered modern architecture to be stark and repetitive and the modernist vision of the city was too restrictive (see Chapter 7). Team 10 was an evolving group which proposed a new approach to architecture and urbanism. The group disbanded in 1981.

The key members of Team 10 were Alison (1928–1993) and Peter (1923–2003) Smithson, Aldo van Eyck (1918–1999), Jacob B. Bakema (1914–1981), Georges Candilis (1913–1995), Giancarlo De Carlo (1919–2005), and Shadrach Woods (1923–1973). They were joined by an international group of like-minded architects who were experimenting with new approaches to urban form and architectural expression. Against the universal utopianism of modernism, Team 10 emphasized local and regional contexts, including the "a profound interest in the historical and social dimensions of architecture and urbanism."[2]

The Smithsons had established themselves as leaders of the New Brutalist group in Britain. They placed an emphasis on straightforward building assemblies such as those used in their Hunstanton School (1954) in Norfolk, England. This project was inspired by Mies van der Rohe's Illinois Institute of Technology campus (1939–1958) in Chicago. The Smithsons wrote and theorized a great deal, and they designed a small number of provocative buildings. The Robin Hood Gardens housing complex (1972) in London is a controversial example of their thinking about mass housing.

A diverse group that generally lacked a central thesis, Team 10 nevertheless produced some of the most compelling architecture of the 1960s. Interested in developing more community-responsive projects, Team 10 members were involved in the study of traditional settlements. They devised an idea of the city that unified the house, the street, the district, and the city. Noteworthy projects included the contextual Economist Building (1964) in London by the Smithsons; the Collegio del Colle student accommodations (1966) integrated into Urbino, Italy by Giancarlo De Carlo; the Free University (1973) in Berlin by Candilis-Josic-Woods (with Manfred Schiedhelm) that employed a mat-plan;[3] and the Byker housing estate (1981) in Newcastle-upon-Tyne, England by Ralph Erskine which involved extensive community consultation. The *Team 10 Primer*, initially published in an architecture journal in 1962, was edited by Alison Smithson and subsequently republished in 1968 as a book. The document was a collection of texts and projects by the group that expounded on the role of the architect, the infrastructure of the city, and the arrangement of dwellings.[4]

The Dutch members of Team 10 were particularly active. Aldo van Eyck established himself in the late 1940s when he began a project to design hundreds of playgrounds for the city of Amsterdam (1947–1978). Later, using his interests in children's play, community, and the building as a city, he designed the Municipal Orphanage (1960) in Amsterdam based on a repeating structural and spatial system.[5] This led to his architecture being labelled "structuralist." The same label applies to works by Herman Hertzberger (1932–), including his Centraal Beheer corporate offices (1972) in Apeldoorn, Holland, which treated the building like a small city.

The emergence of Team 10 coincided with the appearance of Brutalism, somewhat different from British New Brutalism, as a post-war phenomenon. Brutalism was initially linked to Le Corbusier and his Unité d'Habitation housing scheme (1954) in Marseilles, in which he "abandoned the pre-war fiction that reinforced concrete was a precise, 'machine-age' material."[6] This building triggered a wave of imitators, built of rough cast-in-place concrete (*béton brut*) and employing bold forms. Most of Le Corbusier's post-war projects were Brutalist in their execution (see Chapter 10). In the 1950s and 1960s, Brutalism was a widely practiced style evident in projects such as Atelier 5's Siedlung Halen housing project (1961) in Berne, Switzerland, and Boston City Hall (1968) by Kallmann McKinnell and Knowles. Reyner Banham defines Brutalism as:

1. the building as a unified visual image, clear and memorable,
2. clear exhibition of its structure,
3. a high valuation of raw, untreated materials.[7]

Ultimately, Brutalist architecture was not well-received by the public, and its influence waned.

A peripheral member of Team 10 was the Scottish-born architect James Stirling (1926–1992), who began his career as an admirer of Le Corbusier. Stirling established a partnership (1956–1963) with James Gowan (1923–2015). The firm produced a number of New Brutalist designs, including the Ham Common housing project (1958) in

London. During the early 1960s, Stirling drew inspiration from a wide range of historical sources, including Russian Constructivism. This influence is reflected in the highly sophisticated Leicester University Engineering Building (1963), with its dramatic forms expressing various functions. The material palette is brick, tile, and glass. Stirling, a complex and enigmatic architect, steadily evolved his design approach. After a brief foray into High Tech architecture, he became a leading proponent of postmodernism. In the mid-1970s, Stirling executed a series of designs for museums in Germany, culminating in his winning entry for the Neue Staatsgalerie (1984) in Stuttgart. This building, an eclectic and playful assemblage of elements and references, is still seen as a leading example of postmodern contextualism.[8]

★ ★ ★

Louis I. Kahn (1901–1974), the Estonian-born Jewish-American architect, was a pivotal figure in the transformation of 20th-century architecture away from modernism. Trained at the University of Pennsylvania during the 1920s in the Beaux-Arts style, Kahn pursued his career in Philadelphia. In the 1930s and 1940s, he worked in partnership with various Philadelphia architects, mainly on modernist housing projects. Finally, in 1947, he established his own office.[9] It was at this time that Kahn became disillusioned with orthodox modernism and began a search for a new "monumentalism." During a short stint at the American Academy in Rome in 1950–1951, he had the opportunity to study the ruins of Roman, Greek, and Egyptian architecture. This experience had a dramatic impact on his subsequent architectural designs. Architectural historian Vincent Scully argues that Kahn, in his mature work, was returning to the 19th century to start modern architecture over again, to give it more weight, more order, and more mystery.[10]

In his essay entitled "Monumentality," published in 1944, Kahn writes, "monumentality in architecture may be defined as a quality, a spiritual quality inherent in a structure which conveys the feeling of its eternity, that it cannot be added to or changed."[11] The search for a monumental architecture preoccupied Kahn for the rest of his career. His architecture would be of mass and light, built primarily of brick and concrete, based on an order informed by his Beaux-Arts training and passion for Roman architecture. Despite this, his buildings were not nostalgic, traditional, or authoritarian in their execution.

Beginning in the 1950s, Kahn brought a refreshing sense of order to his mature architecture. His first major building, the Yale University Art Gallery addition (1953), is described by Reyner Banham as a key work of Brutalism.[12] The distinctive geometrical order in Kahn's work was in part inspired by the input of his associate Anne Griswold Tyng (1920–2011), who joined his office in 1945. Tyng was a pioneering woman in American architecture (see Chapter 17); she worked with Kahn until 1964.

Following the completion of the Yale Art Gallery, the Jewish Community Center (1959) near Trenton, New Jersey, established Kahn's use of "compartmented" space and his concept of "served" and "servant" spaces.[13] This success was followed by the Richards Medical Research Building (1965) at the University of Pennsylvania. The design features glazed laboratories spanning between brick-clad service towers. As Kahn's work became more refined, his exterior walls became thicker and openings more distinctive. The First Unitarian Church and School (1969) in Rochester, New York, was his first church and consolidated his new approach to mass and light.[14] At this point, by "reconnecting architecture with the fundamentals of history, he revitalized its primary forms and principles, and he awakened an entire generation of architects who followed."[15]

With his reputation secure, Kahn produced several significant commissions through the 1960s until his premature death in 1974. Several projects stand out: the Salk Institute for Biological Studies (1965) in La Jolla, California; the National Assembly Building (1983) in Dhaka, Bangladesh; the Phillips Exeter Academy Library (1972) in New Hampshire; the Kimbell Art Museum (1972) in Fort Worth, Texas; and the Yale Center for British Art (1974). The Salk Institute was commissioned by medical pioneer Jonas Salk (1914–1995) as a research centre. Here, Kahn organized open laboratories and offices around a tranquil courtyard overlooking the Pacific Ocean. The Kimbell Art Museum was designed with a repeating concrete vault that allowed the controlled entry of light into the gallery spaces. The building itself is surrounded by a generous greenspace. The Yale Center for British Art was Kahn's last major project, one that allowed him to refine his ideas about the display and viewing of art in top-lit rooms in an urban building at the heart of the Yale campus.

Importantly, Kahn was a teacher and source of inspiration for a younger generation of architects, including the Team 10 group, who became the leaders of the postmodern movement.[16] He also inspired others through short statements that poetically described his vision of architecture.[17]

★ ★ ★

A movement consistent with postmodernism, and the celebration of pluralism and diverse approaches, involved a group of architects in the United States, including Robert Venturi (1925–2018), Denise Scott Brown (1931–), Charles Moore (1925–1993), Michael Graves (1934–2015), and Robert A.M. Stern (1939–). They each proposed an architecture informed by history and the appreciation of popular culture. The work of American postmodernist architects would have links to similar architects in Europe and elsewhere, who often eclectically borrowed from the history of architecture. The emergence of Pop Art in England and America at the same time, with artists like Andy Warhol (1928–1987) and Roy Lichtenstein (1923–1997), was no coincidence.[18] Pop Art in the 1960s derived much of its imagery from popular culture and advertising.

Arguably, the most influential postmodernists were Robert Venturi and Denise Scott Brown, who operated a practice together for many years and were married. Venturi briefly worked for and taught with Kahn. Venturi outlines his ideas in his book *Complexity and Contradiction in Architecture*, published in 1966. It is an articulate challenge to modern architecture and one of the most important 20th-century books on architecture. In formulating his argument, Venturi acknowledged the influence of Scott Brown, Vincent Scully, and Robert Stern, among others.

In the text, Venturi's admiration for certain architects is evident in the many images he uses to support his arguments, including works by Michelangelo, Francesco Borromini, John Soane, Frank Furness, Edwin Lutyens, and Alvar Aalto. Venturi emphasizes the articulation of the visual languages, along with the notion of "meaning," in architecture. He praises concepts such as ambiguity, "both-and," contradiction, complexity, the double-functioning element, the inside and the outside, the obligation to the difficult whole, and many others. In the opening section entitled "Nonstraightforward Architecture: A Gentle Manifesto," he writes:

> Architects can no longer afford to be intimidated by the puritanically moral language of orthodox Modern architecture. I like elements which are hybrid rather than "pure," compromising rather than "clean," distorted rather than "straightforward," ambiguous rather than "articulated,"

perverse as well as impersonal, boring as well as "interesting," conventional rather than "designed," accommodating rather than excluding, redundant rather than simple, vestigial as well as innovating, inconsistent and equivocal rather than direct and clear. I am for messy vitality over obvious unity.[19]

Venturi's theories are well-illustrated in his famous early house for his mother, the Vanna Venturi residence (1962) in Chestnut Hill, Pennsylvania, which plays with and modifies conventional ideas about the American house. In partnership with John Rauch and Scott Brown, Venturi had a successful career as a practicing architect and continued to write, teach, and lecture. Various projects can be singled out as a testimony to the ideas of the firm, including Gordon Wu Hall (1983) at Princeton University. Together, Venturi and Scott Brown demonstrated a fascination with popular culture and how buildings can be read as symbolic and linguistic statements.[20]

Charles Moore was an influential architect, educator, and writer who emerged in the 1960s as an important advocate for postmodern

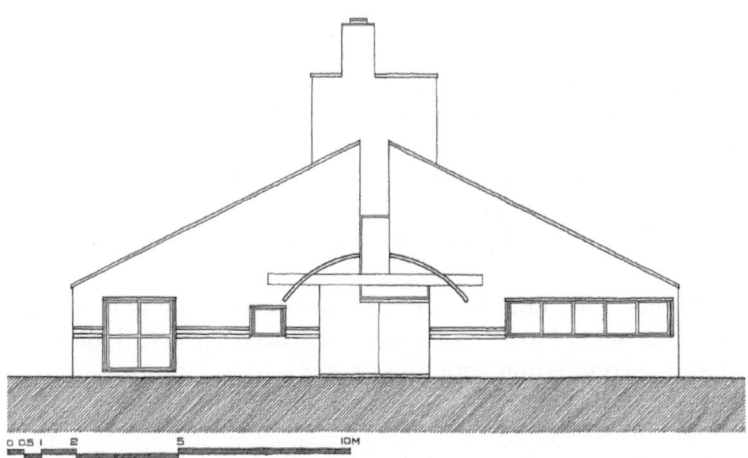

Figure 18.1 Main Elevation, Robert Venturi, Vanna Venturi House, 1962, Chestnut Hill, Pennsylvania, USA. The simple house-like façade is broken in the middle by the entrance and slot above; Mannerist elements include an oversized window to the left, a strip window to the right, and an arch motif in the middle. Drawing by Mohammad Moezzi.

architecture and the concept of place-making. His early projects demonstrate some influence by Kahn (under whom he studied at Princeton University) and an interest in vernacular architecture. His most important early project was the well-known Sea Ranch Condominium in northern California (1965) by Moore, Lyndon, Turnbull, and Whitaker (MLTW). Subsequently, Moore's work became more postmodern, often engaging in interpretations of architectural history and popular culture. This is explicit in the notorious Piazza d'Italia project (1975) in New Orleans, with its whimsical use of a classical language outlined in neon lights and bright colours. Moore's legacy rests primarily on his many houses and thoughtful books such as *The Place of Houses*.[21]

Michael Graves was a Princeton-based architect who began his career with the New York Five, a group of New York architects devoted to the works of Le Corbusier. The informal association included Richard Meier, John Hejduk, Charles Gwathmey, and Peter Eisenman.[22] Graves's early projects, such as the Hanselman House (1967) in Fort Wayne, Indiana, demonstrated his affiliation with Le Corbusier. However, by the mid-1970s, he embraced a new attitude to classical architecture supported by his distinctive drawing style. Arguing for a return to "figurative" or poetic[23] architecture, Graves introduced a new formality into his planning and an exaggerated approach to classical elements. In 1980, his design for The Portland Building in Portland, Oregon, an ordinary office building clothed in Grave's idiosyncratic architectural language, had a controversial impact on the world of architecture. His most successful project remains the Public Library (1980) in San Juan Capistrano, California, which presents a convincing interpretation of the California Mission Style.

By the 1980s, disillusionment with the often superficial and gimmicky designs of many postmodernists effectively ended the interest in strong connections with history.

★ ★ ★

The American critic and historian Charles Jencks (1939–2019) championed postmodern architecture in his book *The Language of Postmodern Architecture* (1977). In the sixth edition of the book (1991), Jencks identifies his key categories of postmodern architecture:

> The characteristics of the Post-Modern come from an attempt to cut across the spectrum of tastes with a variety of styles: thus it seeks a *radical*

eclecticism, or a multiple-coding, as well as the double logic I have already mentioned . . . as well as the other key definers: *historicism*, *contextualism*, the new *complex post-modern space*, *metaphor* and *abstract representation*. The motives extend beyond this to the search for a *relevant ornament*, a *contextual symbolism*, an *anthropomorphism* – in short, to the search for a *suitable content* to represent.[24]

NOTES

1 Paolo Portoghesi, "What Is Postmodern?" in *Postmodern: The Architecture of the Postindustrial Society* (New York: Rizzoli, 1983), p. 32.

2 Dirk van den Heuvel and Max Risselada, "Introduction: Looking into the Mirror of Team 10," in Dirk van den Heuvel and Max Risselada, eds., *Team 10, in Search of a Utopia of the Present* (Rotterdam: NAi Publishers, 2005), p. 13.

3 See Alison Smithson, "How to Recognize and Read Mat-Building: Mainstream Architecture as It Has Developed Towards the Mat-Building," *Architectural Design*, no. 9 (September 1974), pp. 573–590.

4 See Alison Smithson, ed., *Team 10 Primer* (Cambridge, MA: MIT Press, 1974).

5 See Liane Lefaivre and Alexander Tzonis, *Aldo van Eyck: Humanist Rebel* (Rotterdam: 010 Publishers, 1999).

6 Reyner Banham, *The New Brutalism: Ethic or Aesthetic?* (New York: Reinhold Publishing, 1966), p. 16.

7 Ibid., p. 127.

8 See John Summerson, "Vitruvius Ludens," *Architectural Review*, vol. 173 (March 1983), pp. 18–21. See also Peter Arnell and Ted Bickford, *James Stirling: Buildings and Projects* (New York: Rizzoli, 1984).

9 See David B. Brownlee and David G. De Long, *Louis I. Kahn: In the Realm of Architecture* (New York: Rizzoli, 1991), pp. 20–49.

10 Vincent Scully, "Introduction," in Brownlee and De Long, *Louis I. Kahn*, p. 13.

11 Louis Kahn, "Monumentality," in Paul Zucker, ed., *New Architecture and City Planning: A Symposium* (New York: Philosophical Library, 1944), p. 577.

12 Banham, *The New Brutalism*, p. 44.

13 Brownlee and De Long, *Louis I. Kahn*, p. 58.

14 See Ibid., pp. 65–68.

15 Ibid., p. 71.

16 See Scully, "Introduction," in Brownlee and De Long, *Louis I. Kahn*, pp. 12–14.

17 See Richard Saul Wurman, ed., *What Will Be Has Always Been: The Words of Louis I. Kahn* (New York: Rizzoli, 1986).

18 See Lucy C. Lippard, ed., *Pop Art* (New York: Frederick A. Praeger Inc., 1966).

19 Robert Venturi, *Complexity and Contradiction in Architecture* (New York: Museum of Modern Art, 1977), p. 16.

20 See Robert Venturi, Denise Scott Brown, and Steven Izenour, *Learning from Las Vegas: The Forgotten Symbolism of Architectural Form* (Cambridge, MA: MIT Press, 1977).

21 See Charles Moore, Gerald Allen, and Donlyn Lyndon, *The Place of Houses* (New York: Holt, Reinhart and Winston, 1974).

22 See *Five Architects: Eisenman, Graves, Gwathmey, Hejduk, Meier* (Oxford: Oxford University Press, 1975).

23 See Michael Graves, "A Case for Figurative Architecture," in Karen Vogel Wheeler, Peter Arnell, and Ted Bickford, eds., *Michael Graves: Buildings and Projects, 1966–1981* (New York: Rizzoli, 1982), pp. 11–13.

24 Charles Jencks, *The Language of Postmodern Architecture* (New York: Rizzoli, 1991), p. 13.

SUGGESTED READING

Banham, Reyner. *The New Brutalism: Ethic or Aesthetic?* New York: Reinhold Publishing, 1966.

Ghirardo, Diane. *Design After Modernism.* New York: Thames and Hudson, 1996.

Heuvel, Dirk van den and Max Risselada, eds. *Team 10, in Search of a Utopia of the Present.* Rotterdam: NAi Publishers, 2005.

Jencks, Charles. *The Language of Post-Modern Architecture.* New York: Rizzoli, 1991.

Venturi, Robert. *Complexity and Contradiction in Architecture.* New York: Museum of Modern Art, 1966.

19

REGIONALISM AND TECTONICS

As architectural theorist Liane Lefaivre demonstrates, "regionalism" has been an undercurrent in modern architecture since its inception in the 1920s. It gained strength after World War II. Prior to this, the concept of regionalism can be found in the Arts and Crafts movement (see Chapter 8) and the work of Frank Lloyd Wright (see Chapter 10). Lefaivre notes that the Museum of Modern Art in New York, which opened in 1929, showed regionally themed exhibitions throughout its early history despite also advocating fiercely for modernism. She emphasizes the ideas of the prominent American writer Lewis Mumford (1895–1990), who promoted the virtues of regionalist designers in an article in 1947.[1] Lefaivre acknowledges that it was Mumford who developed the concept that "regionalism becomes a constant process of negotiation between the local and the global on the many different issues that traditionally make up regionalism."[2]

Lefaivre and architectural theoretician Alexander Tzonis coined the term "critical regionalism" in an important 1981 essay entitled "The Grid and the Pathway." In it, they examine designs by the Greek architects Dmitri Pikionis and Dimitris and Suzana Antonakakis. They take a long view of regionalism, invoking such traditions as the English Picturesque movement of the 18th century and the concept of *genius loci* or the "genius of the place" (see Chapter 3).[3] The willingness to be self-critical results in a "critical" regionalism, with an emphasis on community and multi-culturalism rather than nationalism and parochialism.

DOI: 10.4324/9781003403975-19

The concept of critical regionalism was then elaborated upon by the historian and theoretician Kenneth Frampton in his influential text "Towards a Critical Regionalism: Six Points for an Architecture of Resistance," published in 1983. Invoking the theories of philosophers Martin Heidegger, Hannah Arendt, and Paul Ricoeur, he gives the concept a phenomenological interpretation (see Chapter 21). Frampton argues that there has been a "victory of universal civilization over locally inflected culture."[4] He notes the rise of universalism (or globalization), placelessness, technology, commodification, and the populism of the postmodern era. Frampton argues that a critically regional architecture would avoid the modernist obsession with progress, focusing instead on the "tectonic . . . as a potential means for distilling play between material, craftwork and gravity."[5] Later, in a refinement of his argument, Frampton developed seven tenets that define critical regionalism as operating in the margins, being carefully bounded and sited, focused on tectonics, tactile, as opposed to a "sentimental" vernacular, and attempting to "escape the optimizing thrust of universal civilization."[6] In the 1990s, Frampton made a strong case for a tectonic approach to architecture in his book *Studies in Tectonic Culture: The Poetics of Construction in Nineteenth and Twentieth Century Architecture* (1995).

The rise of thoughtful regionalism in architecture was one response to the failings of the International Style (see Chapter 12). Attacks on the International Style often focused on the United Nations Building (1952) in New York, which was designed by an international team of architects including Le Corbusier, Oscar Niemeyer, and Wallace Harrison.

★ ★ ★

The northern European countries (Denmark, Norway, Sweden, and Finland) have had a strong history of architecture and design throughout the 20th century. Traditions that have become known as National Romanticism and Nordic Classicism dominated the region during the early part of the century. Several important architects emerged from these movements, including Erik Gunnar Aspund (1885–1940) and Sigurd Lewerentz (1885–1975) in Sweden and Alvar Aalto (1898–1976) in Finland.

Aalto was one of the dominant figures of modern architecture, famous for his buildings rooted in Finnish landscapes and cities. The Norwegian architectural theorist and historian Christian

Norberg-Schulz (1926–2000) has described northern European landscapes, in contrast to those in southern Europe, in the following terms:

> [I]n the North, the sun does not rise to the zenith but grazes things obliquely and dissolves in an interplay of light and shadow. The land consists not of clear massings and distinct spaces; it disperses as fragment and repetition in the boundless. The vegetation is not characterized by particular species . . . but is instead network and thicket. And buildings lose much of their figural effect; houses lie scattered and hidden.[7]

The characteristics of climate and landscape that Norberg-Schulz describes defined Aalto's architecture, even though Aalto also had a deep fondness for Mediterranean environments.

Aalto was born in Jyväskylä in central Finland and studied architecture in Helsinki, graduating in 1921. Two years later, he opened an office in his hometown. He married Aino Marsio (1894–1949), an assistant in his office, the following year. She was his partner in life and in architecture until her early death. In 1952, he married another architect, Elsa Kaisa Mäkiniemi (1922–1994), who was also key to the success of his practice.

Following his early career in the classicist tradition, Aalto made a radical change in direction when he designed several projects in the late 1920s, including the Paimio Sanitorium (1933) for tuberculosis patients; Aalto functionally organized the building into several wings (including sun-terraces) and provided thoughtful details throughout. The Paimio project was widely considered a prime example of the new International Style.[8] Another important early project was the Viipuri Public Library (1935) which balanced classicism, functionalism, and Aalto's emerging personal style.

During the 1930s, the Aaltos moved their practice to Helsinki and established the Artek company to manufacture furniture and other works of industrial design. Aalto's mastery of wood in both his architectural projects and furniture designs is an outgrowth of his Finnish background. His mature work is characterized by a distinctive approach to form that played rational elements against expressive ones. Also, in the 1930s, Aalto designed important projects such as the Villa Mairea at Noormarkku (1941), which is one of the great modernist villas of the period. An exceptionally complex project that draws from Finnish vernacular traditions and modernism, the L-shaped house is organized around an outdoor space containing a

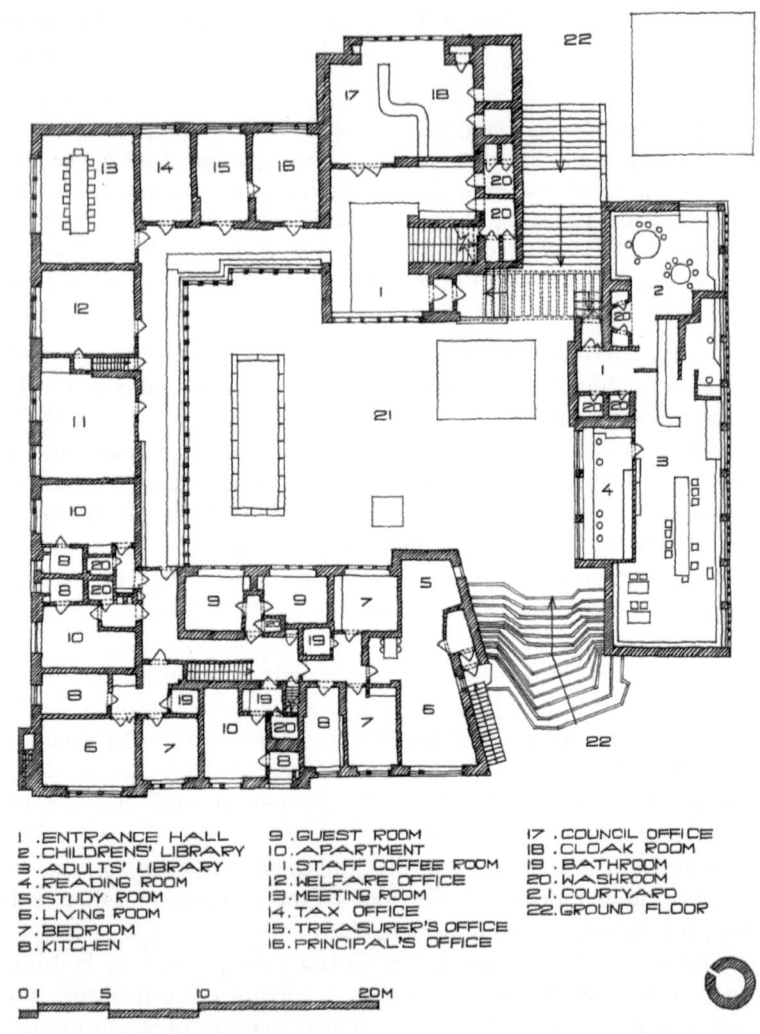

1 .ENTRANCE HALL	9 .GUEST ROOM	17 .COUNCIL OFFICE
2 .CHILDRENS' LIBRARY	10 .APARTMENT	18 .CLOAK ROOM
3 .ADULTS' LIBRARY	11 .STAFF COFFEE ROOM	19 . BATHROOM
4 .READING ROOM	12 .WELFARE OFFICE	20 .WASHROOM
5 .STUDY ROOM	13 .MEETING ROOM	21 .COURTYARD
6 .LIVING ROOM	14 .TAX OFFICE	22 .GROUND FLOOR
7 .BEDROOM	15 .TREASURER'S OFFICE	
8 .KITCHEN	16 .PRINCIPAL'S OFFICE	

0 1   5   10   20M

Figure 19.1 Courtyard Level Plan, Alvar Aalto, Town Hall, 1952, Säynätsalo, Finland. The design is organized by an elevated courtyard accessed by two major stairs; around the courtyard are apartments (bottom), administrative offices (left and top), and library block (right). Drawing by Mohammad Moezzi.

swimming pool. Juhani Pallasmaa, the noted Finnish architect and theorist, describes it:

> The Mairea presents the entire spectrum of Aalto's image play. The house is a combination of different volumes that appear to have grown around the courtyard through time. Scenes of deliberate artistic intention are juxtaposed with items that appear as products of timeless traditions. The wealth of materials and formal variations tends to break the whole into independent episodes.[9]

After World War II, with his international reputation consolidated as one of the "masters" of modern architecture, Aalto designed buildings such as the Säynätsalo Town Hall (1952), the National Pensions Institute (1956) in Helsinki, the Seinäjoki town centre (1958–1987), and the Church of the Three Crosses (1959) in Vuokkseniska, Imatra. Although he was an architect intimately linked to a Nordic region, Aalto had a wide-ranging impact on architects around the world.

★ ★ ★

After World War II a new generation of Italian architects came to the fore, following hard on the heels of the Italian rationalists of the Fascist era. These include Pier Luigi Nervi (1891–1979), Gio Ponti (1891–1979), Luigi Moretti (1907–1973), and Ernesto Rogers (1909–1969). Although Carlo Scarpa (1906–1973) stood outside the main developments in Italian architecture during this period, he would eventually receive much international attention. In the 1960s, a younger generation, including Aldo Rossi, Giorgio Grassi, Vittorio Gregotti, and Carlo Aymonino, put forth an agenda to restore connections to the history of the European city (see Chapter 5).[10]

Scarpa depended upon surviving craft traditions that allowed him to execute a unique body of work. Despite the influences of Frank Lloyd Wright, Josef Hoffmann, Piet Mondrian, and Japanese design, Scarpa was first and foremost an architect of the Veneto region of Italy. Scarpa was born in Venice and studied at the Royal Academy of Fine Arts for six years. He did not formally study architecture, nor did he ever become licensed. He began his working career in the mid-1920s, and throughout his life he taught at the Instituto Universitario di Architettura, Venezia (or the School of Architecture at the University of Venice). His distinctive approach to architecture started in the 1950s, with works such as the Venice Biennale ticket office (1952).[11]

Scarpa is known for his heavily layered pencil drawings that record his labourious and iterative design process. These drawings rarely employed perspective, instead relying on orthographic methods. His drawings guided the design development and the eventual construction process. Scarpa also worked closely with builders. He employed a wide range of materials, often in unusual ways. He is known for his tectonic language and the "celebration of the joint," as architectural historian Kurt W. Forster writes:

> If one were to single out an aspect of Scarpa's architecture that more than any other reveals the defining trait, it would have to be the edge, the border, the outermost limit. Be it merely the edge of a slab, the dividing lines among floor boards, the corner of a room, the gap between steps, or the narrow slot separating two different materials, Scarpa never overlooked the precariousness of the gap or underestimated the threat of an abyss opening within it.[12]

The renovation of the Castelvecchio Museum in Verona (1975) was one of the crowning achievements of Scarpa's career. It is an exemplary example of working with the existing fabric of a building to permit new uses. The site is a medieval castle situated on the Adige River adjacent to a historic bridge. Scarpa both removed and added layers to establish a remarkable coherence throughout the complex. He meticulously installed each artefact, subtly underscoring the interface between historic and modern architecture and between construction details and large urban gestures. He carried this out with "surgical" precision.[13] The later Banco Popolare di Verona (1981) project involved a sizable addition to an existing bank headquarters and its sensitive integration into the urban fabric of Verona.

Scarpa designed several relatively small interventions in the city of Venice, including the Olivetti Showroom (1958) and the Querini-Stampalia Foundation (1963). The second of these involved the transformation of the ground floor and courtyard of a 16th-century Venetian palace. Accessed by a small bridge designed by Scarpa, the interiors account for the periodic flooding typical of Venice. Scarpa choreographed movement towards the courtyard that he designed as a garden.

The Brion Family Cemetery (1978) in the small town of San Vito d'Altivole was designed for a prominent couple involved in the electronics industry as both a private tomb and a public place on the edge of a small town. A veritable "city to the dead," the walled L-shaped compound includes the tomb, a chapel, a meditation pavilion, a shrine, a garden, and two reflecting pools. Here, one of Scarpa's favourite devices, a stepped ziggurat motif, is used throughout the project to unite the disparate parts of the scheme. Two canted tombs for the clients are covered by an arched form and act as a hinge in the overall composition. The main reflecting pool and associated structures create a place for contemplation.

As architect George Ranalli points out, it was Louis I. Kahn and Scarpa who, in the late 1950s, forged a new approach to architecture, distinct from the prevailing modernism. Ranalli argues that they established "a dialogue with the history of architecture, entering a new realm of thinking about interventions into the historic fabric, and returning to the idea of craft, construction method, and on-site invention as the ultimate creative acts in architecture."[14] Working closely with skilled craftsmen, Scarpa's projects tend to contain concentrated moments within a relatively casual spatial order.[15]

★ ★ ★

The development of modern architecture in Australia after 1945 occurred due to both external forces and regional approaches that emerged in the major cities. An important architectural event in Australia occurred in 1957 when the Danish architect Jørn Utzon won an international competition to design the Sydney Opera House. The result is an iconic building that opened in 1973. Initially, Melbourne was the cradle of modernism in Australia, but impetus soon shifted to Sydney, where work by Sydney Ancher (1904–1979), Harry Seidler (1923–2006), and Philip Cox (1939–) garnered attention. John Andrews (1933–2022) first made his reputation in Canada and the United States before returning to Sydney in the 1970s, where he executed a series of important commissions. Richard Leplastrier (1939–) and Glenn Murcutt (1936–) emerged in the late 1960s as Sydney-based regional modernists. Subsequently, regionalist firms developed elsewhere in the country.[16]

Glenn Murcutt, the award-winning architect, is internationally renowned for his carefully executed projects that address the challenges of climate and context. He studied architecture at the Sydney Technical College and worked for various Sydney firms before setting up his own small office in 1969. Because of his unusual dedication to working alone and using traditional design methods, most of his projects are small-scale, either houses or modest institutional works.

Growing up in Sydney, Murcutt was exposed to the early modernist architecture in the region, much of it inspired by Mies van der Rohe, the Case Study houses in Los Angeles, and the Maison de Verre in Paris. Murcutt's early work is clearly derived from these sources; however, eventually, he became interested in local agricultural structures and Australian indigenous cultures. Murcutt's mature work is distinguished by the clarity of the planning and the precision in the way that structure and materials are handled.[17]

The Marie Short house (1980) at Kempsey, New South Wales, was an important "turning point" in Murcutt's work. The open rural site inspired the use of a curved roof, verandahs, timber structure and detailing, louvred glass openings, corrugated metal, and exposed service elements. An emerging regionalism in his architecture interpreted vernacular building methods and responded carefully to site factors. Agricultural buildings that were unpretentious and precise in the way they were constructed were particularly important. Murcutt's use of corrugated metal as a lightweight and durable cladding material is a distinctive aspect of his architecture. Drawing from the functional aspects of common buildings, he became adept at siting his buildings to take advantage of the environment.[18] As architect Françoise Fromonot writes, "He developed what might be termed a *logical reinvention* of tradition . . . Murcutt does not see vernacular architecture in terms of a tradition to be copied, but as a manifestation of knowledge acquired through experience which is worth meditating upon, maintaining and renewing."[19] In the early 1980s, Murcutt became more aware of Australian indigenous cultures and has attempted to adapt some of their teachings to his own work, to produce a "light touch" on the landscape. The movement and catching of air, inspired in part by his longstanding interest in sailing and flying, has been an important aspect of his architectural expression; the same commitment applies to the handling of water and light.[20]

Designed typically for clients from Sydney, Murcutt's houses are often vacation homes sited in dramatic landscapes. The Magney House (1984) at Bingie Point, New South Wales, is located on a site with dramatic ocean views. The plan employs a series of rooms arranged *enfilade*. The section reveals an unusually responsive approach to air movements and allows for the collection of rainwater. The Simpson-Lee House (1994) at Mount Wilson, New South Wales, is located on a wooded site. Two pavilions are separated by a reflecting pool. The slight offset in the plan was driven by the client's demand that Murcutt refine his approach to environmental factors. The Marika-Alderton House (1994) in the Yirrkala Community in the Northern Territory was designed for an indigenous artist and her husband. The steel and timber building was prefabricated in Sydney and shipped in pieces to the remote site, where it sits above the ground plane.

Murcutt has also designed larger buildings such as the Bowali Visitor Information Centre (1994) in Kakadu National Park, Northern Territory, and the Arthur and Yvonne Boyd Art Centre (1999) in West Cambewarra, New South Wales. Winner of the Pritzker Prize in 2002, Murcutt has inspired a younger generation of like-minded architects around the globe.

★ ★ ★

Modern architecture first arrived in Canada on the West Coast in the 1930s. By the 1940s and 1950s, various modernist practices were established across the country. In the 1960s, regionally specific architecture emerged in the various parts of the country.[21] The international career of Arthur Erickson (1924–2009) figures large in the Canadian context, starting with his West Coast modern houses (with Geoffrey Massey) from the 1950s and 1960s. Erickson eventually produced a host of major institutional and commercial commissions, including the Museum of Anthropology (1976) at the University of British Columbia and Robson Square (1983) in Vancouver. More recently, several Canadian firms have achieved widespread recognition, including Saucier + Perrotte architectes in Montreal, Shim-Sutcliffe Architects in Toronto, and Patkau Architects in Vancouver.

Patkau Architects was formed by John Patkau (1947–) and Patricia Patkau (1950–) in Edmonton, Alberta, in 1978. They moved to Vancouver, BC, in 1984 and have since then established a body of work that carefully negotiates between local and international factors. Both original partners grew up in Winnipeg, Manitoba, and studied at the University of Manitoba (Patricia Patkau subsequently studied at Yale University). The work of the Patkaus has undergone an evolution as they have consistently challenged both themselves and architectural norms. The earliest phase in their career is captured by the urbane Pyrch House (1984) in Victoria, BC, which is carefully set on a rocky site exploiting distant views of the ocean. The scheme features a simple plan bent to create a sheltered terrace space.[22]

The next phase featured an intense focus on tectonics or the thoughtful assembly of building systems. This is evident in the Seabird Island School (1991) at Agassiz, BC, designed for an indigenous community east of Vancouver. The form of the multi-purpose community building hints at local zoomorphic forms. Responsive to the site, a covered porch runs the length of the building, providing an urban gesture and referencing traditional indigenous structures. The Canadian Clay and Glass Museum (1992) in Waterloo, Ontario, continued the exploration of tectonic themes, with building assemblies revealed throughout. Kenneth Frampton states:

> The Clay and Glass Gallery explicitly announces the emerging importance of expressive construction in the Patkau practice, not only in relatively small-scale joints – brackets, hinges, pivots, etc. – but also in the articulation of larger components, such as the interface of servant and served spaces. This the museum visitor is presented with an assembly of readily identifiable archetypes, for example, stylobate, vestibule, lobby, stair hall, corridor, patio, terrace, wherein each successive element is rendered as a tectonic feature.[23]

The Barnes House (1993) in Nanaimo, BC, the Strawberry Vale School (1996) in Victoria, and the Grande Bibliothèque du Québec (2005) in Montreal extended the Patkaus's thinking across other architectural scales. Their commitment to tectonics during this period is captured in a sequence of post-occupancy analytical models built by the firm. Acknowledging the complexity of projects such as the Strawberry Vale School, more recent projects are formally and tectonically simpler. In the last decade or so, the Patkaus have also invested significantly in materials research.[24]

★ ★ ★

The works by the architects discussed here show that critically regional architecture, while always locally specific, can also derive inspiration from a wide range of sources, including the intelligent reinterpretation of vernacular precedents and moments in modern architectural history. Arguing against the "scenographic" nature of many recent postmodern buildings, Kenneth Frampton writes:

> building remains essentially *tectonic* rather than scenographic in character and it may be argued that it is an act of construction first, rather than a discourse predicated on the surface, volume and plan, to cite the "Three Reminders to Architects," of Le Corbusier.[25]

NOTES

1 See Liane Lefaivre, "Critical Regionalism: A Facet of Modern Architecture since 1945," in Liane Lefaivre and Alexander Tzonis, eds., *Critical Regionalism: Architecture and Identity in a Globalized World* (Munich: Prestel, 2003), pp. 24–31.

2 Ibid., p. 34.

3 See Alexander Tzonis and Liane Lefaivre, "The Grid and the Pathway," *Architecture in Greece*, no. 15 (1981).

4 Kenneth Frampton, "Towards a Critical Regionalism: Six Points for an Architecture of Resistance," in H. Foster, ed., *Postmodern Culture* (London: Pluto Press, 1987), p. 17.

5 Ibid., p. 28.

6 See Kenneth Frampton, *Modern Architecture: A Critical History* (London: Thames & Hudson, 2020), pp. 365–366.

7 Christian Norberg-Schulz, *Nightlands: Nordic Building* (Cambridge, MA: MIT Press, 1997), p. 1.

8 See Richard Weston, *Alvar Aalto* (London: Phaidon, 1995), pp. 40–60.

9 Juhani Pallasmaa, "Image and Meaning," in Juhani Pallasmaa, ed., *Alvar Aalto: Villa Mairea* (Helsinki: Alvar Aalto Foundation, 1998), p. 89.

10 See Diane Ghirardo, *Italy: Modern Architectures in History* (London: Reaktion Books, 2013).

11 See F. Dal Co and G. Mazzariol, eds., *Carlo Scarpa: The Complete Works* (New York: Rizzoli, 1985).

12 Kurt W. Forster, "The Architect of the Incalculable," in G. Beltramini and I. Zannier, eds., *Carlo Scarpa: Architecture and Design* (New York: Rizzoli, 2007), p. 24.

13 Licisco Magagnoto, "The Castelvecchio Museum," in F. Dal Co and G. Mazzariol, eds., *Carlo Scarpa: The Complete Works* (New York: Rizzoli, 1985), p. 159.

14 George Ranalli, "History, Craft, Invention," in N. Olsberg et al., eds., *Carlo Scarpa, Architect: Intervening with History* (New York: Monacelli Press, 1999), p. 40.

15 Ibid.

16 Philip Goad, "Edge of Centre: Architecture in Australia and New Zealand after 1965," in Haddad and Rifkind, eds., *A Critical History of Contemporary Architecture*, pp. 437–459.

17 See Françoise Fromonot, *Glenn Murcutt: Buildings + Projects, 1962–2003* (London: Thames & Hudson, 2005), pp. 18–25.

18 Ibid., pp. 33–34.

19 Ibid., p. 36.

20 Ibid., p. 47–49.

21 See Elsa Lam and Graham Livesey, eds., *Canadian Modern Architecture, 1967 to the Present* (New York: Princeton Architectural Press, 2019).

22 See Brian Carter, ed., *Patkau Architects: Selected Projects 1983–1993* (Halifax: Tuns Press, 1994).

23 Kenneth Frampton, "Reflective Practice," in *Patkau Architects* (New York: The Monacelli Press, 2006), p. 9.

24 See Patkau Architects, *Material Operations* (New York: Princeton Architectural Press, 2017).

25 Kenneth Frampton, "Rappel à l'ordre, the Case for the Tectonic," in Kate Nesbitt, ed., *Theorizing a New Agenda for Architecture: An Anthology of Architectural Theory, 1965–1995* (New York: Princeton Architectural Press, 1996), p. 520.

SUGGESTED READING

Frampton, Kenneth. *Studies in Tectonic Culture: The Poetics of Construction in Nineteenth and Twentieth Century Architecture*. Cambridge, MA: MIT Press, 1995.

Haddad, E.G. and D. Rifkind, eds. *A Critical History of Contemporary Architecture, 1960–2010*. London: Routledge, 2014.

Lefaivre, Liane and Alexander Tzonis. *Critical Regionalism: Architecture and Identity in a Globalized World*. Munich: Prestel, 2003.

Tzonis, Alexander and Liane Lefaivre. "The Grid and the Pathway." *Architecture in Greece*, no. 15 (1981).

Weston, Richard. *Alvar Aalto*. London: Phaidon, 1995.

20

PLACE AND INVENTION

The emergence of Japan as an economic and cultural power after World War II catapulted modern Japanese architecture into the forefront of global architecture. Japan began a modernization programme under the rule of Emperor Meiji (1852–1912). This period of intense change was characterized by the adoption and adaption of Western construction technology and forms of architecture. Initially, Dutch, American, British, and German architects provided designs for Japanese buildings and infrastructure and often trained young Japanese architects. The British architect Josiah Conder (1852–1920), for example, went to Japan in 1877, where he designed many buildings, influenced education, and shaped the beginning of the architectural profession in Japan. By 1890, Western influence was diminished, and Japan forged ahead with its own programmes. In this period of transition, Japanese architects produced designs in various European styles and also employed a Japanese revival style, which fused modern building typologies with traditional Japanese architectural elements. Examples of this idiom include Tsumaki Yorinaka and Takeda Goichi's Kangyo Bank (1899) in Tokyo and Tatsuno Kingo's Nara Hotel (1908). The Meiji period remains a controversial period in Japanese history, but it was important in establishing the evolution of Japanese society during the 20th century.[1]

From 1913 to 1945, following the Meiji era, major Japanese cities expanded, triggering the need for new infrastructure.[2] One project that was important was the design and construction of the Imperial

DOI: 10.4324/9781003403975-20

Hotel in Tokyo (1923) by Frank Lloyd Wright. Despite Wright's claims that his architecture was influenced by his strong interest in Japanese art and culture, the elaborate hotel he designed for Tokyo showed little direct reference to Japanese architecture.[3] The Czech-American architect Antonin Raymond (1888–1976), who worked for Wright and spent a year assisting on the Imperial Hotel, remained in Japan except during World War II. He continued to practice in Japan over the next 40 years. His own house in Tokyo (1924) was an early example of a modern building in Japan. Built-in mono-lithic poured-in-place concrete, it featured a complicated massing and allusions to Wright's architecture.

During the 1930s, Japan was increasingly imperialistic, engag-ing in wars with China and Korea. Allied with Nazi Germany, Japan became involved in World War II following the attack on Pearl Harbor (December 7, 1941) in Hawaii. During this period of expansionist nationalism, Japanese architects worked in the Imperial Crown style, a form of architecture that incorporated tra-ditional Japanese roofs and elements. One example is Jin Watanable's Imperial Museum (1937) in Tokyo.[4] During the same decade, mod-ern buildings designed by Japanese architects who were familiar with European developments also began to appear in major cities. Several projects by Tetsuro Yoshida (1894–1956) demonstrated a sophisti-cated modern approach; these include the Osaka Higashi Post Office (1931) in Osaka. Further, several schools in Tokyo were designed in this period in the International Style.[5] Kikuji Ishimoto (1894–1963) studied with Walter Gropius in the early 1920s. His Shirokiya Department Store (1931) in Tokyo seemed to be a reference to Erich Mendelsohn's streamlined department stores in Germany.[6] Antonin Raymond and his wife Noémi designed a number of key International Style buildings, including several large and elaborate houses that combined both modern and traditional Japanese spaces. Togo Murano (1891–1984) and Sutemi Horiguchi (1895–1984) also designed substantial houses for the Japanese elite.[7] However, by the end of the 1930s, the International Style effectively disappeared in Japan.

★ ★ ★

World War II ended with the surrender of Japan in August 1945, following the atomic bombing of Hiroshima and Nagasaki by US forces. The reconstruction of a world devasted by war was an enormous undertaking. The rebuilding heralded a new era in modern architecture in Japan, initiated by several key build-ings. The Raymonds returned to Japan in 1947. Shortly thereaf-ter, they designed the Reader's Digest Building (1951) in Tokyo. Executed with a discipline that acknowledged the work of Mies van der Rohe, the long linear scheme shares some similarities with the Atomic Memorial Museum at Hiroshima (1955). This commemo-rative building was designed by the emerging early hero of postwar Japanese architecture, Kenzo Tange (1913–2005).

Tange grew up in Hiroshima and Shanghai, China, and stud-ied architecture at the Imperial University in Tokyo where he was inspired by Le Corbusier. After graduation, he worked in the office of Kunio Maekawa (1905–1986). In 1942, he returned to univer-sity to study urban environments. After the war ended, Tange began to establish himself. He won the 1949 competition to design the Peace Park at Hiroshima with the museum at its heart. During the 1950s, Tange was immersed in urbanism and functionalist architec-ture; however, by the early 1960s, he embraced a more expressive and brutalist form of architecture. During this decade, Tange exe-cuted a series of daring and evocative projects, many built in con-crete, which had become the modern material of choice in Japan. Of note are his Kagawa Prefectural Office (1958) in Takamatsu, the Toksuka Country Clubhouse (1961), and the Yamanashi Press and Broadcasting Headquarters (1966) in Kofu. Arguably, his most intense reconciliation of modern architecture with Japanese tradition were his designs for the Yoyogi National Indoor Stadiums in Tokyo for the 1964 Olympic Games.

The Metabolist movement was launched in 1960 with a manifesto and a series of evocative conceptual projects by a new generation of young Japanese architects. Tange was not officially a member of the Metabolists, but several of his projects were influential to them, including his "Tokyo Plan: 1960," which included a comprehen-sive traffic system and numerous structures floating in Tokyo Bay. Members of the group included Kiyonori Kikutake (1928–2011), Kisho Kurokawa (1934–2007), and Fumihiko Maki (1928–). They launched their manifesto at the World Design Conference held in Tokyo in 1960. This event proved to be a turning point in modern Japanese architecture. The following describes the basic principles of the group:

> Metabolism's name stressed the basic idea of an endless change that occurs within an organism and its nearby environment. The Japanese architects that joined under the name promoted flexible architecture and

dynamic cities that could develop and grow through eliminating their exhausted parts and regenerating new components according to the needs of the socioeconomic environment. The city is conceived of as a metaphor of the human body.[8]

The Metabolists envisaged high-rise megastructure systems that relied on advanced technology to create large transformable modular environments (see Chapter 13). This was a response to shortages of suitable land for settlement and a drive for industrialization.

Early schemes by the Metabolists include Kikutake's "Marine City" (1958) and Kurokawa's "Agricultural City" (1960). Built projects by the group that demonstrated its concepts include Kikutake's remarkable Sky House (1958) in Tokyo, Maekawa's Harumi Apartments (1958) in Tokyo, Tange's Shizuoka Press and Broadcasting Centre (1967) in Tokyo, and Kurokawa's Nakagin Capsule Building (1972) in Tokyo. The Nakagin Capsule Building famously employed small prefabricated living units attached to a vertical service core. The Metabolist group was one of the important architectural movements of the 1960s. Their efforts culminated in the Osaka '70 exposition, where they designed several projects within a master plan by Tange. Afterwards, Kurokawa had a prolific career during which he promoted Metabolist ideas and developed the concept of "symbiosis." These ideas were promoted in books such as *Metabolism in Architecture* (1977) and *The Philosophy of Symbiosis* (1994). Maki also had a highly successful career. His early research into the city was captured in his book *Investigations in Collective Form* (1964). Important buildings by Maki include the Fugisawa Municipal Gymnasium (1984) and the Spiral (1985) in Tokyo.

Arata Isozaki (1931–2022) began his career studying and working with Tange; this is reflected in formative projects such as the Oita Prefectural Library (1966). Early projects such as "City in the Air" (1962) and "Future City" (1962) demonstrated an affinity with the Metabolists. However, Isozaki quickly diverged from them, displaying an interest in both Japanese architectural traditions and quoting Western architectural sources. By the 1970s, his work took on a distinctly postmodern character, captured in his use of cubical forms and square shapes. This was evident in his Gumma Prefectural Museum of Modern Art (1974) in Takasaki. He synthesized many of his themes in his Fujimi Country Club (1974) in Oita. His interest in Western postmodernism culminated in his Tsukaba Centre Building (1983), with its overt references to Michelangelo. Isozaki was a prolific architect who designed projects around the world. His thoughts on architecture are captured in his book *Japan-ness in Architecture*.[9]

★ ★ ★

Experiments in working with traditional Japanese methods and forms occurred in the 1930s and after World War II, particularly in the design of the house. Architects during this period also recognized the historic importance of the Ise shrine, the ancient Shinto holy site, and the Katsura Palace (mid-17th century) in Kyoto. Architects such as Kazuo Shinohara (1925–2006), in his first important period, represented by the House in White (1966), designed provocative interpretations of traditional Japanese houses.[10] Shinohara's career took a shift between 1970 and 1973, which was captured by the Uncompleted House (1970). In 1974, he produced the Tanikawa House (1974) in Naganohara, which was organized around a large pitched-roof space supported by dramatic structural elements covering a sloping earthen floor. Shinohara's architecture is defined by a distinctive approach to space and form and by inventive responses to the context. Shinohara continued to design highly unusual projects for the remainder of his career, including larger commissions.

Itsuko Hasegawa (1941–) graduated in architecture from Kanto Gakuin University (Yokohama) in 1964 and has since established herself as one of the most important architects in Japan. She followed her education with stints in various firms, including the Kazuo Shinohara Atelier (1971–1978). Hasegawa opened her own office in the 1970s. Since then, she has developed a substantial portfolio, taught at various universities, and won many awards.[11] Known for her often whimsical architecture and experimental use of form, Hasegawa combines concrete with a lyrical use of metal, especially perforated metal. These qualities are evident in her Atelier in Tomigaya (1986) in Tokyo. One of her most significant commissions, obtained through a design competition, was the Shonandai Cultural Centre (1990) in Fujisawa. Concerned about modernization in Japan, she has focused her design work on references to nature, which is found in larger projects such as the Yamanashi Museum of Fruit (1995).

Tadao Ando (1941–) was born in Osaka, where he grew up in modest circumstances. He started his career as a professional boxer. A self-taught architect, he opened his own office in 1969. He made his early reputation with a small and austere row house (1976) in

Osaka, constructed in exposed and precisely executed concrete. Known for his use of simple geometries and minimalist spaces that respond to changing light conditions, Ando has created an internationally recognizable approach to contemporary architecture; he has built projects across the world. Representative projects include the Koshino House (1984) in Hyogo, the Church on the Water (1988) in Hokkaido, the Naoshima Contemporary Art Museum (1995) in Kagawa, and the Museum of Wood (1994) in Hyogo. In his work, Ando has captured the essence of Japanese culture while employing modern materials and methods. His architecture provides an experience of calmness separated from the chaos of the world.[12]

Toyo Ito (1941–) is an architect whose work is very different from Tadao Ando's. Ito studied architecture in Tokyo and then worked for Kiyonori Kikutake from 1965 to 1969. In 1971, he established his own practice. His early house for his sister, known as the White U (1976) in Tokyo, demonstrated an inventive use of space in a concrete

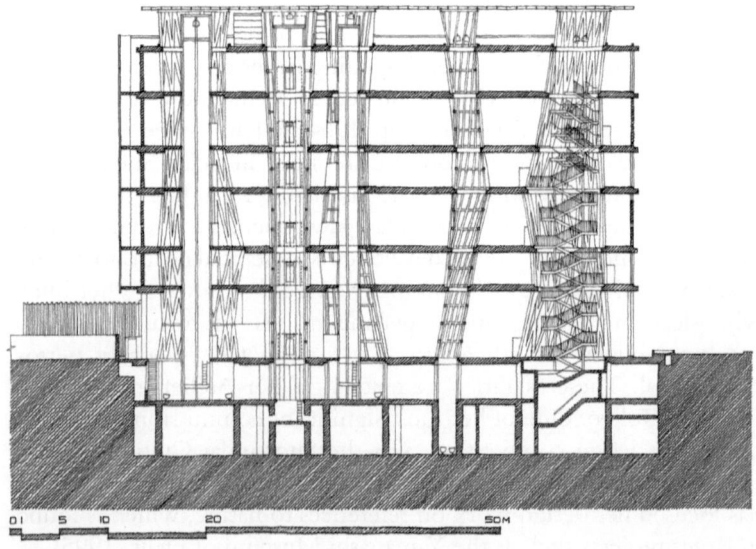

Figure 20.1 Section, Toyo Ito, Sendai Mediatheque, 2000, Sendai, Japan. The building uses varying heights for the location of floor slabs and the inventive use of bundles of steel columns to support them; functions and circulation elements are dispersed as required. Drawing by Mohammad Moezzi.

building shaped around a courtyard. However, as his designs evolved, he became more interested in an architecture of openness, fluidity, and lightness. This is captured in his Tower of Winds (1986) project in Yokohama. Of his many projects, the most outstanding is the Sendai Mediatheque (2000), a media-focused library and art gallery in which the floors of the building are supported by open bundles of structural tubes. The design can be understood as a contemporary essay on Le Corbusier's Maison Dom-Ino concept drawing of 1915.

In the 1980s, Shin Takamatsu (1948–) executed a series of highly idiosyncratic buildings in Kyoto. Built precisely and predominately in concrete and metal, the projects have a very machine-like quality. Buildings such as Origin I (1981), Ark (1983), Pharoah (1984), and Syntax (1988) demonstrate theories of materiality, form, and expression that were circulating in the period.

SANAA is a Tokyo-based firm established by Kazuyo Sejima (1956–) and Ryue Nishizawa (1966–) in 1995. Known for daringly light and airy designs, SANAA has produced a number of notable projects. These include the 21st Century Museum of Contemporary Art (2004) in Kanazawa, the New Museum of Contemporary Art (2007) in New York, and the Rolex Centre (2009) in Lausanne, Switzerland. SANAA are known for their distinctive use of glass, often employing fluid and rounded shapes. They also use minimal structure and predominantly white surfaces. Describing their Glass Pavilion for the Toledo Art Museum in Toledo, Ohio (2001–2006), architect Ronnie Self writes:

> The Glass Pavilion is an intriguing blend of the serious and the playful. It appears restrained and serene, but also fanciful – more like a garden folly set within its treed site than an addition to the existing architecture. . . . Inside it evokes reason and rigor combined with the sensations of a fun house or a house of mirrors. The plan is reasoned but appears diagrammatic. The construction demands extreme precision and integration yet it appears effortless.[13]

Shigeru Ban (1957–) established his office in 1985 after studying at SCI-Arc in Los Angeles and the Cooper Union School of Architecture in New York. His work is divided into two approaches: first, an inventive minimalism, rendered in a monochromatic white, and, second, a commitment to the use of paper, cardboard, bamboo, and wood, especially in projects designed for disaster relief. Examples of the first approach include the Curtain Wall House (1995) in Tokyo and the Naked House (2000) in Saitama. The second approach, with its emphasis on innovative materials, led to his involvement in post-disaster architecture after seeing the effects of the Rwandan Civil War in 1994. His non-governmental organization has been involved in constructing temporary facilities for numerous situations. Well-known examples are the Paper Church (1995) in Kobe, Japan, and the Cardboard Cathedral (2013) in Christchurch, New Zealand, both built after significant earthquakes. His pioneering use of paper and wood systems has earned him widespread recognition.

Since World War II, Japanese architects have realized many remarkable buildings. They have seized upon Western influences but ultimately have drawn from the rich architectural traditions of Japan to define unique interpretations of modernism.

★ ★ ★

Modern architecture in China by Chinese architects has a relatively short history. In the late 1970s, the Chinese Communist Party launched a series of economic and trade reforms that resulted in changes to agriculture and rapid large-scale urbanization. The policies launched a building boom in the 1980s.[14] This led to the emergence of Chinese architectural practices despite the closure of schools of architecture from 1966 to 1976. A debate ensued between the roles of modernism and tradition in a complex and ancient society. A vital example of a work balancing modernity and tradition can be found in Feng Jizhong's Songjiang Square Pagoda Garden (1987), which was treated as an open-air museum of ancient elements in a contemporary landscape. As China opened up to the world in the 1980s, internationally-based architects executed many projects in the country. The work of Chinese-American architect Ieoh Ming Pei (1917–2019) and his Fragrant Hill Hotel (1982) outside Beijing was particularly important.[15]

In the 1990s, following the incidents at Tiananmen Square in 1989, and as China shifted to a market economy, many more Chinese architectural firms were established. Yung Ho Chang (1956–), who trained in the United States, was a leader of this movement. Wang Shu (1963–), whose office Amateur Architecture Studio is located in Hangzhou, also began to build a strong reputation; in 2012, Shu won the Pritzker Architecture Prize. Much of this period falls under "experimental" architecture (aligned with Experimental Art), influenced by contemporary developments in the West.[16] Two important projects from this period reflect the transformations in China resulting from massive change. The first is the Luyeyuan Stone Sculpture Museum (2002) in Chengdu by Liu Jiakun (1956–). Using concrete in a cluster of pavilions, he blends both Western and Chinese sources in a refreshing way that points forward to further developments in Chinese architecture in the 21st century. The second is Wang Shu's China Academy of Art (Xiangshan Campus, 2007).

★ ★ ★

In Asia, architects digested the influence of Western modernism and then returned to local architectural traditions to create a distinctive approach to a revitalized modern architecture. As Tadao Ando writes in 1991:

> The most promising path open to contemporary architecture is that of development through and beyond modernism. This means replacing the mechanical, lethargic, and mediocre methods to which modernism has succumbed with the kind of abstract, meditative vitality that marked its beginnings, and creating something thought-provoking that will carry our age forward into the twenty-first century.[17]

NOTES

1 See Dallas Finn, *Meiji Revisited: The Sites of Victorian Japan* (New York: Weatherhill, 1995).
2 See David B. Stewart, *The Making of a Modern Japanese Architecture* (Tokyo: Kodansha International, 2002), pp. 90–91.
3 See Ibid., pp. 77–89.
4 See Ibid., pp. 107–100.
5 See Ibid., pp. 111–118.
6 See Ibid., pp. 118–123.
7 See Ibid., pp. 129–146.
8 Raffaele Pernice, "Introduction," in Raffaele Pernice, ed., *The Urbanism of Metabolism* (Abingdon: Routledge, 2022), p. 3.
9 See Arata Isozaki, *Japan-ness in Architecture* (Cambridge, MA: MIT Press, 2006).
10 See Stewart, *The Making of a Modern Japanese Architecture*, pp. 192–205.
11 See Maggie Toy, ed., *Architectural Monographs No. 31: Itsuko Hasegawa* (London: Academy Editions, 1993). See also *Island Hopping: Crossover Architecture* (Rotterdam: NAi Publishers, 2000).
12 See Masao Furuyama, *Tadao Ando: The Geometry of Human Space* (Cologne: Taschen, 2022).
13 Ronnie Self, *The Architecture of Art Museums: A Decade of Design: 2000–2010* (London: Routledge, 2014), p. 136.

14 Tao Zhu, "Architecture in China in the Reform Era: 1978–2010," in E.G. Haddad and D. Rifkind, eds., *A Critical History of Contemporary Architecture, 1960–2010* (London: Routledge, 2014), p. 401.

15 See Ibid., pp. 402–406.

16 See Ibid., pp. 406–408.

17 Tadao Ando, "Beyond Horizons in Architecture," in C. Jencks and K. Kropf, eds., *Theories and Manifestoes of Contemporary Architecture* (Chichester: Wiley-Academy, 2006), p. 256.

SUGGESTED READING

Bognar, Botond. *The New Japanese Architecture*. New York: Rizzoli, 1990.

Isozaki, Arata. *Japan-ness in Architecture*. Cambridge, MA: MIT Press, 2006.

Koolhaas, Rem and Hans Ulrich Obrist. *Project Japan, Metabolism Talks*. Cologne: Taschen, 2011.

Tange, Kenzo. *Katsura: Tradition and Creation in Japanese Architecture*. New Haven: Yale University Press, 1960.

Tanizaki, Jun'ichiro. *In Praise of Shadows*. New Haven: Leete's Island Books, 1977.

21

THEORY AND PRACTICE

Structuralism is generally associated with the work of Ferdinand de Saussure (1857–1913), a Swiss linguist and philosopher who developed a method that analyzed the internal structures of language. Saussure developed semiology as the science of signs. Structuralism "looks for the deep and often hidden structures beneath the surface manifestations of meaning."[1] Many concepts utilized by later thinkers were devised by Saussure, including distinctions between language (*langue*) and speech (*parole*), signifier and signified, synchrony and diachrony. He would also influence a wide range of disciplines. For example, the French anthropologist and ethnologist Claude Lévi-Strauss (1908–2009) used Saussure's structural methods to study the "mythic, symbolic, and kinship codes"[2] of traditional indigenous societies. Jacques Lacan (1901–1981) was a French psychiatrist who united the theories of Saussure with a radical interpretation of psychoanalysis, first developed by Sigmund Freud (1856–1939). The French philosopher and cultural critic Roland Barthes (1915–1980) applied structuralism to society, often examining the "myths" of popular culture.[3]

Architectural theorists such as George Baird, Charles Jencks, Diana Agrest, Mario Gandelsonas, and Geoffrey Broadbent took up the theories of structuralism and applied them to architectural "meaning."[4] According to structuralism, a building has meaning in how it describes its function and how it participates in a "system of signs." Affirming this idea, the Italian semiotician and writer Umberto Eco distinguishes between two types of "function" when discussing architecture:

DOI: 10.4324/9781003403975-21

> This continuous oscillation between primary function (the conventional use of an object, or its most direct or elementary meaning) and secondary functions (its related meanings, based on cultural conventions, and mental and semantic associations) forms the object as a system of signs, a message. The history of architecture and design is the history of the dialectic between these two functions.[5]

Structuralism had an impact on the Team 10 movement (see Chapter 18) and on the work of the Dutch architects Aldo van Eyck (1918–1999) and Herman Hertzberger (1932–), particularly in their development of an architectural language based on repeating spatial and building units.[6] Peter Eisenman (1932–) is the leading interpreter of European philosophy; he applied structuralism and subsequent theories to architecture. Eisenman's early investigations into structuralism and the linguistic theories of Noam Chomsky (1928–) led him to design a series of highly theoretical houses in the 1960s and 1970s that manipulated conventional concepts of function, structure, and language.[7] In a short essay published in 1976, entitled "Post-Functionalism," Eisenman argues that contemporary architecture has moved beyond the dualism of form and function that was the basis of modern architecture.[8]

★ ★ ★

Phenomenology is a 20th-century philosophical movement that was founded by the Moravian-German philosopher Edmund Husserl (1859–1938), who introduced concepts such as "intentionality" and "essence" in his writings. Phenomenology evolved into a comprehensive philosophy with an emphasis on human experience, existence, place, meaning, and authenticity. Phenomenology presents a radical critique of the work of the French philosopher René Descartes (1596–1650) and the tendencies of modernity.

Martin Heidegger (1889–1976) was an important student of Husserl's. However, their relationship ended in bitterness after Heidegger joined the Nazi party in Germany during the 1930s. Heidegger remains one of the most influential and controversial figures in 20th-century thought. In his work, he focussed on a primary understanding of "Being-in-the-World," which is reflected in his major text *Being and Time* (1927). His later work featured an increasing emphasis on interpreting language and poetry. The publication of his important essay "Building Dwelling Thinking" in 1954 (published in English in 1971) outlines his notions of "dwelling," the "fourfold," and "locations" in space. According to Heidegger, the rise of modern technology has resulted in a loss of authentic "dwelling."[9] The Norwegian architect and theorist Christian Norberg-Schulz (1926–2000) was a dedicated interpreter of Heidegger, particularly in a series of books that include *Intentions in Architecture* (1965), *Meaning in Western Architecture* (1974), and *Genius Loci, Towards a Phenomenology of Architecture* (1980).

Two phenomenologists who had a particular impact on architecture were Gaston Bachelard (1884–1962) and Maurice Merleau-Ponty (1908–1961). Bachelard's book *The Poetics of Space* (first published in French in 1958 and in English in 1964) is an examination of the human imagination as it pertains to the house and its contents. Informed by phenomenology and psychoanalysis, the text relies heavily on the work of poets.[10] Merleau-Ponty concentrated his thinking on the notion of "perception" and the body immersed in the world, captured in detail in his major text *Phenomenology of Perception* (first published in French in 1958 and in English in 1962). Merleau-Ponty is critical of modern science, especially with regard to the human body in the world. According to Richard Kearney:

> For Merleau-Ponty phenomenology made possible the recognition that the body is not an object among objects, to be measured in purely scientific or geometric terms, but a mysterious and expressive mode of belonging to the world through our perceptions, gestures, sexuality and speech.[11]

The Finnish architect and theorist Juhani Pallasmaa (1936–) has been a leading advocate for phenomenology and architecture, especially in books such as *The Eyes of the Skin: Architecture and the Senses* (1996) and *Encounters: Architectural Essays* (2005). In his writings, Pallasmaa has challenged the modern emphasis placed on vision and the eye, at the expense of the other bodily senses. He argues that architects like Frank Lloyd Wright and Alvar Aalto produced buildings that respond to the full range of human experience.

Several contemporary architects have been inspired by phenomenology. The Chapel of St. Ignatius (1997) in Seattle by the American architect Steven Holl has been described as "seven bottles of light in a stone box."[12] The design, among many others, demonstrates Holl's ongoing commitment to phenomenology.[13] Peter Zumthor, a Swiss architect, has written about his own practice in several thoughtful books and has produced many carefully executed buildings, including the much-celebrated Therme Vals (1996) in Vals, Switzerland. The

American architects Billie Tsien and Tod Williams are also linked to phenomenology. This allegiance was evident in the American Folk Art Museum (2001, demolished in 2014) in New York.

Since the 1960s, several prolific and influential architectural theorists have promoted phenomenology. These include: Joseph Rykwert, Dalibor Vesely, Alberto Pérez-Gómez, David Leatherbarrow, and Marco Frascari. Pérez-Gómez's book *Architecture and the Crisis of Modern Science,* originally published in 1983, is a study of architectural history from the 17th to early 19th centuries that employs a phenomenological approach.

★ ★ ★

Poststructuralism links together several recent philosophers, including Michel Foucault (1926–1978), Jacques Derrida (1930–2004), and Gilles Deleuze (1925–1995), each of whom has significantly impacted architecture. Foucault, the French philosopher, historian, and advocate, began his career influenced by structuralism. As his thinking developed, he moved towards poststructuralism. He applied the term "archaeology" to his early approach to the "hidden structures of knowledge."[14] In a series of famous books he analyzed the institutional history of madness (asylums), medicine (hospitals), incarceration (prisons), and sexuality in ways that focused on his concept of "power" as a universal force. His book *Discipline and Punish: The Birth of the Prison* (published in French in 1975 and in English in 1978) examines the prison and the history of punishment. In a well-known discussion, Foucault examines Jeremy Bentham's concept for a circular model prison called a Panopticon, published in 1791 with drawings by the architect Willey Reveley (1760–1799). According to Foucault, the Panopticon is based on visibility and surveillance and creates a power relationship between the prisoners and the guards; it is a "marvellous machine."[15] Foucault recognized that institutions, corporations, and governments wield power and that "power relations" are rooted in societies, in individuals, and in group actions.[16] His work in these areas has had a significant influence on architectural scholars examining the role of architecture and the history of institutions.

The French–Algerian philosopher Jacques Derrida developed deconstruction as a method for reading texts that results in a plurality of interpretations. He devised working concepts such as *différance* or the "universal system of differences," the reversal of traditional hierarchies, the exchange of the centre for the margins, the iterability of meaning, grafts and grafting, erasure, and so on.[17] Deconstruction was applied as a method across many disciplines, including architecture. The French philosopher Gilles Deleuze is a complex thinker who developed many popular concepts including smooth and striated space, the diagram, the fold, assemblage theory, rhizomes, and territoriality. The concepts are found in books such as *A Thousand Plateaus: Capitalism and Schizophrenia* (authored with Félix Guattari and first published in French in 1980 and in English in 1987) and *The Fold: Leibniz and the Baroque* (first published in French in 1988, and in English in 1993).[18] In the 1990s, Deleuze's theories affected a generation of young architects, particularly those who were experimenting with new digital design platforms.

★ ★ ★

The Deconstructivist Architecture exhibition held at the Museum of Modern Art in New York in 1988 featured the work of seven avant-garde architects: Frank O. Gehry (1929–), Daniel Libeskind (1946–), Rem Koolhaas (1944–), Peter Eisenman, Zaha M. Hadid (1950–2016), Coop Himmelblau (established in 1968), and Bernard Tschumi (1944–). The exhibition was curated by Philip Johnson and Mark Wigley, who recognized that the seven architects formed a loose group connected by their attacks on modernist form. At the time of the exhibition, the seven architects were relatively unknown; however, shortly afterwards, they became internationally renowned "starchitects" recognized for their distinctive approaches to architecture. Deconstructivism, as a term, blends both Russian Constructivism (see Chapter 14) and deconstruction. Describing Coop Himmelblau's dramatic rooftop remodeling project (1985) in Vienna, Austria, Wigley writes:

> The form is distorting itself. Yet this internal distortion does not destroy the form. In a strange way, the form somehow remains intact. This is an architecture of disruption, dislocation, deflection, deviation, and distortion, rather than one of demolition, dismantling, decay, decomposition, or disintegration. It displaces structure instead of destroying it.[19]

This description effectively described all the work in the exhibition.

Frank Gehry was born in Toronto, Canada. He moved with his family to Los Angeles when he was 16. His unique architecture was not born from theory but from his own experiences and his connection to the Los Angeles art community of the 1960s. He came to prominence with the design of his own house (1978) in

Santa Monica, which wraps an existing house in exuberant forms made from inexpensive and ordinary plywood, chain link fencing, corrugated metal, and glass. Through the 1980s, he continued to work with this palette of materials; however, as the projects got larger and more complex, Gehry began to experiment with more complex sculptural forms. This resulted in his firm adopting advanced computer software from the French aerospace industry and pioneering its use. The extensive use of computers is fully evident in two major commissions: the Guggenheim Museum (1997) in Bilbao, Spain, and the Walt Disney Concert Hall (2003) in Los Angeles. The Guggenheim Museum project has become celebrated as one of the most important buildings of the late 20th century due in part to its impact on the city of Bilbao.[20] Employing structurally complex forms clad in titanium and novel construction methods, the building evokes the forms of ships that used to be built in Bilbao.

Daniel Libeskind was born in Poland and emigrated to the United States in the late 1950s. His early career was mainly academic, demonstrated by teaching, writing, and the production of "theoretical" projects. In 1989, he won a competition to design the Jewish Museum in Berlin. The completed museum, his first major commission, opened in 2001. It features a zigzagging form that evokes the Jewish history of Germany and Berlin, including the cultural remembrance of the Holocaust (see Chapter 14). The design is intended to invoke feelings of disorientation, claustrophobia, and absence as visitors progress from spectators to participants.

Rem Koolhaas is an influential Dutch architect who studied at the Architectural Association in London. In 1975, he established The Office for Metropolitan Architecture (OMA) with Madelon Vriesendorp and Elia and Zoe Zenghelis. Koolhaas has published a series of books throughout his career, beginning with *Delirious New York* (1978). A student of the contemporary city, Koolhaas created an enormous compendium of his work (with the Canadian graphic designer Bruce Mau) entitled *S, M, L, XL* (1995). In the book, he describes his interest in concepts such as "bigness" and the "generic city." Among OMA's many projects, the Kunsthal (1992) in Rotterdam, the Maison à Bordeaux (1998), and the Seattle Central Library (2005) stand out. During his career, Koolhaas has embraced Surrealism, reexamined the history of modern architecture, employed cheap and generic materials, and played in the world of high capitalism.

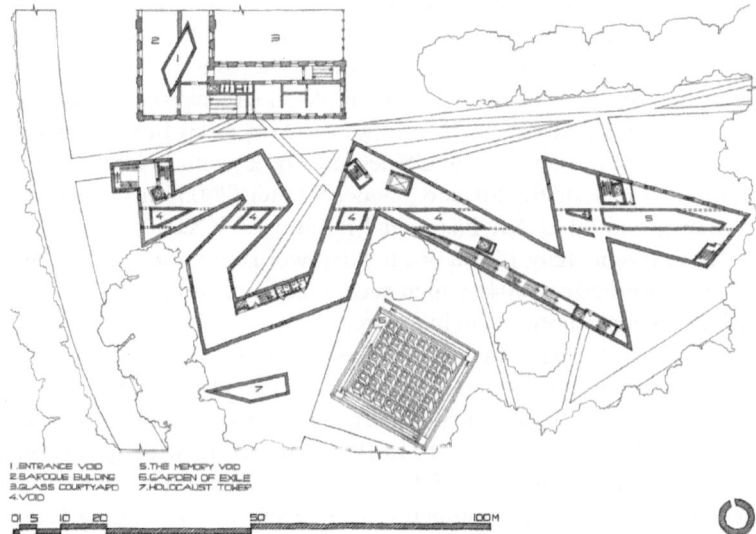

1.ENTRANCE VOID   5.THE MEMORY VOID
2.BAROQUE BUILDING 6.GARDEN OF EXILE
3.GLASS COURTYARD 7.HOLOCAUST TOWER
4.VOID

0 5 10 20   50   100 M

Figure 21.1 First Floor Plan, Daniel Libeskind, Jewish Museum, 2001, Berlin, Germany. The zigzag form of the building is bisected by a linear void space that is crossed by numerous bridges; circulation and service elements are integrated into the whole. Drawing by Mohammad Moezzi.

Peter Eisenman's work, after his initial phase influenced by Chomsky and structuralism, entered a phase from 1978–1988 that used a method that can be called "artificial excavation." This entailed interpreting and translating urban sites through the use of fiction, layering, shifting grids, and "scaling."[21] The phase demonstrated an interest in Foucault's notion of "archaeology,"[22] with projects such as the Cannaregio West design (1978) for Venice, Italy, and the Wexner Center for the Visual Arts (1989) in Columbus, Ohio. A shift towards deconstruction occurred in the 1980s, as Eisenman embraced the computer in his practice. In the 1990s, he incorporated the theories of Deleuze into his work; this can be seen in the Berlin Memorial to the Murdered Jews of Europe (2005) and the City of Culture project (2013) in Santiago de Compostela, Spain.[23]

Zaha Hadid was born in Baghdad, Iraq, and studied at the Architectural Association in London. She worked and taught with Rem Koolhaas before launching her own firm in 1980. She established her early reputation with projects such as the Hong Kong Peak

Competition (1983), which featured her Russian Constructivist-inspired paintings. Eventually, her firm embraced the use of computers and "parametricism" under the leadership of her partner Patrik Schumacher. Hadid gradually took on larger projects, such as the Rosenthal Center for Contemporary Art (2003) in Cincinnati, Ohio, the first museum in the US designed by a woman. Other notable projects include the Phaeno Science Center (2005) in Wolfsburg, Germany, and MAXXI: National Museum of XXI Century Arts (2010) in Rome, Italy. Hadid was the first woman to win the Pritzker Architecture Prize (2004) which recognized her distinctive contributions to contemporary architecture.[24]

Swiss-born Bernard Tschumi has been a notable educator, writer, and practitioner. His interest in the "event" and "effect" in the 1970s, inspired by the Situationist movement in France, is evident in The Manhattan Transcripts project (1981), culminating with his design for Parc de la Villette (1998) in Paris.[25] The design for the park was the result of winning a competition. The scheme occupies a large site that formerly housed a slaughterhouse. The design is based on a "system of dispersed 'points' – the red steel *folies* that support different cultural and leisure activities – is superimposed on a system of lines that emphasize movement through the park."[26] The design reflected Tschumi's interest in the event, cinema, Russian Constructivism, and poststructuralism. Since, he has executed a small but carefully considered body of work.

Other noteworthy architecture firms of the period not included in the MoMA exhibition include Morphosis, Herzog & de Meuron, Jean Nouvel, MVRDV, UN Studio, Foreign Office Architects, and various contemporary practices in Japan (see Chapter 20).

★ ★ ★

During the last decades of the 20th century, architects demonstrated a radical interest in theory as they grappled with the complexities of new technologies, particularly the impact of computers and rapidly changing urban realities. Sometimes projects remained unbuilt, or "theoretical," but most architects wanted to translate their ideas into built form. Architectural theorist K. Michael Hays provides a provocative take on theory when he writes:

> But if theory's vocation is to produce the concepts by which architecture is related to other spheres of social practice, architecture, too, can be understood as the construction of new concepts of space and its inhabitation;

which is to say that buildings and drawings can be theoretical, seeking a congruence between object and analysis, producing concepts as fully objective and material as built form itself.[27]

NOTES

1 Richard Kearney, *Modern Movements in European Philosophy* (Manchester: Manchester University Press, 1986), p. 240.

2 Ibid., p. 252.

3 See Ibid., pp. 319–331. See also See Roland Barthes, *Mythologies* (New York: Hill and Wang, 1972).

4 See Charles Jencks and George Baird, *Meaning in Architecture* (New York: Brazilier, 1970); Diana Agrest and Mario Gandelsonas, "Semiotics and Architecture: Ideological Consumption of Theoretical Work," *Oppositions*, no. 1 (September 1973); and George Baird, "Semiotics and Architecture, 1998," in *Writings on Architecture and the City* (London: Artifice Books on Architecture, 2015).

5 Umberto Eco, "How an Exposition Exposes Itself," in Neil Leach, ed., *Rethinking Architecture* (London: Routledge, 1997), p. 203.

6 See Wim J.A. van den Heuvel, *Structuralism in Dutch Architecture* (Rotterdam: 010 Publishers, 1992).

7 See Peter Eisenman, "Cardboard Architecture: House I and House II," in *Eisenman Inside Out: Selected Writings 1963–1988* (New Haven: Yale University Press, 2004).

8 See Peter Eisenman, "Post-Functionalism," *Oppositions*, no. 6 (Fall 1976).

9 See Martin Heidegger, "Building Dwelling Thinking," in *Poetry, Language, Thought* (New York: Harper & Row, 1971). Heidegger's essay "The Question Concerning Technology" from 1953 is a sustained attack on modern technology.

10 See Gaston Bachelard, *The Poetics of Space* (Boston: Beacon Press, 1969).

11 Kearney, *Modern Movements*, pp. 73–74.

12 See https://www.stevenholl.com/project/st-ignatius-chapel/. Accessed September 15, 2023.

13 See Steven Holl, Juhani Pallasmaa, and Alberto Pérez-Gómez, "Questions of Perception: Phenomenology of Architecture," *Architecture and Urbanism* (July 1994).

14 Kearney, *Modern Movements*, p. 284. Foucault outlined his methods in the texts *The Order of Things: An Archaeology of the Human Sciences* (New York: Vintage Books, 1994) and *The Archaeology of Knowledge and the Discourse on Language* (New York: Pantheon Books, 1972).

15 See Michel Foucault, *Discipline and Punish: The Birth of the Prison* (New York: Vintage Books, 1995), p. 202.

16 See Michel Foucault, "The Subject and Power," in James B. Faubion, ed., *Essential Works of Michel Foucault 1954–1984: Power* (New York: The New Press, 2001), pp. 326–348.

17 See Michael Benedikt, *Deconstructing the Kimbell: An Essay on Meaning and Architecture* (New York: Sites Books, 1991), pp. 9–51.

18 See Gilles Deleuze and Félix Guattari, *A Thousand Plateaus: Capitalism and Schizophrenia* (Minneapolis: University of Minnesota Press, 1987); and Gilles Deleuze, *The Fold: Leibniz and the Baroque* (Minneapolis: University of Minnesota Press, 1993).

19 Mark Wigley, "Deconstructivist Architecture," in Philip Johnson and Mark Wigley, eds., *Deconstructivist Architecture* (New York: Museum of Modern Art, 1988), p. 17.

20 See Mildred Friedman, ed., *Gehry Talks: Architecture and Process* (New York: Rizzoli, 1999). See also, Mildred Friedman, ed., *The Architecture of Frank Gehry* (New York: Rizzoli, 1986).

21 See Jean-François Bédard, ed., *Cities of Artificial Excavation: The Work of Peter Eisenman, 1978–88* (New York: Rizzoli, 1994).

22 See Stefano Corbo, *From Formalism to Weak Form: The Architecture and Philosophy of Peter Eisenman* (London: Routledge, 2016), pp. 39–51.

23 See Ibid., pp. 123–127.

24 See Philip Jodidio, *Zaha Hadid: Complete Works, 1979–2013* (Cologne: Taschen, 2013).

25 See K. Michael Hays, "The Autonomy Effect," in Giovanni Damiani, ed., *Bernard Tschumi* (New York: Rizzoli, 2003), pp. 7–16.

26 See Bernard Tschumi Architects. https://www.tschumi.com/projects/3. Accessed September 27, 2023.

27 K. Michael Hays, "Introduction," in K. Michael Hays, ed., *Architecture Theory Since 1968* (Cambridge, MA: MIT Press, 2000), p. xii.

SUGGESTED READING

Bachelard, Gaston. *The Poetics of Space*. Boston: Beacon Press, 1969.

Benedikt, Michael. *Deconstructing the Kimbell: An Essay on Meaning and Architecture*. New York: Sites Books, 1991.

Corbo, Stefano. *From Formalism to Weak Form: The Architecture and Philosophy of Peter Eisenman*. London: Routledge, 2016.

Koolhaas, Rem and Bruce Mau. *S, M, L, XL*. New York: The Monacelli Press, 1995.

Leach, Neil, ed. *Rethinking Architecture: A Reader in Cultural Theory*. London: Routledge, 1997.

22

POSTCOLONIALISM AND HYBRIDITY

The colonial era involved various European countries (colonizers) controlling and exploiting a large portion of the globe, including peoples (the colonized), land, and resources. Much of the world, except for parts of the Middle East and Asia, was directly colonized by European powers.[1] In the Americas, Africa, and Australia, this often resulted in genocidal action against indigenous peoples. Modernity and colonialism were linked together as colonies provided resources, labour, and markets for colonial regimes. At the same time, modernity was also imposed on colonized nations. Nevertheless, as historian C.A. Bayly points out, modernity also developed in the non-Western world despite its beginnings in the West.[2]

The postcolonial era refers to the period when nations, typically conquered by or created by the colonizers, gained independence from colonial rule. For most colonized countries, this period only starts in the 20th century. Postcolonialism is a concept theorized by various thinkers, including Edward Said, Gayatri Spivak, Homi K. Bhabha, and Stuart Hall, whose writings often employ poststructuralist theory (see Chapter 21). As former colonies secured independence, they usually attempted to reconnect with their own cultural traditions and histories. Most postcolonial countries had endured a long period of subservience to the colonizer's culture, often imitating it as a means of economic survival. One of literary theorist Bhabha's concepts is that of "mimicry," which can be defined as:

> Mimicry in colonial and postcolonial literature is most commonly seen when members of a colonized society (say, Indians or Africans) imitate

DOI: 10.4324/9781003403975-22

the language, dress, politics, or cultural attitude of their colonizers (say, the British or the French). Under colonialism and in the context of immigration, mimicry is seen as an opportunistic pattern of behavior: one copies the person in power, because one hopes to have access to that same power oneself. Presumably, while copying the master, one has to intentionally suppress one's own cultural identity.[3]

Mimicry occurred both during colonial rule and for a period after independence. Another of Bhabha's controversial concepts is "hybridity." It is influenced by the thinking of philosopher Jacques Derrida and other writers, which suggests the creation of a hybrid condition in the space between the culture of the colonizer and that of the colonized. In practice, there was some kind of symbiosis: the colonizer often borrowed from the colonized culture, and the colonized likewise adapted elements of the imposed culture. Bhabha proposes hybridity as a forward-looking and evolving condition.[4] Like the blending of local and global in critical regionalism (see Chapter 19), hybridity accepts the complex realities of globalization.

In the case of architecture, the colonizing power usually imposes its own methods on the colonized. The colonizers also imported architects to the colonies, who often employed locals. When the colonizing power leaves, the institutions and instruments of the colonizing nation usually remain in place. It takes time to re-establish local cultural practices.

★ ★ ★

The development of modern architecture in India was complicated by the reality that India is a complex society with a long history of architectural tradition. India was subject to colonial rule by the British from 1757 (the Raj beginning in 1858) until 1947, when it became an independent nation. The establishment of Pakistan and Bangladesh occurred at the same time. The architectural legacy of British rule can still be seen in surviving examples of railway stations, educational centres, governmental buildings, colonial institutions, etc., designed primarily by British engineers and architects.[5]

Architecture supported the control of India by the British. For example, in 1911, it was announced that a new imperial capital city would be built in New Delhi, south of the old city of Delhi. The plan of the monumental city was devised by the British architect Edwin Lutyens (1869–1944), who had no prior experience in urban design. Derived from Garden City and City Beautiful planning principles (see Chapter 7), the plan perpetuated colonial stereotypes.[6]

Lutyens also designed the Viceroy's House (1931) as a synthesis of European and Indian Moghul traditions for the dominant site in the scheme. Herbert Baker (1862–1946), along with the Public Works Department, designed many other structures in New Delhi during the period.

Beginning in the early 20th century, previously suppressed Indian architects began to find a voice as educational and professional opportunities expanded. An outspoken advocate for Indian-based architecture was the engineer and architectural educator Sris Chandra Chatterjee (1890–1966), a member of the emerging Congress party, the political party of Mahatma Gandhi (1869–1948).[7] His interest in tradition was contrasted with some of his contemporaries, who explored more modern Western architecture, such as Art Deco. In the 1930s and 1940s, Indian architecture was also impacted by various Western figures working in the country, including Walter Burley Griffin (1876–1937), Marion Mahoney Griffin (1871–1961), and Antonin Raymond (1888–1976).[8] This continued in the early postcolonial era, during which the influence of Le Corbusier and Louis I. Kahn on Indian architects was profound.

Jawaharlal Nehru (1889–1964), India's first prime minister (1947–1964), sought to create a modern nation-state by building the economy and new infrastructure. This drive for modernization was captured in the development of Chandigarh, the new capital city of the Punjab region, designed by Le Corbusier, with Maxwell Fry, Jane Drew, Pierre Jeanneret, and a team of Indian architects (see Chapter 7).[9] As various regions in India vied for authority, the new state of Gujarat, centred on Ahmedabad, emerged as an architectural centre after Le Corbusier was commissioned to undertake four key projects there in the 1950s. Wealthy mill-owning families commissioned him to design a new headquarters building for Ahmedabad Textile Mill Owners' Association (1956). Along with two noteworthy houses, these projects are among Le Corbusier's most accomplished works from the 1950s. In the designs, he demonstrated his continuing interest in Brutalism (see Chapter 18) and adjusting his work to specific locales.[10]

The cultural challenges facing postcolonial Indian architects were captured in the design for the Gandhi Ghat memorial (1949) in Bankipore (West Bengal) following the assassination of Gandhi in 1948. Designed by Western-trained Habib Rahman (1914–1996) and the West Bengal Public Works Department, the monument was an awkward hybrid of historic Indian and modernist architectural references.[11] Rahman later joined the Central Public Works Department in Delhi, where he played a prominent role in designing many modernist projects. He continued in his attempt to develop a national style in his unbuilt design for the Indian Pavilion for the New York World's Fair in 1964.[12] The continuing influence of modernism was felt during the 1950s and 1960s as Indian-based firms actively designed International Style buildings throughout the country; this included work by firms such as Joseph A. Stein (an ex-patriot American), Chatterjee & Polk, Achyut Kanvinde, Shivnath Prasad, and S.L. Chitale.

The American architect Louis I. Kahn (see Chapter 18) designed the Indian Institute of Management (1974) in Ahmedabad and the Capital of Bangladesh project (1983) in Dhaka. Anant Raje (1929–2009) collaborated closely with Kahn and carried on his work and design approach after Kahn's death. In the 1960s and 1970s, Indian architects began to forge a distinctive interpretation of contemporary architecture, no longer solely influenced by Western modernism. This was in part because the International Style proved difficult to implement in the face of local building, cultural, and climatic conditions. Achyut Kanvinde (1916–2002), who had trained at Harvard under Walter Gropius, demonstrated this trend in his Gujarat state guesthouse (1969) in New Delhi and the Dudhsagar Dairy complex (1974) in Mehsana, Gujarat. Kuldip Singh's DDA Housing scheme (1976) in New Delhi is another example of modernism thoughtfully adjusted to a local context. It was part of an ambitious initiative to undertake urban planning and construct affordable housing throughout the country. As architectural historians Peter Scriver and Amit Srivastava write, architects in India were "in a conscious struggle to build the physical infrastructure of a modern society with limited technical means."[13] Despite the constraints, there was also a lot of structural experimentation. For example, Raj Rewal's (1934–) exhibition facility at Pragati Maidan (1972) in New Delhi employed a bold space frame system constructed of poured-in-place concrete.[14]

★ ★ ★

A new generation of Indian architects emerged in the 1960s, which included Charles Correa (1930–2015) and Balkrishna V. Doshi (1927–2023). Correa studied at the University of Bombay, followed by stints at the University of Michigan and MIT. Returning to India, he started his own practice in 1958 and, beyond his architectural work, was heavily involved in the replanning of Mumbai (formerly Bombay) over the course of many years. Correa, initially inspired by the work of Le Corbusier, later integrated traditional Indian architectural features into his designs. An important early work is the Gandhi Smarak Sangrahalaya (1963) in Ahmedabad, a museum dedicated to Mahatma Gandhi's life and located adjacent to Gandhi's ashram. Correa and Pravina Mehta's Kanchanjunga Apartments (1983) in Mumbai is a distinctive interpretation of Le Corbusier's housing ideas organized in a dramatically shaped tower. The Vidham Bhavan (1997) in Bhopal houses the legislature for Madhya Pradesh state, with a plan based on a nine-square mandala. In his work, Correa often integrated carefully designed pathways, courtyards, metaphors, climate controls, and references to Indian cosmology.[15]

The work of Doshi must be considered among the most important architecture in the region. He studied at the famous Sir J.J. College of Architecture in Mumbai before moving to Britain and France. Doshi worked in Le Corbusier's office in Paris from 1951 to 1955 and contributed to the design of Chandigarh, among other projects. In 1956, he established his own practice in Ahmedabad, where he began to synthesize his experiences working for Le Corbusier with a growing interest in local traditions. His own house (1962) in Ahmedabad was a laboratory for testing his ideas on climate issues and low-cost housing.[16]

In the 1960s and 1970s, Doshi and his firm, Vastu-Shilpa Architects, designed several townships for large companies as part of a programme promoted by the Indian government to develop regional economies. His design for the Gujarat State Fertilisers (1969) in Baroda is an example of this work. Later, he designed innovative communities for the resettlement of impoverished populations. Doshi's urban designs resonate with two influences: the organization of traditional Indian villages and urban schemes by the Team 10 group in Europe (see Chapter 18). Countering Doshi's township design were a series of commissions for larger projects, including the Institute of Indology (1962) in Ahmedabad, the daring Premabhai Hall (1972) in Ahmedabad, and the Indian Institute for Management (with Stein, Bhalla, Kanvinde, 1979) in Bangalore.[17] Doshi reconciled his essential ideas in the design of his own studio (1981) in Ahmedabad, known as Sangath. Located on the edge of the city in a garden compound, the site was carefully landscaped to accommodate a series of partially subterranean vaulted spaces.

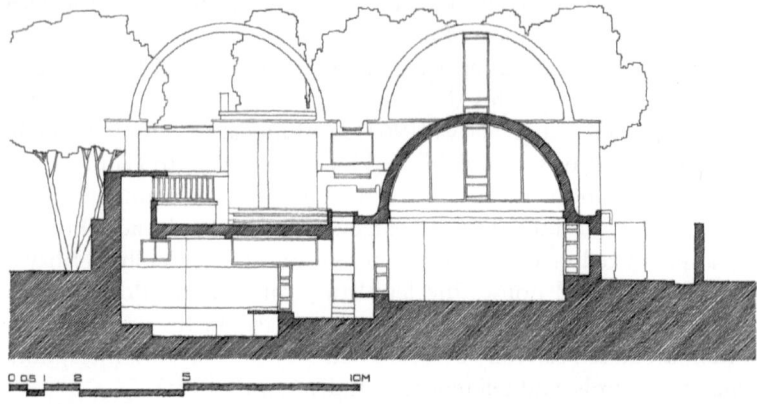

Figure 22.1 Section, Balkrishna Doshi, Sangath, 1981, Ahmedabad, India. The drawing shows a lower-level meeting area to the left and vaulted studio space to the right; upper-level vaulted spaces are shown in the background. Drawing by Mohammad Moezzi.

Following the completion of his studio, Doshi continued to develop designs for significant buildings. He was recognized with the Pritzker Architecture Prize in 2018 and the RIBA Gold Medal in 2022. Other noteworthy architects from the period include Laurie Baker (1917–2007) and Uttam C. Jain (1934–), both of whom were committed to employing local traditions.

Beginning in the 1940s, several important women architects in India were role models for the younger generation. Urmila Eulie Chowdhury (1923–1995) was a pioneering Indian architect who pursued a varied education, including an architecture degree from the University of Sydney obtained in 1947. After gaining work experience in the United States, she returned to India in 1951 to work on the Chandigarh project with Le Corbusier's team. Chowdhury would become the senior architect for Chandigarh (1951–1963) and then chief architect for Chandigarh (1971–1976). She oversaw the second phase of the city's planning and designed many buildings for the city and surroundings, including the Government Polytechnic for Women (1961) and the Government Home Science College (1961). She also directed the Delhi School of Architecture and Planning (1963–1965) and later taught at the Chandigarh College of Architecture (1966–1971).[18] She was the first Indian woman to qualify as an architect in India and the first to be elected a Fellow of the Royal Institute of British Architects and the Indian Institute of Architects.

Pravina Mehta (1923–1992) grew up in a well-to-do family in Mumbai during a time when Indian nationalism was hotly debated. She was one of the first women in India to study architecture at the Sir J.J. School of Architecture in Mumbai. She pursued further studies at the Illinois Institute of Technology in Chicago. Passionately attached to exploring the complexities of Indian culture, she established her firm, Associated Architects, with an emphasis on socially responsible housing, institutional design, and planning. Along with Correa and Shirish Patel, she developed The New Bombay Plan in 1965, inspired by Garden City planning principles. As architect Madhavi Desai writes:

> Mehta was familiar with classical architecture traditions and craft heritage of India, which influenced her designs. Her main pre-occupation was with re-establishing a link between art and architecture and with Indian values which she felt was missing from contemporary Indian buildings.[19]

Representative projects by Mehta include the Advani Oerlikon Electrodes factory (1962) in Chinchwad and the Shree Kirtan Hendra Housing Project (1989) in Mumbai.[20]

By the 1980s, the work of prominent Indian architects had gained global recognition, beginning to redress the imbalances created by European colonialism. Architects were at the forefront of India's efforts to define its nationhood or "Indianness" by merging tradition and modernity, often in a postmodern way.[21] Since the 1990s, a return to traditionalism has been evident in the work of various Indian architects, defining another phase in the postcolonial history of the country.

* * *

Modern architecture arrived in Sri Lanka in the 1930s; by the late 1950s, the local architectural scene was small, dominated mainly by ex-patriots. However, a different modern tradition emerged with the work of Minette de Silva (1918–1998), who was the first woman architect in Sri Lanka, and Geoffrey Bawa (1919–2003), a much-celebrated figure. Da Silva came from a family dedicated to the establishment of a postcolonial state. Following Sri Lanka's independence in 1948, she trained as an architect in Sri Lanka, India, and at the Architectural Association in London. Although influenced by figures such as Jane Drew and Maxwell Fry, who had worked in Africa and India, de Silva evolved her own approach to regionally and culturally appropriate architecture, which involved blending modernist influences with local traditions. Early projects such as the Karunaratne House (1951) and the Senanayake Flats (1957) in Colombo demonstrate her fusion of Western and Asian traditions by using moveable screens and verandahs to manage the effects of a tropical climate.[22]

Geoffrey Bawa was born into a wealthy family of Sri Lankan and European heritage. Initially, he studied at Cambridge University. He was called to the Bar in London in 1944. He returned to Sri Lanka in 1946 to practice law. This was followed by a period of travel and the purchase of an important piece of property he called Lunuganga. It was here he undertook experimental projects throughout his life. A growing interest in architecture and landscape design led him to obtain work in a local architectural office, Edwards, Reid, and Begg. He also began to secure his own commissions. Realizing he needed formal training, he enlisted in the Architectural Association in London, graduating in 1957.[23] Returning to Sri Lanka, he rejoined his former firm. By 1968, he was in charge.

Early on, Bawa collaborated with the Danish architect Ulrik Plesner. The two men developed a tropically suitable architecture with pitched roofs and overhanging eaves, built of local materials and using traditional construction techniques. Early experiments include the A.S.H. de Silva House (1960) in Galle and the Ena and Osmund de Silva House (1962) in Colombo. Subsequently, Bawa executed several projects for the Catholic church in Sri Lanka and began to develop expertise in the design of hotels for the tourism industry.[24]

The Bentota Beach Hotel (1969) is an artfully designed building "that offered subtle hints of a lost world of ancient palaces, medieval manor houses and colonial villas while still addressing the needs of the modern traveler."[25] The design created an enchanting environment out of local materials and established an authentic direction for modern architecture in a tropical situation. In 1979, Bawa was awarded the commission to design a new Parliament complex at Kotte, inland from the heart of the capital city of Colombo and adjacent to the ruins of a historic citadel. Inspired by various traditional precedents, the design features a group of copper-roofed pavilions located in an artificial lake. Completed in 1982, the parliamentary complex was intended to express national democracy, although this has been challenged by tension and violence between Sri Lanka's various ethnic and religious communities. Important late works include the Kandalama Hotel (1994) in Dambulla and the Pradeep Jayewardene House (1998) in Mirissa, where Bawa returned to a more modernist expression. Bawa's architecture is casual and carefully choreographed, responsive to climate and site, and engaged in local and global themes.[26] Bawa's knowledge of Sri Lanka's precolonial and colonial history allowed him to establish himself as one of the most influential Asian architects of his generation.

★ ★ ★

The postcolonial era has resulted in numerous interpretations of modernity throughout the world. In both India and Sri Lanka, architects have successfully established locally appropriate forms of architecture while engaging with tradition and modernism. Nevertheless, the postcolonial still exists in those countries that were colonized.

> The objective of the postcolonial critique, in this sense, is not to overthrow or disband modernism but to destabilize and begin to dismantle – to decolonize – the stranglehold of the "West" on it and also its stranglehold on the "West." Decolonizing modern architecture will not make it universal; it will make it global. By setting it into a global colonial and postcolonial historical field – which is to say by replacing it back into the field that was always the site of its production and reproduction – modern architecture has the potential to continue to further develop as a vital force for change in the world, today and tomorrow.[27]

NOTES

1 Ania Loomba, *Colonialism/Postcolonialism* (Abingdon: Routledge, 2005), p. 3.
2 See C.A. Bayly, *The Birth of the Modern World, 1780–1914* (Oxford: Blackwell Publishing, 2004).
3 Amardeep Singh, "Mimicry and Hybridity in Plain English," see: https://www.lehigh.edu/~amsp/2009/05/mimicry-and-hybridity-in-plain-english.html. Accessed October 2, 2023.
4 See Homi K. Bhabha, *The Location of Culture* (London: Routledge, 1994).
5 See Peter Scriver and Amit Srivastava, *India: Modern Architectures in History* (London: Reaktion Books, 2015), pp. 23–69.
6 Ibid., p. 84.
7 See Ibid., pp. 103–104. See also Samita Gupta, "Sris Chandra Chatterjee: The Quest for a National Architecture," *The Indian Economic and Social History Review*, vol. 28, no. 2 (June 1991), pp. 187–201.
8 See Ibid., pp. 110–119.

9 See Vikramaditya Prakash, *Chandigarh's Le Corbusier: The Struggle for Modernity in Postcolonial India* (Seattle: University of Washington Press, 2002).

10 See Scriver and Srivastava, *India*, pp. 171–184.

11 See Ibid., pp. 129–134.

12 See Ibid., pp. 162–166.

13 Ibid., p. 243.

14 See Ibid., pp. 222–229. See also Vikram Bhatt and Peter Scriver, *After the Masters: Contemporary Indian Architecture* (Ahmedabad: Mapin Publishing, 1990).

15 See Irena Murray, ed., *Charles Correa: India's Greatest Architect* (London: RIBA Publishing, 2013).

16 William J.R. Curtis, *Balkrishna Doshi: An Architecture for India* (New York: Rizzoli, 1988), p. 18.

17 See Ibid., pp. 29–31.

18 See Madhavi Desai, *Women Architects and Modernism in India: Narratives and Contemporary Practices* (London: Routledge, 2017), pp. 54–57.

19 Ibid., p. 67.

20 See Mary N. Woods, "Pravina Mehta: A Woman in Post-Independence India," in D. Fairchild Ruggles, ed., *Woman's Eye, Woman's Hand: Making Art and Architecture in Modern India* (New Delhi: Zubaan, 2014), pp. 184–206.

21 See Scriver and Srivastava, *India*, pp. 289–305.

22 See Liane Lefaivre, "Critical Regionalism: A Facet of Modern Architecture since 1945," in Liane Lefaivre and Alexander Tzonis, eds., *Critical Regionalism: Architecture and Identity in a Globalized World* (Munich: Prestel, 2003), pp. 46–47. See also Minette de Silva, *Minette de Silva: The Life and Work of an Asian Woman Architect*, Volume 1 (Kandy: Minette de Silva Ltd., 1998).

23 See David Robson, *Geoffrey Bawa: The Complete Works* (London: Thames & Hudson, 2002), pp. 12–25.

24 See Ibid., pp. 49–60.

25 Ibid., p. 96.

26 See Ibid., pp. 261–263. See also David Robson, "Genius of the Place: The Buildings and Landscapes of Geoffrey Bawa," in Philippa Baker, ed., *Modernity and Community: Architecture in the Islamic World* (London: Thames & Hudson, 2001), pp. 17–48.

27 Vikramaditya Prakash, Maristella Casciato, and Daniel E. Coslett, "Global Modernism and the Postcolonial," in Vikramaditya Prakash et al., eds., *Rethinking Global Modernism: Architectural Historiography and the Postcolonial* (Abingdon: Routledge, 2022), p. 11.

SUGGESTED READING

Curtis, William J.R. *Balkrishna Doshi: An Architecture for India*. New York: Rizzoli, 1988.

Prakash, Vikramaditya. *Chandigarh's Le Corbusier: The Struggle for Modernity in Postcolonial India*. Seattle: University of Washington Press, 2002.

Prakash, Vikramaditya, Maristella Casciato, and Daniel E. Coslett, eds. *Rethinking Global Modernism: Architectural Historiography and the Postcolonial*. Abingdon: Routledge, 2022.

Robson, David. *Geoffrey Bawa: The Complete Works*. London: Thames & Hudson, 2002.

Scriver, Peter and Amit Srivastava. *India: Modern Architectures in History*. London: Reaktion Books, 2015.

23

RACE AND RESISTANCE

There is no doubt that the evolution of modern architecture since the 18th century has mainly been dominated by developments in Europe and the Americas, predominantly by white male architects. This is evident in racist attitudes towards the architecture of non-white cultures found in the writings of certain 19th and early 20th-century architects and theorists.[1] And yet, as shown elsewhere (see Chapters 15, 19, and 20), after World War II, architects across the world have re-shaped modernism to local conditions as a central aspect of the postmodern age. Even as the world of architectural practice diversifies, "white supremacy" remains pervasive and invasive.[2] As the African American architect Harry L. Overstreet writes:

> When one surveys the landscape of African architecture, it is easy to conclude that little has been accomplished in establishing it in the pantheon of accepted architectural styles. Africa has always been at the mercy of Christian Europe, the leader and keeper of architectural history. Likewise, little has been done to establish the African-American architect in the American community. African-American architects are now faced with the problems of entrepreneurship in a competitive and, unfortunately, largely racist social and political environment.[3]

The history of black architects in America, sub-Saharan Africa, and elsewhere, has not yet been studied in enough detail.

★ ★ ★

The Atlantic slave trade that transported millions of black Africans, mostly from West and West Central Africa, to the Americas began

DOI: 10.4324/9781003403975-23

in 1526 and lasted well into the 19th century. Slavery in the United States of America was not formally abolished until after 1865 when the US Civil War ended. Enslaved blacks played a crucial role in building infrastructure and many notable works of architecture, particularly in the American South. Regardless of the many obstacles perpetuated by racism, African Americans began to be formally involved in architecture in the late 19th century.[4] The emergence of African American architects relied to a large extent on the role of historically black colleges and universities (HBCUs) such as Howard University (established in 1867) in Washington, D.C., Hampton University (founded as the Hampton Agricultural and Industrial School in 1868) in Virginia, and Tuskegee University (founded as the Tuskegee Institute in 1881) in Alabama.

At the Tuskegee Institute, under the visionary leadership of the black educator Booker T. Washington (1856–1915), an early architectural programme for African American students was established. A key recruit to this programme in 1892 was Robert Robinson Taylor (1868–1942), the first black to graduate from architecture at the Massachusetts Institute of Technology. Taylor, over his long career, designed many of the buildings on the Tuskegee campus, including The Chapel (1898), Huntington Hall (1899), and the Carnegie Library Building (1901).[5] Many of the early buildings on the campus were constructed by students. There were several other black architects associated with Tuskegee. Wallace A. Rayfield (1874–1941), who was educated at Howard University and in New York, taught at Tuskegee and eventually practiced in Birmingham, Alabama, where he designed many churches.[6] W. Sydney Pittman (1875–1958), studied at Tuskegee and at the Drexel Institute. He returned to teach at Tuskegee, where he designed several buildings. Later Pittman practiced as an architect in Washington, D.C., where he designed the Negro Building (1907) in Jamestown, Virginia. He ended his career in Texas.[7] Vertner W. Tandy (1885–1949) studied at Tuskegee and Cornell University; he was the first licenced black architect in New York state.[8]

Another important early black architect was Julian F. Abele (1881–1950), who studied at the University of Pennsylvania, where he was the first African American graduate (1902). Abele worked for the Philadelphia firm Horace Trumbauer & Associates. In 1909, he became the chief designer. Abele was responsible for the design of Duke University's west campus; he designed over 30 buildings (1924–1950) for the institution.[9] A very talented designer, he trained in the

Beaux-Arts style but was adept in other styles, including Collegiate Gothic. Clarence W. Wigington (1883–1967) was the first African American municipal architect in the United States. He worked in St. Paul, Minnesota, where he oversaw at least 150 buildings during a lengthy career. Wigington grew up in Kansas and Nebraska. After working as a draughtsman and designer, he moved north to St. Paul, where several of his buildings are St. Paul landmarks.[10] Other pioneering black architects include John Edmonston Brent (1889–1962) in Buffalo, New York; John Louis Wilson Jr. (1898–1889) in New York City; John W. Moutoussamy (1922–1995) in Chicago; Robert P. Madison (1923–) in Cleveland, Ohio; John S. Chase (1925–2012) in Houston, Texas; and, Wendell J. Campbell (1927–2008) in Chicago. The McKissack & McKissack firm was established by two brothers in 1905 in Nashville, Tennessee; it remains the oldest black-owned architecture and construction company in the United States.

Howard University established a Bachelor of Science in Architecture degree in 1911; the institution has educated many important African American architects. Albert I. Cassell (1895–1969) was an influential architect and educator who grew up in Baltimore, Maryland. He was educated at Cornell University, where he graduated in 1919. A year later, he joined the Architecture Department at Howard University, where he was involved in the design of many buildings on the campus and was instrumental in consolidating the architecture programme, which was accredited in 1951.[11] Another prominent member of the Howard University faculty was Hilyard Robinson (1899–1986), who was an early African American graduate of Columbia University's architecture programme. Robinson designed various noteworthy projects, including the Langston Terrace Dwellings (with Paul Revere Williams, 1938), a publicly funded housing project in Washington, D.C.[12]

Paul Revere Williams (1894–1980) was born in Los Angeles. He studied architecture at the University of Southern California and at the Beaux Arts Institute of Design. He was licensed as an architect in California in 1915. After working in various Los Angeles firms, Williams established his own practice in 1923, the same year he became the first black member of the American Institute of Architects (AIA). During his career, he designed over 3,000 buildings. From his mastery of a wide range of architectural styles, he became an accomplished modernist. Williams had many white clients and was famous for designing houses for local industrialists and Hollywood stars, including Cary Grant, Frank Sinatra, and Barbara

Stanwyck. By the 1930s, he was involved in designing public housing projects. He also maintained a longstanding relationship with Howard University. Of his larger projects, Williams's designs for the Music Corporation of America (1938) in Beverly Hills and the Golden State Mutual Life Insurance Company (1949) in Los Angeles are noteworthy. Of his modernist projects, the Palm Springs Tennis Club (with A. Quincy Jones, 1947) and the Theme Building at Los Angeles International Airport (with Pereira & Luckman, 1964) stand out. In 1957, he was the first black architect elected a Fellow of the AIA. Williams received honourary degrees from three HBCUs. In 2017, he was posthumously awarded the AIA Gold Medal, the first African American architect to receive the award.[13]

The first African American woman to become an architect was Beverly L. Greene (1915–1957), who graduated from the University of Illinois at Urbana-Champaign in the 1930s. She worked on large housing projects in Chicago before moving to New York, where she completed a Master's degree from Columbia University in 1945. She was employed by various New York architecture firms, including Edward Durrell Stone and Marcel Breuer & Associates.[14] Other early African American women who practiced architecture include Georgia L.H. Brown (1918–1999), who designed many projects in Brazil; Ethel M.B. Furman (1893–1976), who practiced in Virginia; and Amaza Lee Meredith (1895–1984), who was an art educator at Virginia State University and designed her house "Azurest South" (1938) on the campus. Norma Merrick Sklarek (1926–2012) was a pioneering woman in American architecture who graduated from Columbia University in 1950. She was the first African American woman registered in New York (1954) and California (1962), and a member of the AIA (1959). She worked for several large firms, including Skidmore, Owings & Merrill, and Gruen Associates. There, she became a director and worked on various high-profile projects. In 1985, she co-founded the largest women-owned architecture firm in the United States, Siegel Sklarek Diamond, where she remained for four years. In 1980, Sklarek was the first African American woman elected to the AIA College of Fellows.[15]

The New York-based architect J. Max Bond, Jr. (1935–2009) was a vital leader in the American architecture community. After graduating from Harvard University, he spent several years working in Ghana, where he designed the well-known Bolgatanga Library (1967). He was a partner in the African-American firm Bond Ryder & Associates (1969–1990), which designed projects such as the Martin

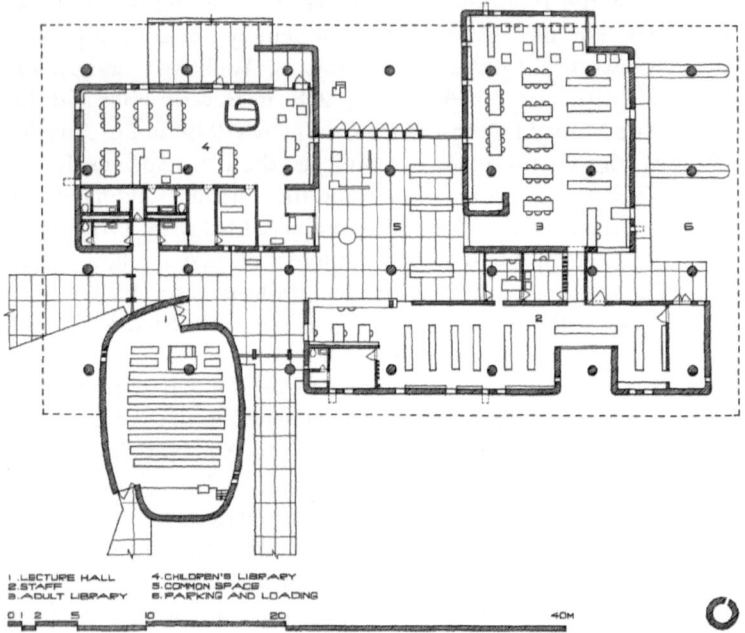

Figure 23.1 Main Floor Plan, Max Bond Jr., 1967, Bolgatanga Library, Ghana. The design features four pavilions of varying sizes and shapes housing an adult library, a children's library, an auditorium, and a staff area; these are interconnected under a large overhanging roof. Drawing by Mohammad Moezzi.

Luther King, Jr. Center for Non-Violent Social Change (1981) in Atlanta, Georgia, and the Birmingham Civil Rights Institute (1992) in Alabama. In 1990, he joined the firm that became Davis Brody Bond. He was also an educator and taught at Columbia University and at City College, New York.[16]

More recently, African American architects Curtis Moody (1950–), Jack Travis (1952–), Phil Freelon (1953–2019), and Mario Gooden (1965–) have been leading figures in American architecture. In particular, the Freelon Group, based in Durham, North Carolina, has designed several important buildings, including the Reginald F. Lewis Museum of Maryland African American History and Culture (2005) in Baltimore, Maryland; the Harvey B. Grant Center for African American Arts and Culture (2009) in Charlotte, North Carolina; and the National Center for Civil and Human Rights (2014) in Atlanta,

Georgia. Together with Sir David Adjaye and J. Max Bond, Jr., Phil Freelon created a consortium (with the Smith Group) to design the National Museum of African American History and Culture (2016) in Washington, D.C. A landmark Smithsonian institution, the design is inspired by both African and African American history.

The formation of the National Organization of Minority Architects (NOMA) in 1971 was an important event in the history of African American architecture in America. Initiated by several prominent black architects, the organization remains committed to combating racism in the profession and promoting equity, diversity, and inclusion. Several prominent African American academics and writers have taught in American schools of architecture outside of the HBCU schools; these include Sharon E. Sutton, Mabel O. Wilson, Craig Barton, Craig L. Wilkins, and Maurice Cox.

★ ★ ★

With the exception of Ethiopia and Liberia, the entire continent of Africa was colonized during the 19th and early 20th centuries by European countries (Britain, France, Spain, Portugal, Belgium, Germany, and Italy). Many modern sub-Saharan African nations gained independence between 1957 and 1966. In the aftermath of colonialism (see Chapter 21), most new sub-Saharan African countries embraced European modernism. Autonomy often came with two struggles: to establish a national identity free of the influence of the colonial power and to secure economic and political stability. Often, the former colonizer remained in control of the economic base. Most works of architecture relied on the designs of white colonial firms who remained. Modernization and development led to the construction of infrastructure and important institutional buildings such as schools, hospitals, and universities. However, by the late 1970s, the promises of modernization for African nations proved to be largely empty.[17]

An example of colonial modernism can be found in the work carried out in West Africa in the 1940s and 1950s, mainly in Ghana and Nigeria, by the British architects Edwin Maxwell Fry (1899–1987) and Jane Drew (1911–1996). They had experience working on a variety of projects in Britain and later worked with Le Corbusier on the design of Chandigarh in India (see Chapters 7 and 12).[18] In West Africa, Fry and Drew designed buildings for 17 educational institutions and were also involved in town planning. Architectural historian Rhodri Windsor Liscombe argues that they combined "altruism and anxiety" in their quest to develop a modernism suitable for sub-Saharan Africa.[19] Drew and Fry focused on the "climatic, geographic, social, and cultural conditions"[20] in their designs, something they also wrote about in their books on "tropical" architecture from the period.[21] However,

> The well-intentioned but residually superior attitude toward African society she [Drew] shared with Fry and the reformist colonial officials they befriended limited the participation of the native population. . . . Neither Fry and Drew nor their colonial and denominational clients fully comprehended the paradox that the new educational construction they were enabling reinforced the hegemony of British colonial rule.[22]

Drew and Fry are representative of the many white firms that worked in sub-Saharan Africa during and after the colonial era. Other European architects in Africa include Ernst May (1886–1970), the German modernist who designed buildings in Kenya and Tanzania towards the end of his career. Henri Chomette (1921–1995), a French-born architect who moved to Africa in 1948, had a prolific career across 23 countries, employing modern architecture carefully adjusted to local traditions.[23]

By the 1960s, sub-Saharan African-born architects began to open offices across the continent. Anthony Almeida (1921–2019) was born in Dar es Salaam, Tanzania, and trained as an architect in India. Upon returning to Tanzania, he established himself as an architect committed to the principles of modernism. John Owusu Addo (1928–) was a pioneering modernist in Ghana who initially trained as a teacher before studying architecture at the Regent Street Polytechnic in London. He returned to Ghana in 1959, shortly after the country had gained independence, where he worked on projects by Kenneth Scott (1918–1982) and at the campus of Kwame Nkrumah University of Science and Technology (KNUST) in Kumasi. He also focussed on innovative housing projects during this period. In 1963, Owusu Addo joined the new school of architecture at KNUST and became the head of the programme. His largest project was a 13-storey office building, Cedi House (1972) in Accra.[24] Oluwole Olumuyiwa (1929–2000) was a Nigerian architect who studied at the University of Manchester and trained in offices in London and Rotterdam. After returning to Nigeria in 1960, he established a firm in Lagos, where he designed many buildings and was active in the profession. His Crusader House project (1958) in Lagos and College of Engineering (1964) in Ibadan are early examples of his approach to fusing African culture with modernism. In Senegal, Pierre Goudiaby Atepa (1947–) had a successful practice, opened in 1977.

Several architects have produced a distinctive sub-Saharan African approach to modern architecture that diverged from the European-influenced style of the 1950s and 1960s. These include the Mozambique-based architect Amancio d'Alpoim Guedes (1925–2015), who was born in Portugal and educated in South Africa. He developed an eclectic style in the 1950s that drew inspiration from many sources, including traditional African practices. Alan Vaughan-Richards (1925–1989) was a British-Nigerian architect who interpreted traditional Nigerian architecture in his designs. The Nigerian artist Demas Nwoko (1935–), whose Cultural Centre (1975) in Benin, Nigeria demonstrates how he has employed local methods and cultural traditions in unique ways.[25]

The 1960s saw the birth of a new generation of important sub-Saharan African architects. Several of them have gone on to international stardom. Effectively, these architects have defined a contemporary sub-Saharan African architecture that is appropriate to the different regions. The oldest of the group is the Lesotho-born Mphethi Morojele (1963–), who has operated MMA Architects in Johannesburg, South Africa, since 1995. His firm has a diverse portfolio of projects, including the Maropeng Cradle of Humankind World Heritage Site (with GAPP Architects, 2006) in Magaliesberg, South Africa. Diébédo Francis Kéré was born in Burkina Faso in 1965 and studied architecture in Berlin, where he completed his studies in 2004. His early project, the Gando Primary School (2001) in Burkina Faso, garnered much attention for the way that it deployed local materials appropriate to the programme, climate, and culture. Since then, he has designed buildings in Africa and elsewhere; he won the Pritzker Architecture Prize in 2022. Other notable projects by Kéré include the National Park of Mali (2010) in Bamako, the Noomdo Orphanage (2016) in Koudougou, Burkina Faso, and the Startup Lions Campus (2021) in Turkana County, Kenya.

The Ghanaian–British architect Sir David Adjaye (1966–) is an international figure in architecture, with buildings designed by him built across the world.[26] Educated in London, he established his firm Adjaye Associates in 2000. Early projects, including houses and small cultural projects, were constructed mainly in England. His first major commission was the Museum of Contemporary Art (2007) in Denver, Colorado. Other distinctive art projects include Ruby City (2019) in San Antonio, Texas. His most significant project is the National Museum of African American History and Culture (see previous). Adjaye has won numerous prizes; he received a knighthood in 2017 and the RIBA Gold Medal in 2021. Other African architects born in the 1960s includes the Nigerian architect Olajumoke Adenowo (1968–) and Issa Diabaté (1969–) from Côte d'Ivoire.

A younger group of sub-Saharan African architects have also developed reputations across the continent. Kunlé Adeyemi (1976–) is a Nigerian who operates his firm NLÉ in the Netherlands. Notable projects by Adeyemi include his Makoko Floating School (2011) in Lagos. Others include Doreen Adengo (1976–2022), who practiced in Kampala, Uganda; Mariam Issoufou Kamara (1979–), who established her firm Atelier Masomi in Niger; Mamy Tall (1986–) in Senegal; and Omar Degan (1990–) who is from Somalia and is the principal of the DO Architecture Group. Despite its colonial history, a thriving approach to contemporary architecture is being practiced across the continent.

★ ★ ★

Regardless of the racist practices of US governments and African colonial regimes, black architects have found ways to practice and theorize about appropriate forms of building. Pioneering architects in the US and sub-Saharan Africa have demonstrated new cultural approaches to design, often against the universalizing tendencies of modernism. As the South African architect Luyanda Mpahlwa writes:

> When looking at the specific conditions of Africa's development over the last centuries, the various colonial influences, and the evolving cultures of the continent, we must acknowledge that specific African approaches to living space and the natural environment have existed. We must begin by understanding this history as well as the underlying characteristics and informants that define the diverse African cultural experiences and practices.[27]

NOTES

1 See Irene Cheng, "Structural Racialism in Modern Architectural Theory," in Irene Cheng, Charles L. Davis, and Mabel O. Wilson, eds., *Race and Modern Architecture: A Critical History from the Enlightenment to the Present* (Pittsburgh: University of Pittsburgh Press, 2020), pp. 134–152. See also Charles L. Davis II, *Building Character: The Racial Politics of Modern Architectural Style* ((Pittsburgh: University of Pittsburgh Press, 2021).

2 See bell hooks, "Overcoming White Supremacy: A Comment," in *Talking Back: Thinking Feminist, Thinking Black* (New York: Routledge, 2014).

3 Harry L. Overstreet, "The Bastion of Hope," in Jack Travis, ed., *African American Architects in Current Practice* (New York: Princeton Architectural Press, 1991), p. 12.

4 See Dreck Spurlock Wilson, ed., *African American Architects: A Biographical Dictionary 1865–1945* (New York: Routledge, 2004), for a comprehensive documentation of early African American architects.

5 See Ellen Weiss, *Robert R. Taylor and Tuskegee, An African American Architect Designs for Booker T. Washington* (Montgomery: NewSouth Books, 2011). See: https://www.blackhistory.mit.edu/story/robert-r-taylor. Accessed November 24, 2023.

6 See Allen R. Durough, *The Architectural Legacy of Wallace A. Rayfield: Pioneer Black Architect of Birmingham, Alabama* (Tuscaloosa: University of Alabama Press, 2010).

7 See Linda Komes, *The Life and Legacy of W. Sydney Pittman* (Charlottesville, VA: School of Architecture, University of Virginia, 1992).

8 See Richard K. Dozier, "The Black Architectural Experience in America," in Travis, ed., *African American Architects*, pp. 8–9.

9 See https://www.aia.org/articles/6306869-julian-abele-honoring-a-legacy-no-longer-i. Accessed November 23, 2023. See Dreck Spurlock Wilson, *Julian Abele: Architect and the Beaux Arts* (London: Routledge, 2019).

10 See https://www.blackpast.org/african-american-history/wigington-clarence-wesley-1883-1967/. Accessed November 24, 2023.

11 See https://www.blackpast.org/african-american-history/cassell-albert-i-1895-1969/. Accessed November 24, 2023.

12 See https://www.arch.columbia.edu/news/hilyard-robinson. Accessed November 24, 2023.

13 See Wilson, ed. *African American Architects*, pp. 619–623. See also Karen E. Hudson, *Paul R. Williams, Architect: A Legacy of Style* (New York: Rizzoli, 1993).

14 See https://pioneeringwomen.bwaf.org/beverly-lorraine-greene/. Accessed November 24, 2023.

15 See https://pioneeringwomen.bwaf.org/norma-merrick-sklarek/. Accessed November 27, 2023.

16 See https://aadn.gsd.harvard.edu/people/j-max-bond-jr/. Accessed November 28, 2023.

17 See Manuel Herz, "The New Domain: Architecture at the Time of Liberation," in Manuel Herz, ed., *African Modernism: The Architecture of Independence* (Zurich: Park Books, 2015), pp. 5–10.

18 See Iain Jackson and Jessica Holland, *The Architecture of Edwin Maxwell Fry and Jane Drew* (London: Routledge, 2014).

19 Rhodri Windsor Liscombe, "Modernism in Late Imperial British West Africa: The Work of Maxwell Fry and Jane Drew, 1946–56," *JSAH*, vol. 65, no. 2 (June 2006), p. 188.

20 Ibid., p. 193.

21 See, for example, Maxwell Fry and Jane Drew, *Tropical Architecture in the Dry and Humid Zones* (London: B.T. Batsford Ltd., 1964).

22 Windsor Liscombe, "Modernism in Late Imperial British West Africa," pp. 193–194.

23 See Léo Noyer-Duplaix, "Henri Chomette: Africa as a Terrain of Architectural Freedom," in Herz, ed., *African Modernism*, pp. 271–281.

24 See https://www.design233.com/articles/john-owusu-addo. Accessed December 4, 2023.

25 See https://www.labiennale.org/en/news/demas-nwoko-golden-lion-lifetime-achievement-biennale-architettura-2023. Accessed December 4, 2023.

26 In 2023, Sir David Adjaye was publicly accused of sexual assault and harassment and creating a toxic workplace by three female employees.

27 Luyanda Mpahlwa, "Reclaiming the Past: Our Heritage, Our Cultures, Our Future," in Philipp Meuser et al., eds., *Theorising Architecture in Sub-Saharan Africa: Perspectives, Questions, and Concepts* (Berlin: DOM Publishers, 2021), p. 154.

SUGGESTED READING

Barton, Craig E., ed. *Sites of Memory: Perspectives on Architecture and Race*. New York: Princeton Architectural Press, 2001.

Brown, Adrienne. *The Black Skyscraper: Architecture and the Perception of Race*. Baltimore: Johns Hopkins University Press, 2017.

Cheng, Irene, Charles L. Davis, and Mabel O. Wilson, eds. *Race and Modern Architecture: A Critical History from the Enlightenment to the Present*. Pittsburgh: University of Pittsburgh Press, 2020.

Herz, Manuel, ed. *African Modernism: The Architecture of Independence*. Zurich: Park Books, 2015.

Meuser, Philipp and Adil Dalbai, eds. *Architectural Guide: Sub-Saharan Africa*, 7 vols. Berlin: DOM Publishers, 2021.

24

ENVIRONMENTALISM AND INDIGENEITY

The impact of climate change began to be felt in the 1960s, at the same time the environmental movement started. Buildings, which consume substantial resources and energy, are a significant contributor to climate change and environmental degradation.[1] The contemporary environmental movement can trace its roots back to the writings of the American naturalist and philosopher Henry David Thoreau (1817–1862), especially his book *Walden; or, Life in the Woods* (1854). The publication of Rachel Carson's *Silent Spring* in 1962 underscored how humans are negatively impacting the planet; the book was vital in launching contemporary environmentalism.

Architecture has always had a relationship to its environment; in indigenous and traditional cultures, buildings were carefully adjusted to local conditions, methods, and materials. However, during the modern era, buildings were often disconnected from their context, a distinguishing feature of the International Style (see Chapter 12). Early efforts to create environmentally responsive architecture occurred in the 20th century with the work of architects such as Frank Lloyd Wright and Alvar Aalto (see Chapters 10 and 19), who paid particular attention to the relationship between a building and its context. This, along with the use of appropriate technologies including vernacular technologies and forms advocated by architects like Hasan Fathy and Balkrishna Doshi (see Chapters 15 and 22), is the basis of what is termed "sustainable" architecture.[2]

★ ★ ★

DOI: 10.4324/9781003403975-24

The first report on the state of the global environment was published in 1951. Since then, many studies, conferences, associations, standards, and declarations have followed, all aspiring to reduce the negative impacts of humankind on the planet. The United Nations was a key sponsor of initiatives like the 1972 UN Conference on the Environment held in Stockholm, Sweden, the 1987 UN Brundtland Commission report, the Earth Summit hosted by Brazil in 1992, and the 1994 UN Framework Convention on Climate Change. These were catalytic in raising awareness about environmental issues and the pending climate crisis.[3] Important in the development of more sustainable buildings are performance standards that govern energy consumption, use of resources, and the production of waste. The United States Green Building Council's Leadership in Energy and Environmental Design (LEED) programme was established in 1998 as one of several green certification programmes. LEED scores projects on factors such as site design, water management, energy consumption, and material use. Another important document is The Hannover Principles (1992), which was authored by the American architect William McDonough (1951–), a pioneering figure in sustainable design.

Beginning in the 1960s, projects like Sea Ranch Condominium (1965) in Northern California by MLTW signalled an emerging "green" architecture, one tailored to lessening the environmental impact of buildings. This was complemented by books such as Ian McHarg's *Design with Nature* (1969), which remains a seminal text that outlines his "ecological planning method."[4] In the 1970s, radical experiments in sustainable architecture, often generated by counterculture groups, occurred all over the world as designers grappled with the emerging energy and environmental crisis. Building upon novel housing experiments in the 1950s, architects in the 1970s placed a particular emphasis on reducing energy consumption in buildings, focused on harvesting solar energy, and sometimes went as far as creating "off-grid" solutions.[5] Projects such as the Ark (1976), built on Prince Edward Island in Canada as a house, greenhouse, and research centre, incorporated solar, wind, and biomass for energy production, along with water recycling and food production, in an innovative design that was based on the "biosphere" concept.[6] The Ark project was supported by the US-based New Alchemy Institute, funded by various Canadian governments, and designed by Solsearch Architects.

Despite advances made in the 1970s in sustainable building design, the 1980s focussed on the aesthetic and theoretical aspects of architecture (see Chapters 18 and 21). However, the decade also saw the rise of conservation and preservation movements, along with historicism and "critical regionalism" as approaches to design (see Chapters 19 and 20). Further, during this period, German architects were particularly invested in developing approaches to green architecture; these included Günter Behnisch (1922–2010), Thomas Herzog (1941–), and Rolf Disch (1944–). Writers such as Christopher Alexander, Amory B. Lovins, and William McDonough also contributed significantly to the concept of sustainable design.[7]

By the 1990s, the use of sophisticated new technologies was the focus of sustainable design, aided by the widespread adoption of CAD (computer-aided design) and digital fabrication in architectural practice. The advent of digital technologies allowed for the modelling and testing of conceptual designs. The British High Tech architect Norman Foster (1935–) has been an important leader in sustainable building design, especially with projects like the Commerzbank Tower (1997) in Frankfurt, Germany. The Italian architect Renzo Piano (1937–), who was a partner with Richard Rogers (1933–2021) on the Pompidou Centre project (1977) in Paris, has also pioneered the use of technology in a search for green architecture (see Chapter 13). This is captured in Piano's projects, such as the Jean-Marie Tjibaou Cultural Centre (1998) in Nouméa, New Caledonia, and the California Academy of Sciences project (2008) in San Francisco, California. The British architect Michael Hopkins (1935–2023) has also applied a High Tech approach to sustainable design, although in projects such as Portcullis House (2001) in London, he introduced traditional materials and forms. The Canadian architect Peter Busby (1952–), who worked briefly for Foster, established his first practice in Vancouver, BC in 1984. Since, he has become one of the leading "green" architects in North America. He joined the US-based firm Perkins + Will in 2004. Important projects designed under Busby's leadership include the Computer Sciences Building (2001) at York University in Toronto, Ontario, Dockside Green (2009) in Victoria, BC, and the VanDusen Botanical Garden Visitor Centre (2012) in Vancouver, BC.[8]

The greening of buildings with vegetation, including green roofs and green walls, has been experimented with by various architects.[9] The Argentinian architect Emilio Ambasz (1943–) fused landscape, vegetation, and buildings together in projects such as the Lucille Halsell Conservatory (1983) in San Antonio, Texas, and the ACROS Building (1995) in Fukuoka, Japan. The Malaysian architect

Kenneth Yeang (1946–) has been a pioneer in the development of "bio-climatic" skyscrapers. Educated in England and influenced by the Japanese architect Kisho Kurokawa, Yeang has practised in Kuala Lumpur since he established a partnership in 1977. Pioneering projects include the Menara Mesiniaga office building (1992) for IBM in Selangor, Malaysia, which uses various passive energy strategies, including façades adjusted to orientation, shading devices, and greenery planted in a spiralling set of sky courts. Yeang has also written extensively on green architecture. The French architect Jean Nouvel (1945–) has employed vegetation in striking ways, particularly at the Musée du quai Branly (2006) in Paris, a museum dedicated to indigenous cultures.

The development of passive and low-tech strategies is important in sustainable design, as is the use of renewable materials and sources of energy. For example, the use of natural ventilation has been explored in both Egypt, where Hasan Fathy resurrected older methods, and in recent High Tech projects such as the School of Engineering Building at De Montfort University in Leicester, England (1993) by Short and Associates. Traditional materials such as brick and wood are also being employed as local solutions to contemporary challenges. Recently, wood has been employed in buildings as a renewable structural material, especially in Europe and North America, where various architectural practices are pioneering in this field. The adoption of green building design methods and technologies has been slow, with some countries showing a stronger commitment than others. This commitment to sustainability will become more imperative as the effects of anthropogenic climate change take hold.

★ ★ ★

Indigenous peoples (First Nations, aboriginals, or natives) are descendants of the first or original people in a territory. Typically, they have experienced forms of colonization and violence, which often resulted in genocide by disease, force, displacement, or cultural deprivation. Indigenous peoples are found on all continents (except Antarctica) and comprise more than 5000 groups in over 70 countries and number over 350 million people.[10] Traditionally, they practised localized forms of architecture; many traditions have been eroded or lost as a result of colonial rule. Despite numerous challenges, including institutionalized racism, various indigenous architects have emerged since the 1960s in countries like Canada, the

United States, Australia, and New Zealand. According to the Maori scholar Hirini Matunga, indigenous architecture is defined as:

> It is architecture from within the people of this place and their relationship with each other, their cultural values, knowledge and principles, their land, environment, geography and climate. It is architecture using their natural resources, materials and construction methods and introduced materials, technologies and approaches adapted, adopted and nuanced to their cultural and social needs. It is also architecture embedded in an ever-evolving Indigenous people and place-based aesthetic using their palette, colours, designs, patterns, geometry, sculptural forms and shapes. In other words, an architecture ultimately redolent of their narrative about their relationships with their place – now, back in time and into the future.[11]

Modern indigenous architecture is specifically designed for indigenous communities and is normally rooted in the concept of "place." The values inherent in indigenous "ways of knowing" align with sustainable design. Historically, most of the buildings designed for indigenous communities were designed by "settler" firms, largely unfamiliar with the cultural traditions of the people they were designing for. However, a growing number of indigenous architects are designing for indigenous communities and beyond.

In Canada, a growing number of indigenous architects are practising across the country, following in the footsteps of Douglas Cardinal (1934–), one of Canada's most distinguished architects. Cardinal, who is of mixed Blackfoot, Ojibwe, Métis, and European heritage, has been a pioneering figure for indigenous architects since he completed his distinctive curvilinear and sculptural design for St. Mary's Church (1968) in Red Deer, Alberta. The design of the church was inspired by prairie landscapes, along with Baroque and Expressionist architecture. He expanded his repertoire with various buildings for the Alberta government before embarking on the Canadian Museum of History (1989) in Gatineau, Quebec.[12] Notably, Cardinal was selected, along with a team of indigenous designers, as the architect for the National Museum of the American Indian (2004) in Washington, D.C., which houses thousands of indigenous artefacts.

Several Canadian architects identify as Métis, which means they have mixed indigenous and European heritage. Often their indigenous heritage was suppressed, which was the case with the noted Manitoba architect Étienne Gaboury (1930–2022).[13] A younger generation of indigenous architects in Canada is being led by Alfred

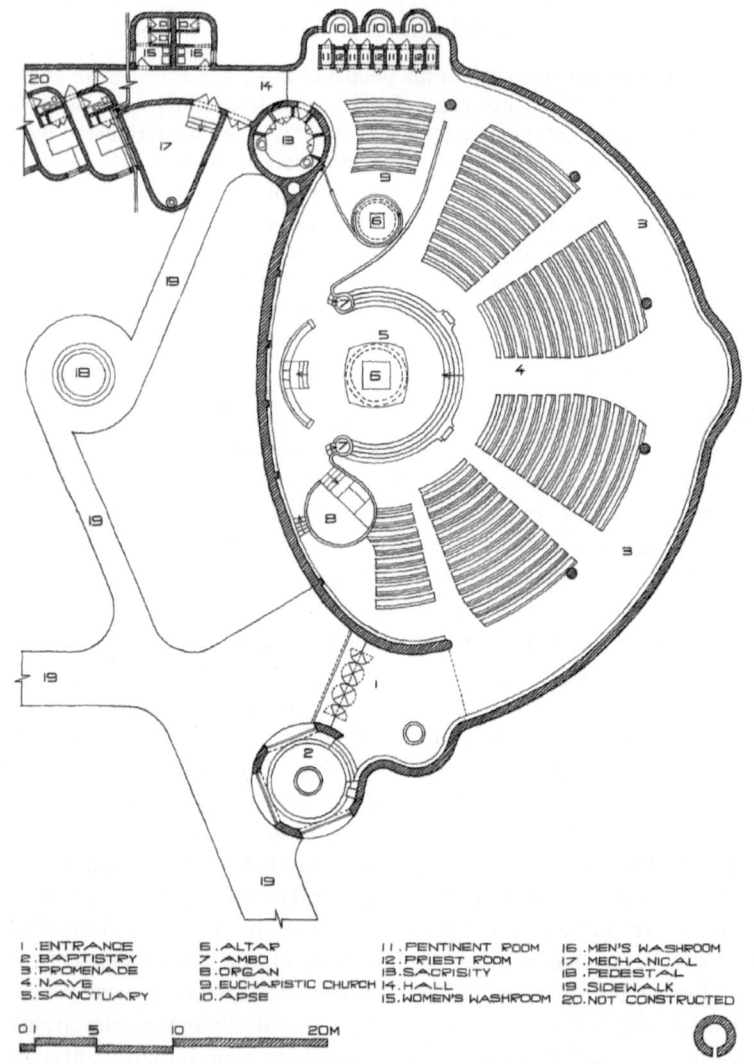

I .ENTRANCE	6 .ALTAR	II .PENTINENT ROOM	16 .MEN'S WASHROOM
2 .BAPTISTRY	7 .AMBO	12 .PRIEST ROOM	17 .MECHANICAL
3 .PROMENADE	8 .ORGAN	13 .SACRISTY	18 .PEDESTAL
4 .NAVE	9 .EUCHARISTIC CHURCH	14 .HALL	19 .SIDEWALK
5 .SANCTUARY	10 .APSE	15 .WOMEN'S WASHROOM	20 .NOT CONSTRUCTED

0 1 5 10 20M

Figure 24.1 Main Floor Plan, Douglas Cardinal, St. Mary's Church, 1968, Red Deer, Alberta, Canada. The curvilinear shape of the building is arranged around an altar facing the nave; the various religious elements, including the baptistery, confessionals, and choir, are carefully integrated into the scheme. Drawing by Mohammad Moezzi.

Waugh (Formline Architecture), Brian Porter (Two Row Architect), and Wanda Dalla Costa (TAWAW). The Truth and Reconciliation Commission of Canada which produced a wide-ranging report in 2015 on the history of indigenous peoples in Canada since colonization, has done much to increase the focus on indigenous issues, including architecture, in the country.

Despite a long and difficult history with colonialism, various indigenous American architects have established practices since Louis L. Weller (1935–2010) was the first Native American to graduate from a school of architecture (University of New Mexico) in 1959. Weller established his practice in 1980 and undertook many projects for indigenous communities. Other American indigenous architects include Denby Deegan (Denby Deegan Associates), Johnpaul Jones (Jones & Jones Architects), and Daniel J. Glenn (7 Directions Architects/Planners), and younger architects such as Tamara Eagle Bull and Chris Cornelius. The Southern Ute Cultural Center and Museum (2011) in Ignacio, Colorado, by Jones & Jones Architects of Seattle, is an important example of architecture by indigenous architects.[14] Many sensitive buildings have also been designed for American indigenous communities by non-indigenous firms, including the First Americans Museum (2021) in Oklahoma City by Johnson Fain Architects, which employs circular and mound forms.

In Australia, a small community of indigenous architects has emerged in recent years, including Kevin O'Brien, Craig Kerslake (Nguluway DesignInc), Jefa Greenaway, and Andrew Lane (Indij Design). Many buildings have been carefully designed for indigenous communities by non-indigenous firms, often employing a process of inter-cultural exchange. Examples include the Brambuk Cultural Centre (1990) in Halls Gap, Victoria and the Uluru-Kata Tjuta Cultural Centre (1995) by Gregory Burgess Architects; the Birabahn Aboriginal and Torres Strait Islander Centre (2002) at the University of Newcastle by Peter Stutchbury Architecture; and the Nyinkka-Nyunyu Art and Culture Centre (2004) in Tennant Creek, NT by Tangentyerre Design.

Since the 1960s, New Zealand has recognized the vital role of the indigenous Maori people in the nation, along with the negative aspects of its colonial history. Like all indigenous peoples, the Maori have various types of traditional architecture, aspects of which have been interpreted and incorporated in modern buildings.[15] Several architects with Maori heritage have practised since the 1950s. One of the first was Wiremu (Bill) Royal (1931–2013), who was the first

Maori to graduate from a New Zealand architecture school and the first to register as an architect (1957). Another pioneer was John Colin Scott (1924–1992), who had the ability to combine modernist and Maori traditions, as is evident in his Fortuna Chapel (1958–1961) in Wellington. Rewi Thompson (1953–2016) established his practice in 1983; among his many works, his own house (1985) in Auckland is particularly well-known for its distinctive use of a stepped form. A younger generation of Maori architects includes Nicholas Dalton (TOA Architects), Elisapeta Heta (Jasmax), Tere Insley (Kauri Architects), and Jade Kake (Matakohe Architecture). An example of an important institution that employed a cross-cultural design process is the Museum of New Zealand Te Papa Tongarewa (1998) in Wellington by Jasmax, which is the national museum and art gallery.

★ ★ ★

Learning from indigenous knowledge and traditions can be a vital contributor to the design of environmentally responsible buildings, landscapes, and cities. With a particular warning to modern societies, Douglas Cardinal writes:

> The earth is sacred. The destruction of the land has meant our destruction. We feel a sense of loss. We feel that the dominant society that is now in control of the land is not a fit guardian of this life source. Its technology is transforming everything, destroying everything, because it is ignorant of the subtle balances of nature. They lack reverence.[16]

NOTES

1 See Barnabas Calder, *Architecture, from Prehistory to Climate Emergency* (London: Pelican Books, 2021); and James Wines, *Green Architecture* (Köln: Taschen, 2000).

2 See Dominique Gauzin-Müller, "A Short History of Sustainable Architecture," in Hans Drexler and Sebastian El khouli, eds., *Holistic Housing: Concept, Design Strategies and Process* (Munich: Detail, 2012), pp. 10–12.

3 See James Steele, *Ecological Architecture: A Critical History* (London: Thames & Hudson, 2005), pp. 165–173.

4 See Ian McHarg, *Design with Nature* (New York: Doubleday, 1969).

5 See Phillip James Tabb and A. Senem Deviren, *The Greening of Architecture: A Critical History and Survey of Contemporary Sustainable Architecture and Urban Design* (Abingdon: Routledge, 2014), pp. 49–74.

6 See Steven Mannell, "Living Lightly on the Earth," in *Building an Ark for Prince Edward Island, 1974–1976* (Halifax: Dalhousie Architectural Press, 2018).

7 See Christopher Alexander, *A Pattern Language: Towns, Buildings, Construction* (New York: Oxford University Press, 1977); Paul Hawkens, Amory B. Lovins, and L. Hunter Lovins, *Natural Capitalism: Creating the Next Industrial Revolution* (New York: Little, Brown & Co., 1999); and William McDonough and Michael Braungart, *Cradle to Cradle: Remaking the Way We Make Things* (New York: North Point Press, 2002).

8 See Perkins + Will, *Busby: Architecture's New Edges* (Seattle: Ecotone Publishing, 2014).

9 See Tabb and Diveren, *The Greening of Architecture*, pp. 75–122.

10 Hirini Matunga, "A Discourse on the Nature of Indigenous Architecture," in Elizabeth Grant et al., eds., *The Handbook of Contemporary Indigenous Architecture* (Singapore: Springer, 2018), p. 307.

11 Ibid., p. 308.

12 See Trevor Boddy, *The Architecture of Douglas Cardinal* (Edmonton: NeWest Press, 1989). See also Odile Hénault, "First Nations Architecture: A Long Journey Forward," in Elsa Lam and Graham Livesey, eds., *Canadian Modern Architecture, 1967 to the Present* (New York: Princeton Architectural Press, 2019), pp. 121–152.

13 See David Fortin, "Mixing It Up: Métis Design and Material Culture in the Canadian Conscious," in Grant et al., eds., *The Handbook of Contemporary Indigenous Architecture*, pp. 253–281.

14 See Joy Monice Malnar and Frank Vodvarka, "Contemporary Native American Projects: Four Studies," in Grant et al., eds., *The Handbook of Contemporary Indigenous Architecture*, pp. 707–804. See also Carol Hershelle Krinsky, *Contemporary Native American Architecture: Cultural Regeneration and Creativity* (New York: Oxford University Press, 1996).

15 See Deidre Brown, "Contemporary Maori Architecture," in Grant et al., eds., *The Handbook of Contemporary Indigenous Architecture*, pp. 107–125.

16 Douglas Cardinal, "The Great White Manager and the Sacred Earth," in Boddy, ed., *The Architecture of Douglas Cardinal*, p. 123.

SUGGESTED READING

Calder, Barnabas. *Architecture, from Prehistory to Climate Emergency*. London: Pelican Books, 2021.

Grant, Elizabeth, et al., eds. *The Handbook of Contemporary Indigenous Architecture*. Singapore: Springer, 2018.

McDonough, William and Michael Braungart. *Cradle to Cradle: Remaking the Way We Make Things*. New York: North Point Press, 2002.

Steele, James. *Ecological Architecture: A Critical History*. London: Thames & Hudson, 2005.

Tabb, Phillip James and A. Senem Deviren. *The Greening of Architecture: A Critical History and Survey of Contemporary Sustainable Architecture and Urban Design*. Abingdon: Routledge, 2014.

INDEX

Note: Page numbers in *italics* indicate a figure on the corresponding page.